Mandy Rice-
the series of scandals surrounding the 'Cliveden Set' ruined the lives of many prominent society figures.

Now, for the first time, here is Mandy's own story; of her introduction to London at the age of sixteen, of the enigmatic Dr Stephen Ward, the society osteopath hounded to suicide; of Peter Rachman, the property speculator, whose friend she remained until his death.

Many, from the notorious to the famous, have been Mandy's friends. For, as she maintains, 'I have been lucky with the people I know'.

Mandy

MANDY RICE-DAVIES with SHIRLEY FLACK

To Roger
With thanks for
my butterfly season at
the Nuffield
Love
Mandy

SPHERE BOOKS LIMITED
30-32 Gray's Inn Road, London WC1X 8JL

First published in Great Britain simultaneously by Michael Joseph Ltd
and Sphere Books Ltd 1980

TRADE
MARK

Printed and bound in Great Britain by
©ollins, Glasgow

1

IT WAS a hot afternoon in July 1963. I bought a seat for the stalls in the Odeon Cinema, Marble Arch, a bar of chocolate and a packet of popcorn. I sat in the dark, staring unseeing at the screen, my head aching with the jumble of thoughts racing round in my mind.

What's happening to me? I kept asking, and why? And whatever it is I want to stop it now. But it was too late for that. I struggled to clear the confusion in my mind. The only certainty in my life on that summer afternoon was the fact that my place in history was already assured as a central figure in the biggest sex scandal of the century. Mandy Rice-Davies, or was it Randy Mice-Davies? Have you heard the one about? . . . Already a stream of Randy Mandy jokes was in circulation, record shops were selling a Mandy-inspired satirical album and cartoonists were stimulated at finding a new character to replace the tired politicians.

Everybody knew me. The girl with the bouffant blonde hair, expensive clothes, audacious hats and enough jewellery to keep the wolf from the door for a few years yet. Invariably they saw me getting out of an expensive car, or arriving at Heathrow. Mandy – always smiling. That was my public image.

But, what about this Mandy? The girl with no make-up, hair tied in two little pigtails, a simple cotton dress and flat-heeled sandals. So anonymous, this Mandy, that two women sitting next to her on the bus could discuss the disgraceful exploits of that other Mandy without the slightest embarrassment.

I took to wearing cotton frocks and pigtails a great deal in the summer of 1963. That was my disguise; it enabled me to move freely without stares and whispers, but it made me vulnerable to hearing what people were saying about me.

And when I became the other Mandy – the public, the notorious one – I had a different camouflage. It was a smile which said I'm confident and happy, and there is nothing you can do to bother me. Like the song we used to sing at school when the bullies were ganging up: 'Sticks and stones will break my bones but names will never hurt me'.

Ah, but they do hurt. The only defence is pretence.

I knew a psychiatrist once, not as a patient but as a friend. 'You know,' he said one day, 'you're a very complex person.'

'No, you're wrong,' I replied. 'I am very simple. I am, in fact, several simple people. And that's the trouble. With so many identities I really wish I knew which one was the true me. Would the real Mandy Rice-Davies *please* stand up.'

2

AS A child I lived with an uneasy sense of being in the wrong place at the wrong time. It is a common childhood fantasy for imaginative girls to daydream about being a princess kidnapped by gypsies and sold to proxy parents. My own confusion was that I had no sense of identity, only a conviction that I was living in the wrong place.

We were neither poor, nor unhappy. Either state might have introduced a welcome note of drama. Life at Blenheim Road, Shirley, Solihull was simply dull. When people talk of boredom my mind flashes back to that three-up-two-down semi where, if it was sausage and mash for tea, it had to be Monday.

I knew what I did not want, that there had to be more to life than what I had. Furs, cars, diamonds (all soon to be mine as it happened) did not figure in my aspirations. Hollywood glamour was no lure. What I needed was adventure, a vaguely defined freedom which I knew might bring excitement and satisfaction if I could find it – I have never stopped looking.

The only tangible element of mystery existing in my young life was the reluctance of my parents ever to discuss their past life. How and where they met, how they came to marry, all this was shrouded in secrecy, so that at an early age I deduced, correctly, that each had been married before and that I was not supposed to know.

Mother was born and grew up in Wales. Her father, a professional soldier in the cavalry who never attained a rank higher than private, died young, leaving his widow to raise the family. Mother was the youngest, and rather pampered I suspect. She was very pretty and this led her to the stage. Briefly. Her career ended with a flop, and as job prospects for a girl from her background were restricted, she married at the earliest opportunity, producing a son and daughter in fairly close succession. During the slump of the thirties, her husband, believing they stood a better chance of survival by leaving Wales, moved the family to the Midlands where opportunities seemed brighter. It was there that she met my father.

His background was completely different. The family can trace their line back through 900 years of Rhyses and Rices, a route scattered with wealthy eccentrics, bishops and even, they claim, a tenuous link with the British monarchy. The family home, where my father grew up, was a large country house in Ponty Yates, South Wales, which has now been absorbed into the spread of the town and become a supermarket.

Great-grandfather (on Father's side) was a gentleman farmer. An odd chap who owned only black animals (it was a local joke that the only white thing on the farm was his wife) and dressed always in a long black coat and a black hat. It was considered quite a good match when his daughter Letitia married David, whose family, though not exactly gentry, were very rich. David's father, an equally weird character, had made his fortune in pit props. Wealth had dried up his work motivation, and as the money poured in he spent it as fast as he could in the local hostelries. He must have been the John Wayne of Llanelly, a lone figure who walked in the middle of the road and, in moods of fierce aggression, would pick fights with the lamp posts – newfangled inventions which he saw as unwelcome strangers.

As is so often the case with peculiar parents, he produced quite gentle and reasonable children. My grandfather – his father's money having provided him with a good education – saw himself as a writer, hobnobbing with whatever local poets could be mustered and penning his own verse in Welsh. He even published, in English, a book of advice to those wishing to invest on the stock market. Its price was sixpence and it became something of a best seller. The last page bore the words God Speed. His own financial dealings were somewhat unreliable. He invested a fortune in Welsh goldmines, which produced very little gold. When the Queen married (as Princess Elizabeth) her wedding ring owed something to my grandfather.

His greatest passion proved his undoing. As an expert in rare books, he devoted many hours searching for items to add to his collection. A visit to Cardiff to buy books proved fatal. He returned that night feeling ill, went into a coma and died.

Wandering along the quayside he had been bitten by a tsetse fly imported in a crate of bananas. In a Welsh village, who could be expected to diagnose sleeping sickness! He died at thirty-five leaving his widow, three sons and two daughters.

Fortunately, my grandmother was not hard up. The boys were shipped off at an early age to Towyn, a boarding school, and Father went straight from school into the police force. Somewhere along the line he married and had a daughter. The break-up of that marriage and his subsequent re-marriage was a fact he found difficult to face for many years. It offended the Puritan streak which characterises the Welsh – I recognise it occasionally in myself and with age increasingly find myself siding with Mary Whitehouse! Recently, curiosity led me into a sex shop, and I found to my horror that I was actually embarrassed, and left in a hurry.

Daddy had been transferred to the Birmingham police force at the beginning of the war and had met my mother. In old age he has taken to making humorous allusions to their meeting. 'She seduced me'; but thirty years ago when the memory was still fresh the immediate past was a forbidden topic.

By the time I was born in October 1944, Daddy had been called up as a radio officer in the Eighth Army. He saw his baby daughter Marilyn once before being sent overseas, and I was already a toddler when we met again. My family circle consisted of me; mother; her daughter, my half-sister, Margaret, who was sixteen when I was born and was a second mother to me (my other half brother and sister were never part of our family); and, for a brief period, my maternal grandmother, a fierce old lady for whom I felt a healthy disdain. My most vivid memory of her is the day my sister had set the table for dinner – china, cutlery, food – and Granny lifted the cloth and shook the lot out of the window. . . .

Father returned from the war, my younger brother David was born, and we settled down to a life of routine domesticity. Father left the police force and went to work for Dunlop, which provided occasional moments of excitement, as testing a new tyre meant a day at Silverstone motor-racing track, having breakfast in Vandervelt's caravan, and everybody fussing over me as a sort of blonde baby-doll mascot.

Once a year the entire family trooped off to stay with

grandmother Rice-Davies in Ponty Yates. I loved the house, its access to animals and farm life (including the gardener's Sunday morning cockfighting, which I was never permitted to watch), the comfort, the huge beds you had to climb up three steps to get into.

Nana terrified me. For health reasons she lived in bed, surrounded by heaps of essential personal possessions: books, writing paper, numerous little silk embroidered pouches and bags, wafted in a cloud of Rose Geranium toilet water which was sent regularly from Floris in London in keeping with her lifelong policy. Everything she bought was good quality and expensive, not because she was a snob, though possibly she was that too, but because she adhered to traditional standards.

She rarely came downstairs, but when she did there were embarrassing consequences for me, usually because I was discovered doing something which was not allowed. I was drawn to one particular room, in which the *pièce de résistance* was a heavy mahogany table fitted with drawers which contained most of her silver. I remember once nosing about in this drawer, which riveted me for hours, when Nana came in looking for her glasses. I dropped like a stone on my knees behind the sofa. To my dismay, she found her glasses, sat down to read and remained there for two hours. I was painfully stiff when she eventually moved.

During the summer visit, I would be despatched to the local cobbler, who would measure me up for sandals. I was permitted to choose my colour, and it was usually red. These I would wear until winter, when my new shoes would arrive (Father having sent in early autumn a drawing of my foot to the shoemaker), hand-made from the finest leather, since Nana only ever bought the best. Along with the winter shoes would come a camel-hair winter coat. Its classic conventionality, always the same style – rather royal family – was a far cry from the children's clothes of the day. I must have looked somewhat old-fashioned among my classmates – but I enjoyed the distinction. This custom continued until she died when I was ten.

I always remember childhood as something I had to get over. I never thought of myself as a child, dependent on adults to care for me and structure my life. School was a tiresome burden simply because I have always felt hemmed in by routine. The discipline I impose on myself is much harder than anything demanded by school or a normal adult working life, but it is positive – sensible. I have never seen the sense of being compelled to study maths. Most of the sums I need to do, I can work out in my head.

I'm not a rebel in the accepted sense, but I must occasionally have seemed anti-establishment because of my refusal to adopt the subservient manner which was expected at Sherman's Cross Secondary Modern. One teacher ordered me in exasperation never to attend her class again, and I concurred with pleasure, spending my time instead in the school gardens. I enjoyed games and art, came top for English composition, but never felt the ambition to excel in order to impress the staff.

My bouts of idealistic fervour, when they came, were religious. Some girls joined the Young Conservatives – I explored religion and flirted with most of the denominations Solihull had to offer. Any spare cash was spent on crucifixes and holy pictures. Attending classes in Roman Catholicism (I never went to confession, it has always struck me as a poor man's psychiatrist's couch), I was simultaneously singing in the choir at the Anglican church. A useful source of income. I had a pure soprano voice – 'Do Greensleeves for us, Marilyn,' the headmistress would say whenever the board of governors came visiting.

I had an over-developed sense of responsibility and this led me into various money-making ventures. At first I started cleaning shop windows. Unable to reach the upper parts, I used to clean all the lower levels and the doors. It was quite a flourishing business. Then there was the greengrocer up the road who used to boil beetroot out the back of the shop. I would go there every Friday night and peel the freshly boiled beetroot. By this time I was nine. It was sixpence here and twopence there. I liked to be busy, my reward was the money I earned.

Soon, however, it became a necessity, for I developed an interest in the most expensive hobby of all – horses. I had always read horsey books, but pursuit of this passion was way out of my parents' budget. They could just about manage the ten shillings (50p) for a half-hour Saturday ride, but I was not content with that. I wanted my own horse.

I began plotting ways to get a horse of my own. Every day I read the *Birmingham Mail*'s pets corner column and eventually a story appeared that the RSPCA were taking over ponies from a redundant pit. They were looking for good homes for the young Welsh mountain ponies. I lost no time in hastening to the RSPCA headquarters to look them over. As I leaned on the fence, one pony, a bay, came trotting over to me. Obviously he thought I was carrying bread – I knew it was love at first sight.

'This is the one,' I told the inspector. All that remained was to find the money to pay for his keep. Undeterred I named him Laddie and went away to work out my campaign. I knew enough from my Saturday riding to see that he was a good sound pony, about eight years old. He would have been unsuitable as a riding-school pony since he was unbroken. He needed an owner like me, an enthusiast who could not afford anything better.

I would need a place to keep him, and enough money to feed him. I was close to my twelfth birthday, the age at which one could legally take on a paper round which would pay me, mornings and evenings, twelve shillings a week. That princely sum would cover his oats and hay. He would need shoeing every six weeks at a cost of £1, and Father was persuaded to increase my pocket money to ten shillings weekly. Then Laddie needed a home. Three miles away was a racing stable. I volunteered my services for Saturdays, Sundays and holidays, mucking out and exercising the horses. Stables always need help and racehorses actually prefer girls, who are more gentle with them, to boys. As I anticipated, the stable manager accepted my deal, and agreed in return to let me keep Laddie there.

I had ten days in which to organise my foolproof scheme before the day appointed for the RSPCA inspector to call and meet my parents – needless to say they were not prepared to give ponies away without checking first.

There was never any question of my parents opposing me. If I wanted something and made up my mind, I always got it. I'm the same today: I have to be very careful about what I want because I usually get it. To this end I was methodical, and I worked hard. My parents have said since, that as a little girl I was quite formidable: 'Nobody could make you do anything'. In fact, I had a nasty temper when thwarted, which I have almost outgrown. I feel that the Welsh are not demonstrative people, you are not encouraged to display your feelings except in song. The atmosphere at home was one of quiet respect and affection, rather than love and kisses. I was never Daddy's little girl curling up on his knee for a cuddle. My small brother was more conventional in the sense of requiring more attention from our parents. Four years my junior, I would try to manipulate and organise him with a certain amount of success. He usually had money when mine had been spent, he was careful and I was over-generous, and he could usually be persuaded to part with it on some pretext.

Basically I am a loner, though somehow I have always managed to collect a following and always seem to be at the hub of a crowd. But then I led quite a solitary life, which suited me because it left me alone to concentrate on my animals: a cat and a dog, guinea pigs and a rabbit – and mice which I kept hidden in my wardrobe in defiance of my mother's rule that mice were not allowed. My favourite white mouse would come riding with me, sitting in my shirt pocket.

Eventually the RSPCA inspector called and, in the formality of the family lounge, met my parents. He asked to see my room and was shown upstairs. One glance showed him all he needed to know about the girl who was to take over the pit pony. No posters of Tommy Steele or Elvis adorned my walls. Instead, a full-page photograph, taken from a magazine, of Colonel Llewellyn on Foxhunter, dominated the montage of cats, dogs and other furry friends. Thoroughly satisfied, he took his departure.

I thrived on hard work, I was stimulated by it. Dashing around with my newspapers morning and night (on foot at first until I could organise a bicycle), and working weekends at the stables. Among the many horses were two so vicious that even the trainer was wary. Gana and Ormond (the latter a famous racehorse) both had the habit of standing back to the door, and lurching out with a hefty kick when anyone entered. Ormond fell passionately in love with me and this became the joke of the stables. 'Your lover is waiting for you,' they would say, and, sure enough, as I came up the drive, there would be a neigh of pleasure from this nasty, vicious horse and the moment he saw me his horsey face lit up. I could get him to do anything, he was putty in my hands.

I saw Laddie every day, cycling to visit him each evening after school to reassure myself that he was not suffering from cold or hunger. It was a four-mile journey through woods. Owls hooted, sometimes the ground would be covered with snow, but it was unthinkable that I should let a day pass without contact with my adored pony.

The local pony club had never had a member quite like me. Solihull is the snobby suburb of Birmingham, more so then than today. My fellow members were rich little girls with blue-blooded show ponies, both rider and pony beautifully turned out at all times. Gradually I collected together my own ensemble of second-hand hacking jacket and jodhpurs, Christmas money provided a hat and yellow sweater and, for a brief and glorious period, I actually owned long black leather riding-boots. I assembled from cast-offs a sort of tack, and rode either bareback or with a borrowed saddle. People in the horsey fraternity are always happy to lend; I was the equestrian second-hand Rose.

Nothing on earth would have persuaded Laddie to jump, but he did turn out to be an enthusiastic gymkhana pony, obedient and good-natured. Together we attended every major pony club event we could possible manage – without the benefit of a horsebox.

Usually little girl riders would be accompanied by admiring mothers and fathers, who would help with the preparation and grooming or generally act as chauffeur or scorekeeper. Mine never showed any inclination to come along, and I was relieved, for in this world I was complete.

On one occasion, however, my father did watch me compete. His great interest was greyhound racing, a field in which he enjoys a certain reputation as a judge of form, and possibly because of what he saw as a similarity of interest and the fact that this pony event (attended by Colonel Llewellyn himself) was to take place at the King's Heath Greyhound Track, he decided to attend.

I could see at once that I was definitely out of my class, the other horses were immaculate, and my poor Laddie had a dipped back! When my race was announced, my name was not called. The semi-finals passed, and I told the organiser I had been left out. 'Don't worry,' he said, 'just join in the finalists.' Four finalists and me lined up. Four beautiful frisky ponies, and poor old Laddie. Sensing my nervousness, he would not budge. I dismounted and gave him a push from behind. By the time he decided to move the others were half-way through the obstacle event and by the time we had moved half round, everyone had finished. He refused to canter, he just did his slow trot. The spectators roared with laughter. I laughed myself. It was the first time I had had an audience, and I was the star. I played to the crowd, everybody was laughing and cheering and I was enjoying it. They gave me a Reserve, a white rosette.

As aware as I was of my financial disadvantages, I was never self-pitying or envious, but, looking back, I realise that many people, specially the adults, probably felt rather sorry for me. This and my dedication towards horses and riding, must have earned their respect.

One Sunday I awoke with a feeling of unease and decided I would not ride that day; I was afraid of an accident, being hit by a car or having a bad fall. Instead I made myself busy in the hay loft above the stables. Suddenly, a rafter cracked and I slipped right through, crashing onto the back of Gana (he had given so many people frights, this time he knew how it felt to be on the receiving end), ending up on the cobblestones. They rushed me to hospital, where my worst fears were confirmed – I had broken my leg and ankle. My screams, which reverberated through the corridors, were not cries of pain (though that was considerable) but anger that the nurses were cutting off my boot. My beautiful riding-boot. Officially, I was off riding for months. However, I managed to move Laddie to a field nearer home and taught myself how to cycle with one leg in plaster, and exercise him without ever putting the injured foot on the ground. It was one of the times in my life when I have experienced premonitions of disaster.

Another strange occurrence happened one morning when I needed to be up early because we were competing in a gymkhana. Not having a horsebox meant a walk of six miles, but first Laddie had to be groomed and plaited. He was in one of the far fields; I knew exactly where because he would go there with some of the racehorses who were turned out. All I had to do was follow the usual track; but, for some odd reason, on this day I took another route, a way I had never taken before or since, and had to fight my way through the hedges. As I scrambled through the second hedge my foot touched something soft. Looking down, it was a man's hand. I looked closer – it was a body.

I ran for help and told one of the stable boys, who was older and I hoped would know what to do. His first reaction was to assume I was joking, his next to run off screaming. We woke the trainer who alerted the police and an ambulance arrived. As the body was lifted on to a stretcher, a bottle of pills rolled out from underneath, followed by a bottle of Lucozade. How strange, I thought. Lucozade's for energy. The ambulance men thought he was dead, but inside the ambulance they managed to resuscitate him. A few weeks later his brother called and gave me £2 for saving his life – I spent it all on Crunchy bars.

My most weird premonition was three years ago in Monte Carlo. Several of us had arranged to play tennis. We assembled in the hotel foyer waiting for the car to take us to the tennis club. It arrived, we all piled in and just as it was my turn, I drew back.

'Sorry, changed my mind,' I said. I felt myself go hot, then cold. 'Come on,' my friends said, and a large American girl started to push me into the car.

'It's the car,' I said. 'I can't travel in this car.'

They refused to take me seriously, and jokingly pulled and pushed me in. There I sat in mute terror, as the car made its way through the heavy traffic to the club. After our game we drove back for lunch in the same car. Again I sat knotted with anxiety and tension until we pulled into the forecourt of the hotel and my ordeal was over.

Next day I was due to leave for Israel, but the French announced a lightning strike. Everything was to close down, including the airports. I had no choice but to drive to Milan and fly from there to Zurich. I ordered a car, now at a premium because everybody had the same idea. The car arrived – the same big black American limousine. I had no choice. It was imperative I get to Milan. During the four-hour drive, expecting disaster round every twist and turn of the coast road, my heart pounding with fear, I learned that the driver was an Englishman who had gone to live in France fifteen years before. He talked of his family, his life there. I felt I knew him well. Our conversation helped pass the time, but I was heartily glad to say goodbye to him and the car at Milan airport. Four days later, a friend telephoned from France.

'Remember that car,' he said. 'The driver went off a cliff into the sea on the way back.'

3

I WAS slower than most finding out about sex. I knew about horses. I had read *Forever Amber* and believed fervently in the agony and the ecstasy of love – red, violent and blood-splashed. I still do.

At Sherman's Cross Secondary Modern many of my class-mates were well into full sexual affairs by the age of fifteen. I had a healthy curiosity and wanted to hear all the details, but, having listened, I was invariably sorry I had asked. It struck me as vaguely distasteful. I objected, too, to the absurd rituals surrounding the boy-meets-girl procedure and would feel comfortably superior to my school friends when, on my evening visit to Laddie, I saw them painted and perfumed in their 'hunting' gear of baggy mohair sweaters, dirndl skirts over multi-coloured nylon net petticoats and white ankle socks all set for an evening's chatting up on street corners or hanging around the juke-box in the overlit one-and-only coffee-bar.

My own head was full of ideas about what was I going to do with my life. I felt I had to get out of this lower-middle-class rut which, for the unwary, could be a lifetime's trap, and that I had to plan the way out. There was no way I was ever going to follow in my half-sister Margaret's footsteps – early marriage, two babies and divorce.

I must have seemed an odd mixture. On the one hand a horsey, sporty fiend, on the other a girl given to hours spent writing poetry. Or is that in fact the truth about adolescence?

My art had always been promising. Now there was talk of an art scholarship and I began to spend a few hours on a Saturday away from Laddie, closeted with an elderly curator at Birmingham Art Museum. Sometimes I sketched, sometimes we sneaked away to a musty back room to surrender to the heady delights of contemplating the pre-Raphaelites. He was a kindly, fatherly old man – was he ever shocked?

The law said that at fourteen a school child was allowed to work half-day on a Saturday. With one stroke I could alter my economic structure, for now that Laddie was living nearer home I was no longer beholden to the racing stables and my weekends were free. A Saturday job would bring in more than the paper round and my various other activities put together.

McConvill's, a Birmingham fashion shop, took me on and I was put in the coat department, under the auspices of an eagle-eyed supervisor with blue hair and diamante-framed glasses. We got on well immediately.

Although I was a mere fourteen year old, I always appeared much older (probably being tall helped the deception – I had never had any difficulty getting into X-certificate films), and I was a useful addition to the staff. After having had to get up at the crack of dawn to work at the stables, taking the bus into Birmingham and spending a few hours in a cosy shop seemed like a day out.

I threw myself with great enthusiasm into this new rôle, possibly too much for my energy did not go unnoticed by the visiting contract window dresser, who wasted no time in enlisting me to help dress the windows. At last, I felt, my artistic flair was being fulfilled, but this state was not to last.

One Saturday I arrived happy and bright to discover that the feud which had been brewing between Diamante Specs and Window Dresser had flared into a battle. A frightful scene was in progress, the most fearful insults and insinuations hurled about. The elderly owner stepped in to effect a sort of truce and I crept about for the rest of the morning like a whipped puppy who was not quite sure what was wrong but knows that somehow he's involved. When it was time to go home, I gave in my notice.

With all of two months' experience in the retail business, I figured I had something to offer and by now I had decided my new policy was to begin at the top. I asked for an interview with the personnel officer at Marshall and Snelgrove, Birmingham's closest thing to Harrods, and offered my services. She hired me on the spot, to my delight and, I confess, surprise, for the store had a reputation for employing only upper-class girls from the better schools.

They started me off in the china department. The buyer

was an elderly gentleman with a genuine love of beautiful things. I was rapidly infected with his reverence and enthusiasm for the china, porcelain and crystal which in those days was the bread-and-butter business of the store, with its vast number of account customers living in the salubrious surrounding areas. Under his wing (I have so many elderly gentlemen to be grateful to), I became engrossed, and when I was offered a full-time job with the prospect of becoming a buyer ten years hence, I was understandably flattered. It was the decisive factor in the should I/shouldn't I? stay-on-for-O-levels debate. I left school.

Meanwhile a major social and cultural event took place in Birmingham – Hardy Amies visited and presented a fashion show.

Sitting in the audience watching the models glide along the catwalk endorsed my own ideas about what looked good. After the show I insinuated myself back stage (proving to myself that if you barge through with your nose in the air nobody ever asks where you are going, a ploy I have never since known to fail), and introduced myself to one of the models, who was very sophisticated, as I imagined a worldly London woman to be, and also very sweet. As we chatted, Hardy Amies himself fluttered by and stopped to say hello. Was I interested in modelling? he asked; and on hearing that I was (which was also news to me) invited me, when I was seventeen, to 'Come and see me in London'. Perhaps he meant it. Perhaps he was merely being polite and kind. I took a bus home, elated with excitement and a sense of adventure. A door had opened.

The fashion world now became an interest. Having bypassed the mad-about-clothes early-teenage stage, I developed an objective approach to the way people dressed and to my own style. I soon discovered that wearing classic clothes made me look older, gave me a classy look, and, in terms of value for money, proved a better investment.

When I heard through the grapevine that Marshall and Snelgrove were putting on their own fashion show to tie up with the première of *Make Mine Mink*, I felt that I should get myself involved. Preliminary sounding out indicated that I was far too young. When I knew the meeting to discuss plans was going on I combed my hair, powdered my nose, absented myself from the china and glass, ran up the stairs to the manager's office, tapped, put my head round the door and, with my widest, freshest, most disarmingly appealing but not too pushy smile, said, Please could I be included? 'Of course,' said the manager.

Dressed from our model gown department, mink-coated from our fur room, bedecked with enough sparkling jewellery (could they actually have been diamonds?) to light up New Street, my crowning glory backcombed and lacquered by Birmingham's top hairdresser into a bouffant extravaganza that added another three inches to my five foot seven inches, I thought I looked stunning as we posed with Terry Thomas and Hattie Jacques, stars of the film, for the photographer from the *Birmingham Mail*.

Mother used to say that when I was a small child, if we were sitting on a bus and there was an old gentleman there he would strike up an immediate conversation with me. Men have always liked me. Women either like me very much or can't stand the sight of me; I'm very strong meat for some of my own sex. I have never done anything to encourage a pass, I have never been a great beauty, at best passingly pretty, yet all my adult life I have fended off men.

These were the discoveries I was beginning to make about myself, and that night I found that chatting to Terry-Thomas and the top executive from Rank, just like chatting to royalty, diplomats, and other famous people I was later to mix with, was not so very different from striking up a conversation with an old-age pensioner on a bus.

At midnight, like Cinderella, I took off the mink coat, the dress and the diamonds and changed into my own clothes, transferring from the black silk evening bag to my own brown leather the business card given to me by one of the Rank executives. 'If I can help in any way . . .' he said. The store laid on a car to take me home, sleek and black. It reminded me of the hire car my grandmother in Ponty Yates once sent for us, when Father caught me waving out of the window like a princess and firmly ticked me off for putting on silly airs and graces.

Life at Marshall and Snelgrove proceeded as betore. Now I modelled in the store on Saturday afternoons. The film première remained a comforting glow in my memory, something to take out and caress on the bus ride home after a day in the store, or during an evening slumped in front of the family television when, conversation non existent, I would remind myself that there was more to life than this. More excitement. I had only to wait.

It seemed then, and it is even more true today, that my life has proceeded in events, each one leading to the next. There have been very few false trails. I never waste time or energy running around trying to drum up a happening. I wait, and it happens.

So it did. Hurrying along the street during my lunch break, I was stopped by a man with a proposition. How would I like to model at the Earl's Court Motor Show? Today I do not remember his name, but his offer was that one stroke that teaches you fate has the upper hand. Businessman, husband and father; grey haired, sober-suited, hardworking, inoffensive and master of my fate. More than Profumo, Ward, Rachman, names shortly to become notorious, he was the man who changed the course of my life.

I was by this time becoming interested in boys. There was the small matter of two who actually fought over who was taking me to a dance. In the event I decided not to go but the flutter their quarrel created was a novel and pleasurable feeling, and the other girls at the youth club viewed me with more interest than previously.

At fourteen I had experienced the first awakenings of what I suppose is physical awareness but at the time I felt it was something spiritual, almost biblical – I was into a deep religious kick at the time. In the field where I kept Laddie, the circus came. I went to help with the horses. The trapeze artist was a young, beautiful Italian called Rocco with curly black hair and soulful eyes and little English. For two weeks we were together, me grooming the horses, he practising his acrobatics; but after only three days, and without either having made a move in the other's direction, he said sadly: 'I think I am in love with you.'

This was better than Romeo and Juliet. That night I watched him performing on the trapeze, heard the crowd gasp at his skill, and my own excitement was sharpened by knowing that though he was the centre of attraction, I had a power over him. The heady wine of reflected glory. . . .

Once we talked about fear. I asked him why he did the job he did. Explaining his feelings to me, he said, 'While I am up there on the trapeze, I am living. The rest is just waiting.'

The circus was due to leave, I was preparing the horses for the show, and afterwards we were to ride them to the station. Rocco came up from behind, put his arms around me and kissed me. I thought it the most romantic moment I could ever imagine, the poignancy, the gentleness. I never saw him again.

Laddie was kept in a field which lay behind the coffee bar, at that time a meeting place for all the Teddy Boys in the district who would come roaring up on their motor bikes and spend the next few hours combing their hair. Visiting Laddie one evening I found him with his nostrils flaring, covered in sweat and frothing at the mouth. Somebody or something had scared him, and instinctively I knew who to blame. I calmed him as best I could, put him into his shed and stormed into the coffee bar.

'Who is your leader?' I demanded, sounding like somebody straight out of a B film. The whole place came to a standstill, and a tall blond youth clad in skin-tight black leather and studs unwound himself from a chair. 'Look,' I said, 'one of your boys has been running my horse around. Rather childish isn't it? I thought you went in for frightening people not animals.'

'Who's dunnit?' he asked.

There was a general movement as they shuffled sheepishly and rattled their bicycle chains.

'Don't worry, luv,' he said, 'it won't happen again.'

Neither did it. He started to come around the back of the coffee bar, watching me as I exercised Laddie. I sensed he fancied me and I reckoned that as long as he did, and as long as I kept him at arm's length, I would have no trouble from the rest of them. I appealed to his purer senses, and I manipulated that, keeping him interested but not too interested. That precarious state continued for six months until I left Solihull.

Fifteen years later, visiting the new Bullring Centre market in Birmingham, there was this good-looking guy selling flowers. Older, but still with a touch of the James Deans.

'Hello, Johnnie,' I said.

'Christ, it's Marilyn. I was really soft on you.' He gave me a bunch of chrysanthemums.

My virginity was discarded in the room above the sweet shop next to the Odeon cinema. Girls talk of lost virginity suggesting something accidentally mislaid – my deflowering was no accident.

I met the handsome Robin when I went into his parents' shop to buy sweets. A graduate at Trinity College, Dublin, he was helping out in the summer holiday. We chatted about this and that, he was remarkably good looking and when he invited me to the pictures, I agreed. It was first love – the weak at the knees, palpitating, nervous kind of love. He was charming, amusing, sophisticated and he knew all the tricks of the game, like making dates and not showing up, being warm one minute, offhand the next. And always cool – no fumbling in the back row, or groping in the car. I lived in a state of delicious anticipation.

Inevitably came the day, early closing, when we were alone in the flat above the shop. There was no hesitation, I was an enthusiastic participant in what struck me as a perfectly pleasant way to spend an afternoon. I had expected, afterwards, to feel in some way fundamentally changed by my experience and in this respect was disappointed. Oh, so that's it, I thought as I set off home.

Robin seemed quite anxious for a repeat performance at the earliest opportunity, which was a few days later. He parked in the woods. Perversely, this time I said no, I would prefer to go home. 'Go on then,' he said. In bravado I got briskly out of the car and, to my horror, he promptly drove off. Staggering home blindly in the dark, I called him all the names under the sun, but knew a sneaking admiration for his style. This was better than a B film. I vowed to level the score, and eventually I did.

When the model agent spotted me in the street, he had already found two girls for the Motor Show and he needed a third. He had been briefed that the new car to be unveiled – very secret – was young in spirit, the girl had to be young too. My parents were wary of the proposition, but after checking it out it seemed an offer there could be no harm in accepting.

Marshall and Snelgrove gave me a week's holiday and, with dresses and shoes provided by local sponsors, I launched myself on Earl's Court.

The Mini was the most photographed, most publicised car ever. My work, if one could call it that, consisted of being decorative and charming and co-operative to the photographers. I was taken to receptions and launching parties, met the designer Sir Alex Issigonis, lunched with Sir David Brown of Aston Martin. At night I returned, chaste, to my room in a small hotel just off Earl's Court, the first time I had ever been on my own. I was in no danger, I was leading a glamorous life and I loved it.

At the end of the week I returned home with the £80 I had earned for one week doing something I enjoyed. Three pounds a week in the china department was now a distinctly unattractive prospect. I suggested to my parents that I should go back to London and try my luck. They were horrified.

I was sixteen, and legally nobody could stop me. I made my plans, gave in my notice, sold the sewing machine which had been last year's Christmas present and packed my bags.

Two people were taken into my confidence. My young brother, who did not believe I would dare, and a current boyfriend. An earnest young man. We had been to the pub for a Sunday evening drink when I broke it to him that this was also goodbye. He was so shocked that I immediately regretted telling him. He left me at the house and ten minutes later he was back, white faced, a reckless look about him. 'There's something I have to say to your father,' he said. Oh no, he was about to tell all. Daddy asked him in and I gave him a withering look. He stood there, stammering painfully. 'What is it?' asked father.

'Oh – just something about the car,' he said. To my intense relief, he had lost his nerve.

After my parents had left for work on Monday morning, and my brother had gone to school, I took my suitacse from its hiding place in the wardrobe and headed for the station. People in Birmingham talked as if London was the other end of the world. I knew it was only two hours away. If it did not work out, I could always come back.

I said no goodbyes, except to Laddie.

4

THE journey was passed in contemplation of adventures yet to come, which, in the event, turned out to exceed even my wildest expectations. I was a girl from the provinces braving the big city and I thrilled to this challenge. The world, even then, did not strike me as a terribly daunting place; I was a traveller setting off in search of an adventure. I have remained so all my life – jet-hopping to the world's sun spots. I have never been a tourist in search of a sun tan.

Confident that I should find modelling work at once, I had left the standard note telling my parents not to worry about me. Included in my ambitious plans for the future was the deep desire to even the score with Robin. He was the spur. After the night he left me in the woods to walk home, I had heard nothing from him, and in my schemes for the future I envisaged inviting him to dinner at my smart bachelor-girl apartment, being totally captivating, making him fall madly in love with me. In a schoolgirl way I was in love with him, but I also had the sense to know that distance is the best cure for heartache. Going into something new creates fresh thoughts and pushes the others into the back of your mind. Put an ocean between you and your heart: good advice for the lovesick.

I lunched on the train. To guard the money and make do with a sandwich would have been the sensible course, but I prefer to live for the moment, and treating myself to a British Rail lunch indicated that I was not worried about the future. Arriving at Paddington, the first thing was to buy the *Evening Standard* and turn to the Sits. Vac. column. Immediately one advertisement seemed to leap from the page. 'Dancers Wanted. Murray's. 4pm audition.'

The name was familiar and I remembered that one of the models who had worked with me at the Motor Show said she also worked as a dancer at Murray's.

It was now three o'clock. I took a taxi to the club, then walked round the corner into Regent Street to kill time until the audition. On impulse I went into a small leather goods shop and bought myself a purse, red leather packed in a box with tissue wrapping. I decided it was my good luck gift to myself. Then I presented myself at Murray's.

I had never seen the inside of a nightclub, unless you count the old Hollywood movies I'd seen on TV. Murray's at night was a place suffused in a potent glow, intimate, rich, glamorous. At four o'clock in the afternoon with the tables stripped bare and the harsh electric spotlights switched on for cleaning, revealing the tattiness of the flocked wallpaper, the only lush features were the numerous huge potted palms and decorative ferns like some succulent jungle. In fact, they served a practical purpose, as dumping ground for the champagne cup which was the obligatory drink for hostesses. The combination of daylight starvation and a liquid diet of champagne and fruit juice proved as unhealthy for the plants as it did for the girls, and their turnover was rapid.

Some thirty would-be's gathered. Seated at a table was a fat, balding man, bespectacled, brisk. His voice impressed me. Clipped, well educated. This was the owner, Percy Murray, who, after the most perfunctory glance, asked, Could I dance? I had in fact started to take ballet classes before my broken leg intervened, so I felt no hesitation in answering yes. 'Let's see what you can do,' he said. I was led backstage by Noelle, the head girl, who in appearance and manner was more like a prefect than a nightclub queen. I was given a skimpy leotard to put on and, lining up with the other hopefuls, filed back on stage.

The reason he had asked whether I could dance was because there existed a distinction between dancers and showgirls. Show girls were taller and appeared topless on stage. Dancers remained covered up and were expected to master a dance routine. The simplicity of the steps we now copied was reassuring. The real object of the exercise was to see how we looked on stage.

Percy Murray was a man of specific tastes in women. His ideal girl had to be tall and thin. So flat-chested as to look boyish. undressed. Tits were vulgar. He abhorred vulgarity.

He liked his girls to look as if they could sit down to tea and cucumber sandwiches with the vicar and feel quite at ease. Happily I was as thin as a rake at that time and so devoid of bosom that even my nipples were invisible! I used very little make-up, and my hair, naturally a light blonde, was recently dyed a dark colour and worn short and curled under with a fringe and two kisscurls on my cheeks. By a happy coincidence I bore a strong resemblance to head girl Noelle, which was a bonus as it meant I could understudy for her. Possibly this tipped the balance in my favour as I was one of only two successful applicants. As the tired pianist closed the lid of the piano and lurched off, I was informed I had the job.

'How old are you?' Mr Murray asked me. I knew the age limit was eighteen.

'Eighteen,' I lied blithely.

He gave me an odd look. 'Of course, I'll need a letter from your parents.'

Later, he told me that he had had his suspicions about my age, and about the neatly forged parental consent I subsequently delivered. During my brief career at Murray's, he kept a watchful eye on me.

He told me I should be paid £25 a week, there were two shows a night, I would start work the next day. Did I have somewhere to stay? I replied that I'd just arrived off the train.

'I'll put you in the Strand Palace for ten days until you find accommodation,' he said.

They sent me by taxi to the Strand Palace Hotel where I was greatly impressed by the red carpet and the chandeliers. Not bad for my first night, I decided.

I unpacked the ancient leather suitcase that had belonged to my grandfather and spread my possessions around the room: a wool dress, two skirts and shirts, three pairs of shoes and a cocktail dress I had bought during the Motor Show week. *Pegasus*, my school anthology of verse, my leather-bound copy of *The Canterbury Tales*, went on the bedside table together with the notebook I had started to keep in which I recorded my Inner Thoughts. The entry for that night was purely self-congratulatory: 'One day in London and already I have a good job and a room in a smart hotel.' I posted a card home saying all was well: 'I have a job. I'll write soon.'

Before going to bed that evening, I returned to Murray's to meet the girls and be fitted for a costume. I was an Indian, with feathered headband, short leather skirt and top, beads and ankle bracelets. Officially I was Noelle's understudy, but within a day of my arrival she was indisposed, and relinquished her starring rôle to me. I can see why. Covered in brown body make-up, I wiggled around the stage and sang, 'She was a big chief of the Navajo tribe, a Redskin girl with fire in her eyes. Boom, Boom, Boom!'

They sent me off to buy false eyelashes and make-up from a chemist next door to Leicester Square underground station. Noelle had suggested a lichen-green eyeshadow; I went one better and bought a black china screwtop jar of Leichner eyeshadow in virulent emerald green. Even the smell was exciting.

I shared a dressing-room with an Italian girl called Martella whose upper-class vowels would occasionally lapse into pure Italian cockney. She helped me apply the lashes, but I needed no help with the make-up. Piling it on was like painting a canvas. We looked like parrots with our brilliant colours, our mouths layered with lip gloss. I was delighted with the result and strutted on stage without a tremor of nerves. Martella's hoarse whisper from the wings almost threw me into hysterics. 'Lick your lips and look sexy!'

Percy Murray was a respectable businessman whose proud boast was that Murray's catered to the upper crust, and most of the 'crowned and uncrowned heads' of Europe had passed through his portals. He referred in reverent tones to the occasions during the war when Winston Churchill had graced Murray's; and certainly during my time there, I saw more titled than untitled clients. The only actual king was Hussein of Jordan, a regular nightly visitor.

As far as we girls were concerned, the place was run like a strict boarding school. Along with the letter of employment we were handed a list of rules, and you stuck to the rules or paid a fine. Unpunctuality, chipped nail polish and ungroomed hair all warranted a fine, deducted from your weekly pay. Noelle checked us all to see that we arrived on time, like a prefect calling the register, and inspected us when we were ready to go on stage. Class distinction divided the lowest order – the hostesses who did not dance – from the middle order – the showgirls – and the top order – the dancers. Showgirls and dancers were allowed – encouraged would be too strong a word – to sit with customers between shows, and for this they earned commission on drinks consumed. They were only permitted to order champagne or champagne cup – a fruit juice and champagne mixture, which was then poured into the potted plants.

Each order earned a £5 commission, and the client invariably added a tip when he paid his bill; but, quite apart from the financial considerations, sitting with the customers was infinitely preferable to sitting backstage in our little rabbit warren. We were all young and easily bored and the two hours between shows in claustrophobic surroundings were the longest two hours of the day.

There was never any hint of impropriety. Percy Murray and his eagle-eyed son could sniff out any hint of a blossoming liaison and stamped it out, fast. Clients at Murray's did not come in looking for a girl to take to bed because Murray's was not that sort of club. It would be like a middle-aged man going down to his local tennis club and making a pass at another member's daughter – everyone knew everyone else. Percy Murray knew that if one of the members got involved with a girl it could cause complications. A lovers' tiff could lose the club a good client, in the same way as an affair between a girl and a waiter. By forbidding romance he was protecting his investment.

A man who asked for a hostess did so because he wanted someone to talk to and invariably it was the same subject of conversation – the wife and children. Out would come the family snapshots. An alternative theme was the job – the problems of the firm, the pressures of business. At the end of the evening the girls would compare notes and add up how many wife stories and how many job stories they had listened to that evening.

Surreptitiously we developed friendships, and broke the rules. There were lunch dates. I heard of after-closing jaunts with King Hussein, who would apparently collect a car full of girls and drive down to Brighton, siren going hell for leather all the way there and back. But it was always made clear to girls and members alike, and we knew the penalties, that sex was out, and if Percy Murray found out about it, it meant the end to membership and to job.

Within a week I felt established. The newspapers always carried columns of flats and bed-sits to let and I found accommodation in a large house in Eaton Avenue, Swiss Cottage. The owner lived on the ground floor and let out the rest of the house as bedsitting rooms. Mine was the most grandiose of them all, it was the first floor ballroom. The furniture was not luxurious or even smart, but the proportions of the room made up for any deficiency, and surpassing all this was the bathroom: a huge room in white marble with the biggest bath I had ever seen – or have ever seen since.

The house contained a library of French classics and this was better than a feast to me. Maupassant, Balzac, Zola became my constant companions. Unsettling, disturbing, inspiring me to dream of intense passions and relationships. Nothing in life has ever quite measured up.

My rent was £9 a week, I had plenty in hand for my initial nest egg and with my first week's wages I went on a small spending spree. From a shop I had earmarked as the last word in chic, Bazaar in Knightsbridge, owned by Mary Quant, I bought a pair of green velvet trousers. From Anello and Davide, where the girls bought their stage shoes, I chose a pair of high black-leather boots. A set of ballet-practice clothes, some records to dance to and I felt deliciously *au fait* with my new rôle as independent girl about town.

I had been at Murray's several weeks when I noticed a girl I had not seen before. Remarkably beautiful with blonde hair, slim but large breasted, the most mesmerising thing about her was the profile. Another girl introduced us. 'Marilyn, this is Christine Keeler.' It was dislike at first sight.

The other girls had gone out of their way to help me settle down, but Christine was always ready with a bitchy remark. She had worked at Murray's on and off for over a year. When finances were high, she was off doing something else. When she ran out of money she would come back to work. They put up with it because, as I was later to learn first hand, everybody put up with Christine.

As much as I disliked her, I had to admit she was astonishingly beautiful. She had the face of Nefertiti – months later I showed her a photograph of Queen Nefertiti's mask, and we compared nose, lips, brow. The similarity was uncanny.

Initially, she used another dressing-room, yet I was aware that many of her most bitchy remarks were directed at me. Once, as I was about to go on stage, I realised I had mislaid the top half of my Red Indian costume. I was going frantic. I am meticulously tidy and I knew I could not have lost it. Muffled giggles coming from Christine and her little set indicated the culprit. Hastily the costume lady improvised with a few strips of leather and I went on.

She went too far, however, the day she made a nasty comment about my green eyeshadow just as I was about to go on stage. Inwardly fuming as I flashed my glossy-lipped smile at the audience, I resolved to retaliate. I waited until just before she was due to go on. Each dressing-room had a ceiling fan. I took a handful of talcum powder, ran into her room and threw the powder at the fan. Sitting at her dressing-table putting the finishing touches to her make-up, she was suddenly coated with ghostly white powder. Her jaw dropped open in amazement and she burst out laughing. From that moment we were friends. Two days later she had fixed me up on my first blind date.

Christine had recently fallen in love with a wealthy Jordanian student, studying at the London School of Economics. There was to be a party at his London house and she asked if I would like to go along. I thanked her for the invitation and made a note of the address. It was Sunday, my day off, and I was pleased to have somewhere to go. The house was an elegant London mansion, and thirty guests, all Arab, were lunching there. Christine's boyfriend, Herman, had a close friend called Aziz and it was he who attached himself to me for the day. When we parted, he said he would come to the club the following evening.

Sure enough the request came, via Percy Murray, for me to join the table. I had never been permitted 'out front' before. Mr Murray was suspicious of my age, but when this request came he knocked on my dressing-room door and asked if I would like to join the two young gentlemen. Acting as if I could not care less, I allowed myself to give a good impression of thinking it over and deciding I might as well and, changing from costume into a dress, I went into the club. The champagne cup flowed, Aziz was polite and attentive, very good-looking and extremely rich. What more could I want? And he was obviously impressed with me. This was infinitely better than waiting backstage. Christine and I arranged to meet them after the second show, thus breaking one of the Percy Murray commandments, and as soon as we had creamed off our make-up and changed, we crept off to where their car was waiting.

In those days the place to go after the clubs closed was Queensway, where the coffee stalls were the meeting place of London's night people. Debs and their escorts coming back from parties in evening clothes, the usual insomniacs, prostitutes taking a breather, all would congregate and chat like long-standing friends, eating hot dogs and drinking coffee. It was another club.

Dawn was breaking when they drove me home to Swiss Cottage. They had wanted us to go home with them, but I had declined. Neither did I want to invite them into my flat, in case the landlady did not approve. Christine asked if she could stay the night with me.

'Why not?' I said. It was cosy having her sleep there that night. I realised that, for all my independence, I had found it lonely living alone.

Having established that I could now sit out with the customers, life became a great deal more interesting. I am a good listener and most people have at least one subject on which to wax enthusiastic and knowledgeable. Murray's clients were all successful and I acquired enough of a working knowledge of stocks and shares, the commodity market, property, income tax, motor cars and golf, to ask the right question in the right place.

One evening a waiter handed me a note written by Walter Flack, inviting me to meet him the following day for lunch. He looked presentable and the girls told me he was a millionaire property speculator. I agreed.

He was waiting for me in the bar at Overton's. Had I ever eaten caviar? he wanted to know. Of course I had not, so that was what he ordered. He was terribly amused when I ate the chopped egg and onion and left the caviar – I grew to like it after that. It was the start of a friendship which meant many delicious lunches in London's best restaurants. He was a kind man, though very sad. His life seemed rather empty, the only time he sparkled with life was when he described his early struggles to make money. Often after lunching together we would go shopping, usually at Harrods, where he haunted the food hall. Invariably there was a gift for me, chocolates or perfume. One day we found ourselves in the pet department watching the playful antics of a litter of chihuahuas. I have never cared for small dogs, but Walter insisted I must have one and promptly bought me, at an exorbitant price, a black and white chihuahua. He insisted that I take it everywhere with me until, in the end, I became quite devoted to it.

His favourite topic of conversation was money and his various business deals. From him I learned always to check bills, never to dip into savings or sell something in order to finance day-to-day living. At times I have been really short of cash and I have scraped by on a pittance sooner than cash in shares or securities. He also taught me never to fold my table napkin at the end of the meal.

To be wined and dined so persistently by a middle-aged millionaire was surely, I thought, leading up to one thing. I waited for him to make the move, but it never came. Gradually I realised that it was important for him to be seen with a pretty girl, that he enjoyed my company but had no desire to take me to bed.

I have always liked older men. As I get older, the age gap is narrowing but I was always attracted to older men for their wisdom and experience. I ask a lot of questions. Most of my best friends have been men, and I have proved that you do not need to be madly in love to have a good relationship. Twice in my life I have experienced what the French call *coup de foudre* (lightning) and both men I married, but I don't kid myself that *coup de foudre* is necessarily a better base for marriage than friendship and respect.

One night after the first show, Percy Murray came back stage to ask me if I would meet 'one of our oldest clients', the Earl of Dudley. We chatted pleasantly for a few minutes and then as I rose to leave, the Earl asked for my address. 'I'd like to send you some flowers.'

Next morning I was summoned out of bed to answer the door to the delivery man from Fortnum and Mason. There was Eric's gift, a vast bouquet of flowers and a case of pink champagne. Shortly afterwards there was a knock at the door.

'I hope you don't mind,' he said. 'I've come to drink champagne with you.'

Of course I invited him in. 'There is nothing like sending yourself champagne, is there?' he giggled as he uncorked the first of several.

Over the ensuing week I grew very fond of him. A large, well-built man in his mid sixties, he could be amusing company and a fund of fascinating information. He had an answer for anything I cared to ask - details of nineteenth-century history, how I should address the Queen should I happen to meet her, gossip about the aristocrasy.

He would sometimes lapse into moods of deep depression which I assumed were caused by his money worries, since he was always complaining about money, and I assumed he was quite hard up. For a start there was the decrepit old Jaguar he drove, our lunches and dinners were invariably in musty old clubs - surely, if he could afford it, he would prefer the Mirabelle or the Savoy? - and I could see he had only one suit and tie to his name. (In fact one of his eccentricities, as I later discovered, was to order a dozen identical suits so that he appeared, with that and his old regimental tie, to be wearing the same clothes all the time.)

He blamed his impecuniousness on his son, Viscount Ednam, and told me that to escape death duties he had made over all his money to him.

It was easy to feel sorry for Eric, who seemed such a lost soul, though had I known it at the time I had no reason to pity him his poverty. He was actually (despite having handed over the estate) still one of the richest men in England.

There were no sexual overtures, merely an affectionate kiss on the cheek, a pat on the hand. Nevertheless, he finally confessed he was in love with me and asked me to marry him.

I told him I would think it over. 'You would have to discuss this with my father, of course,' I said, and could not help giggling at the thought of Lord Dudley sitting down across the table from Daddy requesting my hand in marriage. Eric seemed to think that was quite reasonable. I rather liked the idea of marrying a lord. Although I did not expect to be rich out of it, I could see myself in widowhood as the thirty-year-old dowager countess and it appealed to my sense of the dramatic.

Along with Eric and Walter Flack I had a third gentleman friend. Once again it was lunches only (did all this food explain my developing breasts, this new curviness that was replacing the original boney frame?). Once again he was a middle-aged millionaire. His name was Robert Sherwood. He asked one thing of me - that I pack my bags and go home to Solihull. 'This is no life for you. Go back before it's too late,' he said. I ignored his advice.

The romance with Aziz was warming up. He usually spent the evening in the club then, after the second show, we would take off into the small hours. Although he was studying, he was not about to spend his evenings doing homework and going to bed early. Most of his friends were wealthy Arabs, and with their Harrow and Sandhurst accents were not unlike the British aristrocrats of their own generation although, in the main, Aziz and his friends had ritzier apartments and flashier cars. There were endless parties. At one I smelt hashish for the first time.

'What's that funny smell?' I asked our host, a famous pop star who was passing this fragrant cigarette around.

'It's something we have to take for our asthma,' he said. That struck me as a logical explanation. Afterwards when I smelt the familiar smell I assumed there was an asthma sufferer in the room, a belief that lasted for some months.

Aziz was four years older than I, but unworldly and naïve, particularly regarding sex. A strict Moslem who took out his mat and prayed four times a day, it was unthinkable for him to have sex outside marriage. Alcohol, too, was forbidden, although by now he had crossed that bridge.

I had a healthy interest in sex, fanned by my observation of Christine who quite patently found the whole thing infinite fun. With Aziz there was a fair amount of kissing and cuddling but we never progressed any further, and I realised neither would we unless we could actually get to the stage of taking our clothes off. When the opportunity came, it was late at night after a party, Christine said she did not want to go home and disappeared into Herman's bedroom. Taking the initiative I informed Aziz that I too would stay the night, and I would share his bed. He did not protest.

Naked, and with the lights off, his scruples were overcome but, infuriatingly, I was disappointed. Sex, the idea, was exciting; but sex, the act, left much to be desired. Judging by Christine's enthusiasm, I was missing out on something, but what? This new development in our relationship was obviously a delight to Aziz but unfortunately had the effect of exposing his least attractive trait, his possessiveness. The more jealous he became, the more boring he seemed.

I suspect I am not particularly sexy, certainly not in the sense of being promiscuous. Until recently I was sexually rather naïve, probably because all the men I have been involved with were so intensely jealous that in their company I was never permitted to take part in a conversation that bordered remotely on the sensual or sexual. Men who didn't know me made jokes about me, but men who knew me found they took quite a long time getting me into bed.

Every man's sexual fantasy – it's a curious rôle to play in life. I meet men who were schoolboys when my picture was front page news and they greet me as a figment of an erotic dream. There is nothing I can do about this, it has nothing to do with the real me. That Mandy is a pert blonde who is all things to all men. Perhaps that is her secret — she never disappoints.

I remember an evening spent with a famous singer after I had become 'notorious'. Because we were singing on the same North of England club circuit we met often and liked each other.

One evening we found ourselves alone in our hotel. And he said, 'Would you like to come upstairs?'

'OK, let's have a drink.'

We went up to his room. He looked at me and said, 'I know everybody in the country thinks I'm a huge sex symbol but I don't think I'm very good in bed.'

I looked at him and said, 'I know everybody in this country thinks *I'm* a big sex symbol but I don't think I'm very good in bed, either.'

'Really,' he said. 'Would you like to make love?'

I said 'No, I don't think so.'

He said, 'Neither do I.'

So we sat all evening reciting poetry to each other.

I went home for Christmas. Dressed to kill, armed with gifts including a bottle of sherry and a *Panettore*, the Italian Christmas cake of dry sponge, sultanas, citrus peel and sugar topping. For my sister I took a gold and turquoise necklace. Her marriage had broken up and she and her daughter had moved back home with my parents. I wanted to surprise them. My mother opened the door and burst into tears. Nothing had changed (even my room was exactly as I had left it) except that my parents looked so much older. It seemed years rather than weeks since I had left.

If I had expected Robin to be waiting on the doorstep, I was disappointed. That there was no move from his direction strengthened my resolution to score.

There was a party at a friend's house and I felt terribly superior to them all. I had gone to London, I had a job, a flat of my own (well, bed-sitter really), as much money as I needed, was wined and dined at all the best places, an earl had proposed marriage. Not bad at sixteen. . . .

I am embarrassed at the memory of how much I showed off.

5

VELVET preceded Mandy as my new name. Determined on a modelling career, I wasted no time in finding myself an agent. Another dancer at Murray's recommended her agent, a benevolent man and a pioneer in the business called Pat Glover. Working in clubs was a logical job for aspiring models, since it left the days free and provided a steady income while one waited for the modelling fees to come in – it was not unusual to wait six months to be paid for a modelling assignment.

Pat Glover despatched me to a fashion photographer for the required composite. I had the right measurements for fashion modelling (in those days perfect legs were defined by the capacity to grip four pennies between crutch, knee, calf and ankle) and, despite an overlarge nose, I am photogenic from most angles. Many photographers were later to give me advice about my nose, like having the nostrils reduced by plastic surgery, but I could never quite bring myself to take the step.

My agent was confident I was ideal model material, and began booking me for fashion catalogue work immediately. But Marilyn. . . . He did not care for the name, said it was too old for me. I decided on Velvet, with all its romantic schoolgirly connotations from *National Velvet*, the film that established Elizabeth Taylor as a star. And I still had one foot in the stable. . . . This lasted for two weeks until, sitting in the coffee bar opposite his office in Welbeck Street, Pat Glover admitted he thought Velvet even worse than Marilyn. We ran through a list of likely names, from Patsy, Jo, Vicky to the more upper-class Elizabeth, Victoria, Anne, and then, still film-minded, the name of a new child star flashed into my mind. Mandy Miller.

'Mandy,' I announced triumphantly, to Pat's approval. My new identity was agreed.

One day Pat sent me along to audition for a Pepsodent

toothpaste commercial. 'You need a good smile, and be able to swim and skate.' I had never skated in my life. Not only could I not swim but my school swimming lessons at the local baths had instilled a pathologicl fear of the water. Nevertheless, I could smile very nicely, so I went along to the audition with cheerful optimism – along with what seemed to be hundreds of other toothily smiling girls.

I was the only one wearing a large and flamboyant hat, a detail which must have got me noticed. When it came to my turn, the producer, an American called Cy Enfield, asked me whether I could swim and skate.

'Sure,' I said, flashing my dazzling smile. I could see he was impressed with my teeth.

'And what about your legs?' he said. 'Do you have good legs?'

'I can certainly hold four pennies,' I replied.

He laughed at that and said, 'We'll let you know.' As I left the room, however, he took me to one side and said, 'Don't worry, I think you've got it.'

And I had. The rate for commercials was £20 a day, a small fortune at that time (even the briefest commercial would be stretched to take four days' shooting), plus repeat fees.

The date fixed for the actual shoot was some time ahead and it was my intention to be swimming and skating expertly by then. A session at the Porchester Baths rapidly disillusioned me. If I were going to drown, why do it now, why not at least have a try at the commercial. With luck the cameras would concentrate on the shallow end and I could keep one foot on the ground.

Skating was another matter. I tested the ice at Queen's Ice Rink but could barely stand up, let alone skate. Nobody learns to skate well in a few weeks, especially someone who has absolutely no aptitude for it. I gambled this way – if I can survive the swimming scene I can talk my way through the next hurdle. If I don't survive the swimming scene, I won't be expected to skate.

On a freezing day in March, we assembled at Skindles, a smart country club in Maidenhead. A line-up of girls in bathing suits, an outdoor pool and a biting north wind. As we stepped out of our wraps to take our places by the pool, I saw to my horror that the cameras were positioned at the deep end.

'Now girls,' said the director, 'It's simple. You get into the pool, hold on to the bar and when I saw the word, you give a big smile and push away backwards.' This was even worse than I had dreaded.

'Action!'

I flashed a smile at the camera, and lurched backwards curving up and over and down, and down and down. Panicky, breathless, completely disoriented, I was hauled from the water by a camera operator who was just about ready to jump in and save me. I had in fact actually swum a few strokes, but they were not taking any chances.

'Sorry, Cy,' I gulped through mouthfuls of water, 'to tell you the truth I can't swim very well.'

'Don't worry, we've a great shot of your backward leap. Dry your hair.'

My make-up was redone, and I was recast, walking along the edge of the pool hand in hand with actor John Prebble, but I realised I had to confess before the skating session began in Brighton.

'I have to tell you, Cy, I can't skate.'

Momentarily he was thrown, but immediately he reassured me. 'Never mind. I'll think of something.'

The script called for us to skate forward in a line, do a downward twist then come up with a big smile – except that I didn't skate. His solution worked perfectly. The camera was positioned on the ice machine, the ice machine towed a thin piece of board and I stood on the board, flanked on either side by a line-up of genuine skaters. When the camera zoomed down for a close-up of the twirling feet, they were somebody else's feet. When the camera zoomed up for a close-up it was my very own wide, teeth-gleaming smile.

It was a stunning commercial. For a long time people were stopping me and saying, 'Had no idea you could skate so well.' My parents were thrilled, the neighbours were so impressed.

6

CHRISTINE Keeler was nineteen and had left home, a converted railway carriage near the gravel pits at Wraysbury, Middlesex, three years earlier. I recognised in her a kindred instinct to live for the moment, and to this end she drifted about London, going to parties, staying with friends, moving in with someone for a few weeks now and again.

She had planted the rumour that she was dying of leukaemia, which was given as an explanation for her pale skin, whereas, in fact, without the ivory pancake make-up, her cheeks were ruddy and healthy. Her subsequent recurring 'attacks' of leukaemia were used as an alibi for her gypsy behaviour. Most of the girls at Murray's would say they had been away for an abortion if they wanted three days off, but Christine would cite her 'illness' instead. (When I first started work at Murray's, I was astonished at how frequently the girls seemed to require the services of an abortionist. It struck me as a most hazardous way of life until I realised it was the ultimate in ask-no-questions excuses.)

It is difficult to equate the public image of Christine, as the hard bitten go-getter, with the Christine I knew. She was shy and quiet, domesticated in that she liked to cook and play house, at the same time sweet and amusing company. She had a good sense of humour, not particularly witty because she was never sharp in that way, but light, easy company.

She had not enjoyed a happy childhood, but there was no bitterness about her. She flipped through life, a day, a night at a time, not bothering about what would follow. Had she been an intellectual, you would have said she led a bohemian existence. She had the way of a waif, infuriating yet always making you feel you must help her. Disorganised to the point of helplessness, she attracted people who were the opposite, who felt they could sort out her practical problems and lift her out of her day-to-day chaos. She was an undemanding friend, happiest with people who made no demands on her. I enjoyed her company and learned never to rely on her for anything.

She liked men and had an unerring eye for what women understand as an absolute bastard. We used to joke that Christine would walk into a room with twenty eligible bachelors and make a beeline for the one out-and-out rotter. She fell in love frequently, passionately and unreservedly. She left herself wide open to being treated badly because she did nothing to protect herself. Often her intensity actually scared the man off after a brief fling and Christine would be left lovesick and forlorn and asking where had she gone wrong. But not for long, and then somebody else was on the scene. At one extreme she was impressed by older, successful men, at the other she had an unhealthy penchant for the flotsam of the *demi monde*. It was her predilection for West Indians which had led to her introduction to soft drugs. She had a healthy sex drive and assumed that there was but one logical conclusion to sexual attraction.

Although my own experience, when we first met, in no way matched hers, I never questioned her way of life. In the society in which we moved, people did not question each other's behaviour. She had many men friends, some with whom she had once had an affair and many others who were platonic friends. Men were madly attracted to Christine, and remained close to her long after the passionate interlude, had it taken place, was over.

Her first-ever boyfriend, a young man from her home town, was an occasional visitor and could be guaranteed to help with effort or money any time his services were required. She had, too, an ex-fiancé, rich young publisher, ex-Guards' officer Michael Lambton. Splendidly handsome, he was at his best standing rigidly to attention in the front of the stalls while they played 'God Save the Queen'. Admittedly he seemed to have a drinks problem ('Pass the pottie, dear,' he would say to his passenger after a boozy session, and one would lean over for the baby's pot kept in the back seat of the Bentley like an aircraft sick bag), but he was a sweet and generous man. Their actual romance had cooled, she said, because of his drinking; but in difficult times, like the end of a romance, Christine went back to Michael, who welcomed her with open arms. 'Running home to Daddy,' we called it.

Money had no meaning for Christine. When we shared a flat I would be panicking one week before the rent was due that I had no money, whilst Christine would be totally unconcerned. During one attempt to organise her life, I introduced her to Pat Glover, who was impressed and immediately booked her for work; but after she had turned up for only two out of a string of assignments, he took her off the books. Whatever the urgency of the situation – even with me rampaging round the flat in my determination to be punctual – Christine could sleep in without a twinge of conscience.

When we set up home together later, she brought with her her collection of comics which were her favourite reading matter and would lie in bed for hours with the *Beano* and *Dandy*. She also had a baby's feeding bottle. I, too, bought one, and on quiet evenings we filled our baby bottles with orange juice and sucked and read simultaneously, curled up in our beds.

Her lack of interest in money extended to clothes. Her wardrobe was a haphazard assortment, blended by her extraordinary good looks. Fastidiously clean – she bathed twice a day – she had an unfortunate knack of looking tatty. Having dressed with care for our lunch dates (our housekeeping budget was based on never having to buy lunch for ourselves and organising a full diary of lunch dates was paramount), by the time the taxi had deposited us at the Savoy or the Mirabelle, Christine looked as if she had done a morning's work, with scuffed shoes and invariably a run in her stockings. This puzzled me. I studied her minutely to find the reason for this but remained baffled.

Meanwhile, I parted from Aziz and the Earl of Dudley. The two events coincided.

As Eric's fondness for me persisted so did his marriage proposals. He would plot how this was to be carried out.

'If they get to hear of it,' he said, referring to his son and daughter-in-law, 'they'll have me put away.'

I did not need to believe him to enjoy the melodrama. In fact, there was a half truth, his family were aware of his infatuation with a sixteen-year-old nobody and were, quite understandably, concerned.

One Sunday evening he telephoned. I could tell from his voice he was in a state of excitement. He invited me to dinner.

'I am going to introduce you to some very exciting people,' he said. Just as I was responding to the invitation he added: 'But please don't wear your green eyeshadow, and don't spike your lashes. In fact,' he added, 'don't wear any make-up at all.'

I resented the implied criticism of my appearance, and said that in that case I would prefer not to go at all. Hastily he capitulated, and through his mumblings I realised these had to be important people for him to be so keyed up. I allowed myself to be mollified and said I would join them after dinner. I was slightly worried that perhaps I was being invited to an orgy, one heard about such things, but in Eric's case it hardly seemed appropriate. As a concession I left off my green eye-shadow but did spike (his old-world expression for mascara) my lashes.

I found Eric sitting in the drawing-room of his flat in Dudley Mansions, with an elegant elderly woman. Somehow in my nervousness I missed the introduction, and had no idea who she was except the feeling that I was in august company. She was chatty and friendly, I for once completely gauche and tongue-tied. I even spilled my drink.

What a pity I'd missed 'him', the conversation ran, the 'him' referred to being her husband, who had felt tired and gone to bed immediately after dinner. Tomorrow was to be an important day for them, they were to visit the Queen, and after that spend a few days at Eric's house in the country.

After an hour of polite conversation, Eric drove me home. 'So who is she?' I asked.

'My dear, you have spent the evening with the Duchess of Windsor.'

And to think had it not been for my obstinacy I could have dined with the former King of England.

Aziz, having discovered sex, was now insanely possessive and whenever we were in the same company I could feel his soulful eyes staring at me. At a party one evening where I was deep in conversation with a handsome young Arab prince, Aziz's jealousy boiled over; to interrupt our conversation he burned my arm with his cigarette. I let him know, in no uncertain terms, that as far as I was concerned we were finished. He continued trying to contact me and one evening came into the club to talk things over. Wishing to avoid a scene, I sat down at his table at which point Eric came in, also looking for me, with a woman friend to whom he was anxious to introduce me.

Aziz was not prepared to share my company and made it plain. Eric, at his most aristocratic, drew himself up to his full height and advised Aziz to leave immediately. I too stood up to intervene and, during a ludicrous scuffle, ended up with the contents of the champagne bucket over my head. As if summoned by magic, the club's two heavies appeared and, possibly on the basis of selecting the biggest, picked up Eric and removed him bodily into the street. His stupefied woman guest hastened out after him.

That was my farewell to Aziz.

Later, at home, a chastened and disappointed Eric telephoned me. His friend, he said, was Princess Radziwill. Not only had he wished to introduce us to each other, but he wanted to decide between us – the lucky lady was to be the new Countess, a honeymoon cruise had been planned.

That was my farewell to Eric. He left England two days later, and he married his princess.

Christine's occasional stop-overs with me at Swiss Cottage were strictly unofficial and involved sneaking up the stairs and hoping the landlady did not hear, so, before long, we agreed to find something larger to share. I scouted around and with no trouble at all found a two-bedroomed flat in Fulham at £12 a week.

By this time I was pleading all sorts of excuses for not turning up at Murray's every night. I was busy modelling and when evening came a date was more attractive than working, so I had fallen into the routine set by so many others. However, on the night of our move both Christine and I had been at the club and had agreed to move house as soon as we arrived home – at 3am. For some reason, possibly Christine's idea of something exciting to do and certainly I fell in with it, we planned a moonlight flit. Michael Lambton met us at the club, drove us to Eaton Avenue and waited.

'I'll keep the engine running,' he whispered.

We managed to stifle our giggles as we hastened upstairs, grabbed our belongings and loaded with suitcases, plastic bags and boxes, tiptoed down again. True enough Michael had kept the engine running – and he had draped handkerchiefs over the number plates to disguise the getaway car. We collapsed into the old Bentley with roars of laughter.

The following evening we threw our housewarming party. Catering was simple – a few packets of peanuts, a bottle of whisky and a bottle of sherry. I had left the guest list to Christine, and predictably there were no girls on it. One man I had already met. He was a plump middle-aged property speculator who had been lunching in the Savoy two days previously at a nearby table and Christine had introduced us. His name was Peter Rachman; Christine had once had a brief affair with him. He brought a beautiful blonde girl called Sherry and I assumed, mistakenly, that she was his current girlfriend. Two men came together, long-standing friends of Christine. One, Tim Vigors, a fascinating good-looking man, full of life and humour, a former pilot who bore the scars of being shot up in the Battle of Britain; the other Stephen Ward, society osteopath, artist, a good conversationalist, quite charming. I did not like him, I suspected the charm was superficial, that beneath it he was cold.

It was a pleasant evening – all these people knew each other. There existed a sort of unspoken truce between Rachman and Ward, who had no liking for each other but maintained a polite relationship. Vigors was ebullient, more so that evening because he had just taken delivery of a splendid Lancia which was parked outside, alongside Peter's car, a navy blue Rolls-Royce convertible with white hood. It was in this we all drove off to dinner. When the bill came, it was Peter, peeling off the notes from a thick roll, who paid. Wealth impresses.

I was attracted too by his manner and by the fact that I knew he was attracted to me. He took my telephone number when he dropped me back at the flat and asked if he could call me. It was inevitable that within two days he had telephoned and invited me out to dinner. Almost the first thing Peter Rachman ever did for me was to give me the opportunity to settle my score with Robin.

My father gave Robin my Fulham number and he called me

to say he was thinking of coming to London for a few days and could he drop in. He arrived, handsome as ever, I gave him a drink and we chatted amiably. Christine joined us and I could see she was very taken with him. Pooch the chihuahua took an instant dislike to Robin and kept snapping at his feet. When Robin retaliated with a sharp kick, it made me feel better about what I had planned. Glancing at my watch I said: 'I'll have to be leaving in a few minutes, I'm going out to dinner.' Robin was quite astonished at this. But I played it very cool, saying how sorry I was I had not been able to cancel my date. Peter arrived and I hoped Robin would glance out of the window and see the navy blue Rolls.

I found myself fidgeting. It was one thing to sweep out leaving him frustrated. Quite another to leave him to spend the evening with Christine. Happily Tim Vigors chose that moment to drop in for a chat and Robin took his leave. He got his bags together and as he went down the stairs I felt a pang of pity for him, and almost called him back. I still liked him, although I no longer felt anything more than that. I resisted the urge and watched him go. Five minutes later I heard him calling me. I opened the window. There he stood on the pavement. 'Marilyn,' he said, 'can you lend me a fiver for a taxi?'

Five pounds in 1961 would pay for a taxi and a bed for the night. I threw him down a £5 note scrunched up in a ball. We both laughed.

'Tit for tat,' he shouted as he walked off up the street.

7

CONFIDENT of conquering London, we set our sights on going further afield, Christine and I, and as neither had ever been abroad, we decided to see France.

Having bought our tickets to Paris, it started to get very complicated. I had no passport. In total ignorance I'd imagined you simply collected it at the Customs. Fortunately, I was informed before we set out that this was not the case. Now I needed a passport in twenty-four hours. I told the official at the Passport Office that my beloved auntie was dying in Paris and I must hurry if I was to see her before the end. As I was under twenty-one he required permission from my father – that was easy, I was well-practised in forging Daddy's signature.

There was a £20 limit on cash taken out of the country, and travellers' cheques had to be ordered well in advance. Which was how we came to set out for a holiday in France with only £40 in cash between us, but blithely believing all one needed to do was write a cheque on the other side.

Paris was how we expected it. Funny little houses, geranium pots on the balconies, clean hotel neither chic nor expensive, just ten francs a night between us. After four days we realised we were not going to have enough money to get to Cannes. What was even worse, when I went to the bank they told me it would take four days to get any money through. We didn't want to stay in Paris another four days, so decided to go to the South and wait there for the money, in the hotel and on the beach, where at least it would be sunny – Paris was bleak and wet.

How to get there? Walking around Notre-Dame, we noticed two very good-looking guys walking around as well.

'They're nice,' said Christine.

'Christine, we are in a church!' But I agreed with her.

Eavesdropping, we could tell they were Spanish. They were taking a lot of interest in us, stopping and waiting for us to catch up and we would walk on and they would walk after us, the usual sort of thing. Outside they came over and introduced themselves. One was titled, the other was a surgeon who had just finished his final exams and had given himself a trip to France as a present. They had a hired car and gave us a lift back to the hotel, asking would we like to go out that evening as they had booked a table at the Lido.

We were curious to see the Lido and keen for a good meal, so happily accepted. Meanwhile Christine's plan was we would acquire the keys to the hired car, and use it to drive to the South of France where we could dump it.

'After all,' she said, 'it is just a hired car, it isn't like stealing their car.'

It so happened that the one in charge of the car was the surgeon and he was the one interested in me – not that our preferences or theirs mattered because we were going to clear off. The only thing that mattered was that I had to get hold of the key somehow, and I wasn't very sure how I should go about it.

The car key – because it was rented – was attached to a big rubber ball, and he had put it in his back pocket. My only chance would be on the dance floor. Dinner was served first and then there was time for dancing before the show. I knew I had to get the keys before the show started because when the show ended we would all leave and it would be too late.

Dancing with him I was sliding my hands around him, twiddling with his hair, anything to distract his attention. At the same time I was letting my hands stray to his back pocket, but the rubber ball was wedged and I couldn't prise it out; while Christine was trying to manoeuvre the other one to cover up my movements at the back. At last I succeeded, managed to get the key and we went back to the table.

This called for the Loo Trick. Off to the ladies – out the back door. I couldn't drive at this time so it was then up to Christine. Outside we were in a mad panic, worried in case they came out, guilty at what we were doing, desperate to get back to our hotel and collect our things, fast. If they came and saw their car had disappeared it would not have taken them long to put two and two together, especially as the key was missing.

We got into the car and, of course, Christine could not start it. It was a left-hand drive. She put it into gear and then it jumped. As she struggled a policeman walked over. He asked if we had a problem. 'Oh yes,' we said. 'Big problem. Us English. Car no go.' By this time we were both hysterically nervous. He waited patiently, making soothing noises and giving advice and eventually Christine managed to start the car and, with the policeman holding up the traffic behind to let us out, we set off.

Having collected our luggage, we then had to find our way out of Paris. We had no map, we could not find anybody who knew where Cannes was (it was only a thousand kilometres down the auto-route), but eventually we came to signs for Autoroute du Sud and set off driving all night. We ran out of petrol but still had a few francs left; I also had some pound notes, which we thrust at the garage attendant and shot away while he was still puzzling over it. We didn't branch off after Avignon and eventually the fan belt broke and we came to a stop outside Montpelier. Still in all our finery from the night before, we stood at the side of the road hitching a lift. A lorry driver stopped. There was a half bottle of whisky in the glove compartment of the now abandoned car, which I gave him and he was well pleased. A hundred kilometres on, he left us at a roadside café. I was totally famished and Christine was desperate for a cigarette – I can sympathise today but then I could not understand such cravings. She chose to smoke rather than eat as the money could not stretch to both.

Another guy picked us up, a nice-looking man in a red sports car who waited until we were on a deserted stretch then pointed to the ring on Christine's finger, a ruby and diamond ring, and indicated that if she did not give it to him he would not take us the rest of the way up the mountain. Christine said, '*Non, non,*' so he booted us out of the car and drove off.

Fortunately a little chap came along in a Citroën. How we packed everything in I don't know, but he was going to Toulon and dropped us there on the edge of the town where it was easy to get a lift.

A young naval officer stopped to help. He asked where were

we going, and we told him Cannes, asking him the same question. He wasn't going anywhere in particular but he said he would give us a lift to Cannes. He asked where we were staying and I said the only hotel I had heard of, 'The Carlton, of course.'

By this time we had actually managed to change our clothes but were absolutely filthy. He dropped us at the Carlton and the doorman came to the door and took our luggage. I made a date to see our young officer the following night for dinner and he drove away. The doorman, meanwhile, had carried our baggage in and I had to dash after him and say, '*Non, non,*' and take our luggage back.

It was night, very dark, and we stumbled wearily about until we found a small hotel which seemed not too expensive, where we could at least catch up on our sleep. The next morning, on the beach was a bunch of English chaps, all very friendly and chatty, and among them was Nat Cohen, down there on film business. That evening he took us to the casino – strictly speaking we were under age but did not look it and, as we were with Nat Cohen, nobody queried it. He gave us chips to play with and I put mine on number sixteen for luck because it was my age. I could not stop winning all night. I came out with about 1,000 francs, which was enough to stake us for a few days.

By the time the money had dwindled and I was thinking I had better put my cheque into the bank, it was the start of the Easter Bank Holidays and it would take seven or even eight days to come through. This was worrying. We had hardly any money and Nat Cohen had left. We knew no one who could take us to dinner and we were existing all day on our breakfast of coffee and rolls; we were getting quite hungry. We thought about asking the hotel owner to lend us some money, as he had his eye on us when his wife was not around, but decided against that course of action. We were even debating whether to ask the British Consul to lend us some money, when, out of the blue, as we were sitting on the Promenade des Anglaises, who should come along but Robert Sherwood, the Canadian steel millionaire, whom I had met at Murray's. 'Hello, Mandy,' he said, 'how are you?' It seemed the most normal thing in the world to bump into each other like that. He was staying in Monte Carlo and had come into Cannes to have a flutter at the casino.

'Let's go and have some lunch,' he said. Our eyes lit up. We tried not to look too hungry as we tucked into the delicious meal.

He asked how long I was staying and I answered in a vague way. Before we got up to leave the table he passed me something under the tablecloth, something bulky. I put it in my handbag. I could not imagine what it was, I thought maybe he had given me his address, but then he had never made a pass at me. The moment he had gone, leaving Christine and me at the table, I looked in my bag and there was an envolope. He had gone to the loo at some stage, taking an envelope from the restaurant, and had put 1,000 francs in it. He must have felt I was desperate and in a sticky situation.

I have been lucky with the people I know.

8

DÉBUTANTES of the day were launched into society at a cost of thousands. My own launching pad was Comeragh Road in unfashionable Barons Court, and, instead of the requisite rich daddy and impeccable connections, I had a pretty face, a ready smile and an ebullient spirit. Also I was witty, a characteristic I had never given much thought to, but now I was finding that a ready wit, so long as it is neither spiteful nor tactless, will take you anywhere. My circle of friends and acquaintances grew to a rich mix of aristocracy, diplomatic and showbusiness; London was my village. There was no lack of invitations to country weekend house parties. Had I been a real débutante I would have ended up with a rich young husband, a place in the country, horses, dogs and domestic bliss. Instead I met Peter Rachman.

He came into my life during one of Christine's Savoy Grill lunches, when we were guests of two visiting American surgeons she had known for some time. I was wearing my number one modelling audition outfit – black-and-white Russian-style dress which I had bought from Bazaar, with a black fox hat, and was well aware I looked good. So I was not surprised when, on our way to the powder room, a man stopped and spoke. Short and stocky, balding, it was Christine he spoke to.

'Hello,' he said in a curious high-pitched voice. 'Who is your friend?'

Christine introduced us, exchanged a few pleasantries and ended with the invitation.

'We're moving into a new flat, do join us for a house-warming drink.'

In the ladies' room Christine told me he was Peter Rachman, a very rich property man with whom she had once had an affair.

We returned to our table and I kept glancing at him out of

the corner of my eye. Short, plump and bald he was, but, more than that, he was sun-tanned, gleaming with cleanliness and apparent good health and meticulously well-groomed. Silk shirt, cashmere suit, crocodile shoes added up to a very good look. I wondered if he would turn up at our party.

When Christine described to me their brief liaison it sounded complicated in the extreme. Sometimes she lived with him, sometimes she did not; he gave her a car but kept demanding back the keys – it fizzled out. Christine was flippant about things, it did not suit her to be somebody's live-in girlfriend and having him come round in the afternoons. Then she had to contend with the disapproval of Stephen, who was a snob and as such objected to Peter, a self-made Jewish immigrant. The affair ended acrimoniously, Christine never had a good word to say about him and, later, when I knew him better, I realised that Peter hated Christine totally.

I felt safe with Peter from the first time he took me out to dinner. Our friendship developed over meals at restaurants, selected by Peter because they conformed to his main criterion – that he should be permitted to inspect the kitchen whenever he chose. This obviously eliminated many top restaurants, although he liked the carverie at the Strand Palace because somehow it struck him as hygienic that he could see the meat being sliced. His favourite restaurant was the Polish Daquise in South Kensington, where he not only had lunch but also tea; he had a passion for the rich cream pastries they served.

I was comfortable with him, he was easy to talk to, a good listener as well as a good talker. He had beautiful eyes, usually concealed behind tinted glasses, good teeth and a straight finely-boned nose. Because he was always sun-tanned (he used his sun lamp every day, as well as an expensive tanning cosmetic all the time) his plumpness was minimised. In any case it was his stomach that was large (not his arms and legs) and this is common among people who, like Peter, have been brought to the point of starvation. Many years later in Israel, living among Jews who had suffered similar privations to Peter as children, I recognised the legacy of starvation.

Sexually he was not aggressive. I knew he was attracted to me, but there was no pressure from him. Even when I knew him better sex was not a passion with him, but something functional like drinking a glass of water. I knew that whether I went to bed with him or not I could keep him as a friend because Peter liked to be seen with a beautiful girl on his arm, which, of course, is the big giveaway of the self-made man. Usually they do not begin to make money until they are over thirty-five and at that age to have the company of a beautiful woman is a status symbol. – There is an old Jewish joke in which one wife says to another, 'My husband is richer than yours.' To which the other wife replies, 'Nonsense, mine must be richer, he has a far more beautiful mistress!'

I knew Peter lived in a mansion in Hampstead, bought his antiques at Sotheby's (he was so proud of a recent purchase, a fine Sheraton cabinet which he had converted to conceal the television) and had a mistress called Audrey. He told me they had been together for many years, since she had helped him through the difficulties of his early business struggles and that he would always owe her a debt of gratitude. He said, too, that the arrangement was now one of mutual convenience, there was no physical relationship between them. Audrey spent many months each year in America with her sister and Peter hoped that on one of these trips she might meet and fall in love with another man and want to marry. He told me he believed they were unsuited. Much of what he told me then was lies, but in the beginning that was the carpet he gave me to walk on, and I accepted it.

After my initial reaction to Stephen Ward at our house-warming party, the more I came to know him the more I enjoyed his company. Charming, well informed, well educated, he could talk seriously on any subject and he also had a fund of useless information which makes for inconsequential conversation. He was the perfect dinner guest and socialised assiduously. Many of his friends were also his patients, many patients became his friends and, like dear old Percy Murray, Stephen Ward's appointments book could boast 'the crowned and uncrowned' heads of Europe.

His home territory was the triangle made up of his flat in Wimpole Mews, his consulting rooms in Harley Street and his local coffee bar in Marylebone Lane. Occasionally he used another coffee bar favoured by artists who could sketch the nude model provided by the management while they drank their coffee. He lived in shabby surroundings. The flat was functional, two bedrooms, living-room, kitchen and bathroom, small, sparsely furnished. A few books were littered about, and his own sketch book, but, strangely for an artist, Stephen did not collect art, nor books nor in fact anything except possibly people. There was always a steady flow of people through Wimpole Mews, many just for the stimulating pleasure of his company and the sure chance of meeting others, like a sort of club. Then there were Stephen's lame ducks who, having fallen on temporary hard times, needed a bed for a few nights. As Christine had been used to doing for the past two years.

Stephen was interested in people and gave generously of his time, provided he found some spark there to interest him. He was choosy about his friends. He had, too, a curious attitude to money. It was immediately apparent that he was inclined to meanness. He rarely offered drinks; insisted people paid for their 'phone calls; had a polished knack of never offering a cigarette, which he did by taking a packet from his pocket, slipping a cigarette quickly into his mouth while, at the same time, the packet enveloped in his hand, making a quick gesture and saying, 'Nobody wants a cigarette, then?' Like a magician the cigarette packet had been out and back, the cigarette in his mouth, the question asked, before anyone had time to say, Yes, they would like a cigarette. Yet Stephen was not mean for the sake of acquiring wealth. He had no interest in money, his clothes were any old thing that happened to lie around. He had everything he needed, he could live the life of a millionaire, because he had entry to the homes and lifestyles of millionaires.

He did not like animals and he did not like children. He called me Little Baby, and in fact I think his girlfriends were his children. He listened patiently to your emotional and other problems, gossiped with us the trivial in-chat of the day. He liked to have girls around him, because this ensured there was always something going on – parties, dinners. He got on very well with women but I suspect that secretly he rather despised us. He was not homosexual or even bisexual, as far as I could know, as was later suggested. He had never slept with Christine, theirs was not that kind of relationship, but he had love affairs, although I think sex was not particularly important to him. He liked his women friends to be decorative, amusing, intelligent, an asset to be seen with. Many of his closest women friends married into the aristrocracy, not because of Stephen's influence; he was just a good spotter of that sort of talent. He had been married once, and the marriage lasted six weeks. Now, at forty-eight, he was a confirmed bachelor.

Early in our friendship, Stephen took me to spend a spring weekend at his country cottage at Cliveden, the Berkshire estate of his great friend, Lord Astor. We drove down from London in his white Jaguar convertible, stopping on the way to load up with groceries. The Cottage, for which he paid the humble peppercorn rent of £1 a year, was an impressive gabled residence, built on the banks of the Thames, the upper floor jutting out to overhang the river, which made one feel as if one was on a boat. All around were the magnificent parklands of Cliveden, which boasted the country's finest collection of rhododendrons, and many of the early flowering varieties were then in bloom.

Stephen cooked dinner, which we ate in front of a roaring log fire, and we settled down to chat and plan what we should do the following day. We had both decided to paint. Suddenly Stephen got to his feet and said he had to slip out to the pub for some more wine, he would be about half an hour. I heard the car drive away, and sat happily reading. Then I heard a faint tapping sound. I listened – had I imagined it? Now the cosy cottage seemed quite eerie, nothing but the sound of the wind rustling in the branches and the water lapping a few yards from the french windows. It came again, a definite tapping – from the direction of the window. And then I saw it, a hand gently waving outside the window, and tapping. I was petrified with fright, though, at the same time, some sense told me it could not be a real hand, it was too big! Two minutes later, as I was battling to compose myself, Stephen put his head round the door, laughing at the joke. He had driven away, parked the car and crept back with this grotesque rubber hand on a stick to tap, like some disembodied spirit, at the window.

'I could have had a heart attack. Thank God you're a

doctor,' I said lightheartedly.

But it had unnerved me so much that when we went upstairs to bed I knew there was no way I was going to stay alone that night so, instead of sleeping in the guest room where he had put my suitcase, I crossed the tiny passage, and climbed into bed with Stephen. He was a good lover, but he was not my trip and I was not his. It warmed our friendship, but neither of us had any desire to repeat the performance.

Next day Bill Astor called in to say hello and asked us to tea that afternoon. I liked him at once, it was impossible not to. He was a kind, generous man, wonderfully easygoing, never condescending. A man who could mix on equal terms with people of all types. His aristocratic father had married his mother, a rich American divorcee, and Bill had inherited the best qualities of each. The similarity between him and his mother Nancy, Lady Astor, was remarkable: they had the same sense of humour and warmth at putting people at ease.

There were several people, including Jon and Ingeborg Pertwee, who lived close by, gathered in his drawing-room for tea that afternoon. Cliveden was always crowded, it was a standing joke that all one had to do was turn up at Cliveden on a Friday night, dump your suitcases in the hall and no questions would be asked because everyone would assume someone else had asked you down for the weekend. So there was a constant flow of guests enjoying the lavish hospitality of the house and responding with wit, humour and good conversation.

Later, I read in the newspapers that the parties at Cliveden during this period had assumed the proportions of a long-running orgy. How laughable. Nothing could have been further from the truth. Nancy Astor was there and her sharp eyes missed nothing. She was driven around the estate each day and kept a close watch on affairs, although officially the lady of the house was now Bill's wife, the model Bronwen Pugh. She too was hardly the type to draw a blind eye at impropriety; gracious and kind, certainly, but equally she was aware of her position of importance and authority.

Bill led me on to the balcony. Stretching beneath and beyond was the magnificent sweep of lawns, great oaks, rhododendrons sweeping into infinity. Below the balcony was a wide terrace of stone.

'Close your eyes and make a wish,' said Bill. I closed my eyes. 'Open,' he said.

I did. There in front of us a colonnade of fountains had sprung into life, arcs of droplets shimmering like ribbons in the still wintery sun, against the brilliant green of the lawns. It was a sight I shall never forget.

I went often to Cliveden. Sometimes alone with Stephen, frequently with other friends. Relax, chat, tea or dinner at the house with the Astors, a dip in the pool. Light, amusing, undemanding. I began a very bad painting there which was never finished and it ended up among the paintings Stephen had to sell when he was trying to raise money to pay for his legal costs. A newspaper carried a cartoon of a woman rushing across a street with my painting under her arm saying: 'Wait until I get home and find out how my husband came to be painted by Mandy Rice-Davies.'

I first met Nancy, Lady Astor, in the drawing room at Cliveden, she was standing by the window gazing intently at something below. She beckoned me, and I could see her attention was held by a scene in the swimming pool.

'Is that a bikini I see?' she said, rather as one might say Is that a Martian! I sensed that she liked me, as older women invariably do. I found it easy to talk to her.

It amused Stephen to discover that I was the same girl Lord Dudley had been planning to marry. He knew of the story from the other side (Eric's daughter-in-law, Maureen Swanson, was a friend of many years) and he could not resist the opportunity for making a little mischief. So, during one of our Cliveden weekends, he took me to visit Maureen and Billy, Viscount and Lady Ednam, at their house, which was reasonably close by. Maureen opened the door, took one look, and, before either one of us had opened our mouths, said, 'How dare you bring that girl here!' and shut the door smartly in our faces.

Stephen treated this as a huge joke, and saying, 'Leave it to me,' rang the bell.

After some minutes, a fair amount of raised voices and clattering, the door was thrown open. Lord Ednam stood there. 'Do come in, don't take any notice of Maureen,' he said.

Then calling his wife, he said, 'Maureen, meet Mandy. And mind your Ps and Qs, she might have been your mother-in-law!'

The ice broken, she was perfectly charming to me, serving tea and crumpets in the beautiful drawing-room. How one cuts up and eats a buttery crumpet, standing up and with a cup and saucer in the other hand, I never discovered. At one point I dropped a blob of melted butter on the *petit point* of a chair seat. Should one mention this or pretend nothing has happened? I said nothing. After a while Maureen noticed it herself, fetched a cloth and rubbed it clean.

She was a pretty, dark-haired woman with clear, pale skin and a smouldering vivacity. I noticed her shoes, rather frumpy low heels, I thought. After an hour or so, my own pointed-toe high-heeled shoes looked out of place and hers looked absolutely right. I resolved to get a pair for stalking the country the next day, and that was my introduction to Gucci.

Maureen was pregnant. Lord Ednam had children by his first wife and this was to be his first with Maureen. In fact, the baby was stillborn and Stephen hurried over to the house to draw a picture of the baby before the funeral.

I moved easily in my new circle of friends. Although my own background was humble by their standards, I had mixed with wealthy people at the stables, and I knew from observation the lifestyle that great wealth and position involved. Just up from Birmingham, I mercifully had no accent to eradicate, even the Welsh tones of my parents had not formed in me. In this new circle people accepted you simply because you were there, and there was little snobbism (compared, for instance, to my father's cynical humour who, when he heard one of his nieces had gone to work abroad as an *au pair* said, 'Reduced to charring. That's what our family is coming to!').

My saving grace in life has always been my ability to get on with much older people. In society older people have the last word, they run the houses, they preside over events. If the old mother or grandmother says, 'Bring that amusing young girl along,' then one is in. People who have wealth and power in life can choose whom they befriend. If they like you, if you are decorative, easy company, tactful, discreet and pleasant to have around, then you are accepted. It is still this way for a girl

– it is quite different for a man.

I learned fast. I have always had a keen curiosity about people – so much so that once I actually followed a few steps behind one couple leaving a restaurant in order not to miss the tail-end of their conversation. As a child the height of being posh was going to dinner at the Lyons Corner House, where one had a three-course meal and waiters served at the table. This was a far cry from my first banquet at one stately home, where it was so grand that there was a footman behind each chair. Dress was formal, and long white gloves were obligatory. But what to do with the gloves? I consulted a book on etiquette and learned that you removed your gloves and placed them in your wine glass as a signal to the footman that you did not want wine. Well, I did so. And glancing round the table I saw I was the only woman with her gloves in her wine glass. And then all those knives and forks. I could not work out whether you used the dessert fork to anchor the food and the spoon to bring it to your mouth, or *vice versa*, and was relieved to see everybody simply picked up the fork and ate with that.

The rules matter to people outside society. Once in there are no rules, and certainly nobody takes any notice. I decided my own rule would be when in doubt, don't. Since I was never sure about tipping the household staff after a weekend, I decided it was better not to tip at all and be thought of as mean, than to tip inappropriately and be identified as non-U.

The closest I ever came to making a serious *faux pas* was on a weekend shoot. I was guest of some young Hon whose uncle had a place in the country and it was assumed that I was familiar with the shooting. I genned up on the clothes, made myself completely familiar with the drill, bought the appropriate green line boots and made sure I said all the right things. I even got myself out of bed at dawn without complaint to be at my butt at the first flutter of wings.

Only problem was, I shot a swan! Even I knew that swans belong to the Queen and that it is not done at all to shoot them – even accidentally. My ghillie was a man of few words and prompt action. He quickly dug a hole and buried the unfortunate bird. Honour was saved.

I was working hard at modelling and, presumably, earning a

large amount of money – if the fact that I ultimately had to settle a tax bill for £1,000 for that year is anything to go by – but Christine and I always seemed short of cash. The landlord who lived downstairs would bring up pieces of meat for Pooch, and the moment his back was turned Christine and I would re-cycle it into toasted steak sandwiches for ourselves. Doggy bags were a great boon. After a lunch, during which we had eaten our way through as many courses as were available in order to stay full up longer, we would ask for our doggy bags to be filled up for our pets (Pooch was usually with me as evidence) and the kitchen would produce various titbits which would provide our supper later on. When the *petits fours* were out on the table, we would rush through the lot exclaiming, 'Gosh, how delicious!' and the restaurant would promptly produce a second portion, beautifully wrapped, to be taken home. It was all good for business – it went on the bill.

We were so highly organised at our eating dates that occasionally we double booked. On one occasion I had fixed a foursome at a restaurant with a male model and his pianist brother who lived in great style in Chelsea with a white baby grand, and Christine too had committed us for dinner. Not to miss out, we arranged the first dinner for eight, went into the ladies' room at the end of the meal and skipped out the back way to keep our ten o'clock supper date with Christine's friends.

Were we forced to spend an evening at home, we were sure of company. Our flat became a convenient spot for what seemed like half of London calling in for a drink or a coffee. Stephen, Bill Astor, Tim Vigors were our regulars. Tim was heading a sales company selling small aeroplanes at that time and I remember was anxious to sell one to Paul Getty. We plotted a spectacular sales demonstration. Invited by Getty for tea, it was arranged that we should be sitting on the terrace when Tim would zoom down in his aircraft, and make a big impression. All went according to plan, but when Tim appeared overhead doing his swoops and acrobatics, something went seriously wrong. The engines started to splutter, the plane went out of control and he was forced to crash-land on the lawn. We rushed forward, terrified that he had been badly injured. Tim staggered out, to be greeted by Getty hopping about in rage at the damage to his lawn.

'A phone – I must phone for help,' gasped Tim, staggering towards the house.

And Getty, whose meanness was legendary, directed him to the pay-box telephone to be used by all visitors in the hall.

Poor Tim, bruised and bewildered, stood there fumbling for change to make a call. Getty never bought a plane.

We had been in Fulham three months and the next quarter's rent, £200, was due. Neither Christine nor I had the money. I was owed much more than that but the cheques were slow in coming through. I thought of asking Pat Glover to advance me the money, made the phone call and could not quite bring myself to ask the favour. But I had to ask somebody. The next time Bill Astor called in for a chat, I told him our predicament. Would he be prepared to lend us the £200 so that we could pay the rent on the day it was due?

'Certainly,' he said, took out his cheque book and wrote a cheque for £200. He saved us from immediate embarrassment. Poor, good-hearted Bill, that small (to him) act of kindness cost him plenty when it came out at the trial.

I was seriously thinking of becoming an actress, it was one step on, I thought, from modelling, and making commercials had given me an idea of how to work with cameras and lights. I met Douglas Fairbanks, Jnr. with his wife and daughter Melissa at Cliveden and was able to talk to him about the film business. I was flattered by his interest when he telephoned me a few days later and invited me to lunch at the Dorchester.

Even then, in his fifties, he was a remarkably good-looking man as well as being an amusing companion and I felt strongly attracted to him. After lunch he suggested we go upstairs to his suite there, and I did. We went to bed. There were several of these little afternoon interludes. A pleasant lunch, an hour in bed. I was genuinely fond of him and I imagined he felt something similar for me.

He suggested I went along to see a producer friend of his at Shepperton Studios where they were casting a new TV series called *One Step Beyond*. He went even further, he phoned and booked the appointment for me and paved the way.

However, arriving for the meeting I had a rude awakening. Certainly the producer was interested, but it seemed to me that he first needed an indication of what he could expect in return. That was it. I felt I had been sent as a piece of meat. I pretended to be totally thick and not understand the proposition and left. I felt deeply hurt, I could not disguise the implication. Over our next lunch, I told Douglas what had happened and my embarrassment. We never made love again.

I grew closer to Peter. Our lunch and dinner dates became more frequent, our friendship intensified, though not to the point where I understood completely how he made his considerable income except that he was into property and clubs. I assumed he was building up to the ultimate proposition, to when he thought the time was right to suggest we went back to his place – but where? I knew there was a flat in Bryanston Mews West where Christine had stayed briefly, but this was in the process of being refitted and was swarming with builders. I would not have invited him back to my flat, he knew this, and in any case he would not have accepted; the knowledge of his intense dislike of Christine lay unspoken between us. I was prepared to go to bed with him if he wanted it. Sex brings intimacy into a relationship that can last a lifetime. I knew by then that sex was not dependent on great passion. Twice in my life I have been in love in the way that makes your knees weak, disturbs your thought process, dominates your life; and both of those men I married. But physical passion fades and it seems my most enduring relationships have been less physical, and with much older men.

We had spent a delicious day together. Lunch at the Daquise, a visit to Peter's tailor, Morris Krevatz, to collect two new suits, which always put Peter in a good mood, then along to Queen's Tennis Club for the opening of the season, and finally to Sherry's flat in Knightsbridge for tea. Tactfully, Sherry made her excuses and left. We began manoeuvres on the sofa in the sitting-room, progressed to the bedroom. It was not earth-shattering, but then I didn't expect it to be. This then became a routine: two or three afternoons a week we went back to Sherry's flat to make love.

I was fond of Sherry, she was a beautiful girl from a respectable middle-class background who had had the misfortune to get involved with Peter's great friend and business protégé,

M. – C

Raymond Nash. Married with four children, Nash was a compulsive womaniser who had two mistresses at that time: Sherry and Odette. Insanely jealous and vicious he kept his women in physical fear. When Odette tried to leave him he had beaten her and shaved her head in the shape of a cross as retribution. To cover the stubble she bought a wig, and it was trying on her long blonde wig that inspired me first to buy one like it and then to have Vidal Sassoon bleach my hair back to its original colour. Overnight I was blonde, to Peter's delight.

I learned through Sherry that Peter had another girlfriend, a vivacious Italian called Manuella. I was convinced that the evenings we did not spend together, he spent with her. Everything I heard about Manuella fed my jealousy: she was beautiful, she was extrovert, she had outrageously large breasts which she flaunted by not wearing a bra – in those pre bra-burning days this assured rapt attention in any situation. Then I heard that she had spent an evening flaunting herself with Peter at a disco called La Doubel but that the following day she was due to leave for Rome. Peter was taking her to Heathrow.

That afternoon we spent in bed. I was the loving, compliant female but beneath I was seething with jealousy. Each time Peter murmured he had to leave, I persuaded him to stay a little longer. His time was running out, I could see him getting edgy, trying to talk his way out of the bedroom without actually resorting to telling me the truth. Finally, with minutes to spare, he got up to leave.

'Why the hurry?' I asked innocently.

'Well, I have an important appointment. I have to meet someone, I cannot let them down.'

'You're going to meet Manuella, you mean,' I shrieked. 'And take her to the airport. I know all about it.'

He was so shaken all he could say was: 'How do you know? Who told you?'

'Never mind who told me,' I stormed. I was behaving like an irrational child but I did not care. 'If you leave this flat now, I swear I will never see you again.'

It was a calculated risk. I looked convincing, he hesitated, but only for a moment. Then he laughed, and, beginning to undress, he said: 'I'll stay.'

That evening he asked me to do something for him. 'I don't want you living with Christine,' he said. 'Will you move into my flat in Bryanston Mews?'

He promised not to interfere with my life, or try to control me, he would encourage me with my modelling. Simply, he felt uneasy to know I was living with Christine.

The following day he came with the Rolls to collect my things. The mews was still not ready and the plan was for me to stay for the time being with Raymond Nash's mistress, Odette, where they had a spare room. I agreed – it seemed that one advantage would be to feed back information to Sherry about the goings-on at this second ménage, especially as Sherry had heard a rumour that Odette was pregnant.

I knew Nash's reputation but assumed he would leave me alone because of Peter. False security. One night, after a heavy drinking bout and a row with Odette in the next-door room, they both came into my room and sat, one each side of the bed. I had been asleep until woken by the noise, and was startled and disoriented. Odette held my hand, Raymond took the other and began to stroke my arm. I did not hang around to see what they had in mind. I was no fragile creature; if there was going to be a struggle we would have it now. Pushing past them I stormed out of the room. 'I'm making myself a cup of tea, then I'm going back to bed,' I said. Sheepishly they drifted off.

Thinking it over, I knew it would be unwise to cause trouble by telling Peter of this episode, but since I was equally determined not to spend one night more than was necessary under the same roof as Raymond Nash, I told Peter why. It caused a bitter quarrel, and Nash nursed a deep hatred for me from that moment. But Peter arranged to move me into Bryanston Mews West immediately, although the workmen had not yet completed.

It was the perfect bachelor-girl apartment, close carpeted in soft green with a well-fitted kitchen and luxurious bathroom. Comfortably furnished with the best that money could buy, the sitting-room boasted an antique Welsh harp and an ornate drinks trolley in glass and gilt filigree. There was a huge mirror in the sitting-room which gave a view of the bedroom next door. A two-way mirror, Peter explained, installed by a former tenant, Dennis Hamilton, just like the one he and his ex-wife Diana Dors had had at their home in Maidenhead. This was slightly shocking, in his puritanical view. He did not have long to worry about it. A few months after I moved in we had a fight and I threw my wooden hairbrush at him. He ducked and it hit the mirror, shattering it completely. We hung a painting over it to disguise the mess until it could be repaired, and it never was.

Christine took a typically philosophical stance about my leaving her, and, although I would not have advertised the fact to Peter, we kept in touch. On a visit to London Zoo one day, as we were looking at the animals, Christine said with barely suppressed excitement, 'Guess who I'm having an affair with.'

'Who?' I said.

'Jack Profumo,' said Christine.

'Who's Jack Profumo?' I asked. He was not exactly famous.

'He's the Minister for War, that's all,' said Christine.

'Oooh, how nice for you,' I said. Minister for War. I was quite impressed at that.

9

FOR my seventeenth birthday, Peter gave me a white 3.2 Jaguar. He handed me the keys and the log book. 'It's yours,' he said. The fact that I had never passed a test, or even applied for one, presented no immediate problems, for this car came complete with my very own driving licence. In my naïvety I never questioned the driving licence. I immediately climbed into the driver's seat and took off for Birmingham to visit the family. I considered a few months' lessons at the wheel of Peter's fully automatic Rolls-Royce driving round Regent's Park in the evenings, had been sufficient instruction. Living with Peter was like having the key to your very own Aladdin's cave.

Each week he gave me £80, cash, to spend. He insisted this was fun money, he did not want me to save it because, I suppose, it might have led to my independence. Even I found it difficult to lavish £80 a week on myself, when all the bills were already being picked up by Peter, so I saved some, and sent some home to Margaret, who was now a single parent with one child too young to be left and, therefore, unable to take a job. Margaret and her daughters, Carol and Jackie, would come up for shopping days with me and we would rummage through Harrods, where I could play fairy godmother, buying the children beautiful clothes – a rare treat for a child whose mother was living on £5 social security a week.

Peter need have had no fears as I had no desire to be independent of him. Our arrangement was perfect, I had every possible luxury and comfort, a splendid address, an attentive and devoted lover who encouraged me to work conscientiously at my modelling and liked me to see my own friends – as long as that circle did not include Christine. If he was away, then he made his second Rolls-Royce, dark brown with red-headed chauffeur, available to drive me around London. (I assumed this was Audrey's car, and was available during her long trips to America.) His ambitions for me were almost paternal. He was delighted when I enrolled for a sandwich course in art at the London Polytechnic and impressed at the seriousness I gave to my studies there, and bought me a horse so that I could continue with my riding.

At the beginning he had Morris Krevatz make me two suits – one white, one black – but then I discovered the Dior room at Harrods and decided that was definitely my style. He liked to come shopping with me, and had a novel way of solving the difficult choice between three separate outfits – buying all three! It was a matter of pride that he should be not only rich, but enjoy recognition as a man of substance. And that the recognition should include me. This could sometimes take the form of childish showing-off.

Once, I admired a pretty miniature portrait, set in gold, in the window of an antique shop. When I went in to ask the price, the owner replied: 'More than you can afford,' and turned his back to me. Apart from being offended at his rudeness, Peter, when I reported this back to him, took it as a personal insult that I should appear to be somebody who could not afford the price of an antique miniature. He plotted his revenge. The following day we went back to the shop. I hid outside while Peter went in and asked the price of the miniature. I saw the shopkeeper come to the window, remove the miniature and withdraw into the shop again to show it to Peter. Then Peter opened the door and called me in. In front of the shopkeeper, I opened my bag and counted out from a wad of 500 notes the price of the miniature, which was £120. All this was done with cool disdain. Peter genuinely thought he had scored points, but I do not think the man had even recognised me as the girl he had turned away the previous day.

What had begun as a strictly love-in-the-afternoon friendship, settled into a domestic arrangement. He called me Choochi, and I called him Chich. Gradually he moved his favourite possessions into the flat including his books and his records. He was mad about opera, which at that time I found rather heavy; but as I became used to it I, too, started to enjoy it. His favourite opera was *Don Giovanni*, and today I can sing it from beginning to end.

We always lunched together (unless I was working through the lunch period), then back to the flat, to bed and a rest for an hour or two. Usually he had business meetings, people to meet, then we would dine and begin the tour of *the clubs*, including his own, La Discotheque, and then his favourite gambling places, before falling into bed in the early hours of the morning. Like all active people, he slept very little, four hours a night was sufficient. He got up without disturbing me and drove back to Hampstead in time for a game of tennis and breakfast with Audrey before a morning's business. I fondly imagined that they did not sleep together at all, but was disillusioned by the oldest means of all – reading a letter in his pocket. It was sent to him by Audrey from abroad and contained a loving reference to his bed being lonely without her there. I was jealous of what they had together. Once I rang the house and when he picked up the phone he was laughing and I hated them for being able to joke together. Yet, at the same time, I knew I had the best of the relationship.

Sometimes he asked, 'Would you love me even if I didn't have any money?' It was impossible to imagine Peter poor, although he had known abject poverty. One of his first jobs as an immigrant after the war was to wash up in the kitchens of Bloom's, the Jewish restaurant in London's East End. Now that he was rich he liked to eat there occasionally, parking the Rolls as close to the front door as restrictions would allow. I dreaded these visits and did my best to talk him out of them since I knew they always resulted in him having a severe bilious attack, and not because of the food, which was delicious! I decided there had to be a deep psychological cause for Peter's inability to digest it with comfort.

Sex which, being brutally honest, had begun as my side of the bargain and which at the outset was merely perfunctory routine, blossomed until it was an important part of our relationship and something mutually gratifying to us. I took Peter home to meet my parents, who were somewhat relieved that it seemed at last as if I was settling down. He appeared a most presentable son-in-law, and told them sincerely how much he loved and adored me, and that we were going to be married.

I was curious to learn about his childhood background, but he shrank from telling me, though occasionally, if his mood was right he mentioned his early life. I know now that he was born in Lvov, then part of Poland, to well-off parents and had had a good education. When the Nazis came his parents were dragged away and the young Peter was set to work on a chain gang, building a highway to the Russian frontier. He escaped only to be caught by the Russians and put in a labour camp, where he was frequently beaten up. From snippets I learned what he had been through: how he used to de-lice himself and throw the insects on the fire, listening to them pop as they exploded in the flames; how he made clothes and shoes out of newspapers; how he had joined the Polish Free Army and kept his daily bread ration in his rucksack, never eating more than half, for fear that there would be no more and he might starve, so that the remainder went mouldy.

Even when I knew him he continued to live with the daily reminders of his experiences. He was freaky about cleanliness, took several baths a day using gallons of Dettol in the process. Our flat was stocked with enough food to feed a small army (and we always ate out) and, at Hampstead, one room consisted of floor-to-ceiling shelves stacked with food like a supermarket. He suffered appalling nightmares and he would wake, screaming and sweating with fear, crying for his mother. He had never seen or heard of his parents again after the day the Gestapo took them, and despite the most exhaustive enquiries was never able to discover their ultimate fate.

In my childish ignorance I thought I could help him by bringing all this into the open, and once cajoled him into seeing a film, *Kapo*, which dealt explicitly with life in a concentration camp. During the film he began to tremble. We left the cinema, and he suffered deep depression for several days. I regretted that I had been the cause of his suffering.

Years later, living in Israel, I met many people like Peter and I know they do not discuss their experiences because in order to survive they must shut off their emotions. Only a chance remark gives a clue to the child that was dragged from their arms, or the husband or lover beaten to death before their eyes.

Peter had a curious double-edged response to violence. He

hated and was disturbed by it to the extent that he would cross the road and walk the other way if he saw a scuffle, or even a loud argument in progress. At the same time he could be quite hardened. One of the King's Road characters was a Polish poet, who often shared a coffee or drink with us. For several weeks he was missing and when he reappeared he was dreadfully disfigured. It seems he had squealed to the police, and been found out by the criminal fraternity. Their punishment was to bend a cut-throat razor over the knuckles, punch this into his mouth, leaving a macabre smile and no tongue! I was so horrified by this gruesome sight I could not sleep thinking about it. But Peter, upset to see his friend in this condition, was not shocked by the punishment itself.

If Peter was not very willing to talk about his childhood and adolescence he was happy to talk about his rise to fortune. He spoke of the menial jobs he had done before renting an office and setting up as a flat-letting agent, eventually buying property to let primarily to black immigrants. He was quite proud of this for, unlike the image of Rachman the exploiting slum landlord that later emerged, he believed he was performing a public service.

'This country lets anyone in, including blacks, and then there is nowhere for them to live. At least I give them a roof,' he said. Once he took me on a tour of his property empire, but warned me not to go inside. His tenants, he said, chose to live, frequently, ten to a room and coming from primitive conditions did not know about lavatories and simple hygiene.

Peter's faith in my talents was touching. He encouraged me to take any opportunity that came along and was as delighted as I was when I had a call to audition for a show with Sammy Davis, Jnr. He was appearing at the Prince of Wales Theatre, and during the run he was to do a television special. He needed dancers, and also needed pretty girls who could look like dancers. When I turned up for the audition, wearing my Bazaar dress, the mink scarf with tails and the inevitable hat, the BBC audition room was packed with girls. I did not fancy competing under these conditions, so, approaching the receptionist at the desk, I said: 'I'm sorry, I can't wait here. I don't have the time.' I hoped to give the impression they had better snap me up, and it worked.

'What is your name, how old are you?'

I wasn't yet seventeen, and told her. She gave a little smile, and said, 'Come back at six.'

Returning later, to an almost deserted building, I heard laughter coming from the room I had been told to attend. I assumed they were having a giggle at my expense, a mere sixteen-year-old trying to get on a show with Sammy Davis, Jnr. I decided to brazen it out. Throwing wide the door I announced,

'Hello fans.'

They all thought that very funny. Lionel Blair was choosing the dancers and he could not have been more encouraging. They liked me too because, now with my blonde hair, I looked a little like Sammy Davis's wife, Mai Britt.

He was the most difficult person to work with, improvising as he went along, whilst we all dashed about and tried to keep up with him. Another in the line-up was Pat Booth, who went on to become a model and then a photographer. Sammy Davis's lead dancer was a beautiful black girl, Boots, who stayed on in London and became a close friend for a brief period. He is a remarkable man in many ways, alert, caring, interested in people. Years later, at a government reception in Israel, Sammy was one of the guests of honour. He walked into the room, looked around at the line up of generals and politicians, spotted me in the corner and made straight for me, to throw his arms about me with a big hello, happy at seeing a familiar face amongst so much top brass.

I believe my working contacts were all the more attractive to Peter because his business associates were, in the main, rather shady characters, his immediate contacts and employees being immigrant entrepreneurs like himself. Yet he cared about respectability, was a snob about mixing with the right people and took delight in the fact that we were invited to Cliveden–though such invitations were due more to Bill Astor's good manners than anything else. He was enraged one night at La Discotheque when I innocently repeated a remark made to me in passing by a young man, who leaning close had whispered, 'How does it feel to be a gangster's moll?'

'Peter, what's a gangster's moll?' I asked in all innocence. His reaction scared me. Who said it? he wanted to know.

Where was he? I had no desire for this sort of scene. Peter instructed his bodyguard-cum-sidekick, Jimmy Houlihan, to walk round the room with me, peering into the gloom so that I could find the offender. I made a great show of pretending to identify him, but had to conclude he was no longer in the club.

Peter kept a gun in the glove compartment of the Rolls and explained this was needed for protection as he carried so much money around. He demonstrated the safety catch, and told me: 'If anyone should attack me, don't hesitate to shoot. It's quite all right, I have a licence.' Such dubious instructions I took cheerfully at face value. Another such command was that in the event of anything 'happening' to him, his gold bracelet bore the code for his numbered Swiss account.

Peter was a compulsive gambler. As well as providing kicks, his gambling was also a means of legitimising or laundering large sums of cash that came his way. He gambled at clubs and casinos, also at private parties. One night, he left the table to visit the loo and left me holding his hand of cards; at stake was £20,000. I frequently saw him lose huge sums of money and, after the initial novelty of gambling wore off for me and I began to be bored by it, I tried to talk him out of it. Gambling, like eating at Bloom's, was something that left him feeling ill and dejected.

Gamblers have strange bedfellows and I would amuse myself studying the faces of the characters grouped around the tables. Billy Hill, ex-boss of the underworld, had a beautiful girlfriend called Gipsy, a woman in her forties with thick black hair who believed in keeping her tabs on her jewellery, for she wore it all together – ropes and ropes of long gold chains, round her neck, on her wrists, up her arms, dangling from her ears. As she moved the chains clinked and the gold dangling coins and medallions jangled. When she spoke it was with pure Cockney tones. I was fascinated by her, and she took a liking to me, for one day she turned up at our flat for a game of *chemin de fer*, bringing me a present of a Nina Ricci suit. I was thrilled but Peter was quite jealous.

'Be careful where you wear it,' he said. 'It has probably fallen off the back of a lorry.'

I suspected that a great deal of the jewellery he gave me, whilst not falling off the back of a lorry, had come by way of a bad debt or somebody owing a favour. The first really expensive piece he gave me, though, had been chosen specifically for me. It was a thick gold-mesh bracelet, incorporating a plain strip of gold on which he had intended to bear the inscription 'To Gorgeous Mandy from Peter, July 1961'. Unfortunately he had entrusted the engraving to an immigrant Pole who spoke no English and the words actually came out 'To Gorgeous Mandy from July 1961 Peter'.

La Discotheque attracted a lively crowd, some titled, some very rich, some ascending stars (Julie Christie and Samantha Eggar were regulars there). I danced with them all, after they had first asked Peter's permission. He never danced, he liked me to dance but only with his approval. So I danced with unknowns, Michael Caine, Christopher Courtenay and Terence Stamp, who was, Peter thought, most suitable. Terence, an unknown East End boy at that time, had had his hair bleached blond for *Billy Budd*, which was in the making, and Peter's assessment of anybody who dyed their hair for whatever reason was that they must be homosexual. The most handsome partner of them all was a young society man about town called Johnny Summers, well born but impoverished, whom I found powerfully attractive and who I believed reciprocated. Between dances we would sit and chat, and although neither of us made a move that would in any way appear compromising, I felt sure he really fancied me, and liked me. It was a warm friendship.

One day it stopped abruptly.

It was a habit, late at night when La Discotheque was winding down, to pile into my Jag and drive over to the Café des Artistes in Fulham, stopping on the way at the Chelsea bakery for hot bread straight from the oven. Peter would finish his business and join us there or meet me later at home. One evening my passengers were Christopher Courtenay and Johnny Summers. We chatted at the café for an hour or so and I made my way home as usual. A couple of days later, walking towards me in the King's Road, I saw Johnny. I was sure he had seen me, but he gave no sign of recognition. I waved and shouted, but he steadfastly refused to look at me, then he crossed the road to avoid me. I had no idea what I had done to offend him. It was not until after Peter's death when I caught up with Johnny's life, and asked him outright what had caused him suddenly to cool off, that I found out.

'I'll tell you,' he said. 'Two guys in a big car pulled up beside me late at night and said simply, "Lay off Mandy". 'That was it and that was enough for me.'

I was so accustomed by this time to thinking of myself as Queen Bee that I was suitably curt one evening in the club when a customer asked me to get him a drink. I had left Peter sitting at our table, and had gone to the bar to fetch him a Coke. Peter always insisted that I personally wash the glass, open the can and serve his drink for him, it was all part of his hygiene ritual. But I did not serve drinks to others.

'I don't work here,' I told the customer.

'I don't care about that. Get me a drink.'

As if this was not bad enough, this uncouth lout then grabbed at my wrist. I retaliated, instinctively, with a sharp slap on his ugly face.

The atmosphere, as they say, was electric. Jimmy was at my elbow trying to smooth things down – and trying to placate the man who, in my view, should right now be sailing smartly out of the door to land with a thud on the pavement, as was fairly standard procedure.

Then Peter was there.

'Apologise, Mandy,' he said. I was aghast. 'Please, please, apologise, Mandy, for me.'

I was not about to do any such thing. Peter ushered the outraged customer towards the office, practically grovelling.

Jimmy whispered in my ear. 'That is one of the Kray twins.'

They were at the peak of their reign of terror. Peter, I now know, was terrified of them. It cost him a lot to show how sorry he was.

Although I was expressly forbidden by Peter to see Christine, we kept in touch and whenever the opportunity presented itself I would see her for a gossip. She was full of her affair with Profumo. When Peter, one night, took himself off to a boxing match, I sneaked over to Stephen's flat where Christine was staying temporarily. I found her alone, Stephen had gone to a party. I had not been there long and the telephone rang. It was Stephen.

'This is a lovely party, why not come over,' he asked Christine, 'instead of being alone.'

'Mandy's here.'

'Then bring Mandy, too.'

We drove to the address he had given, an elegant house in Bayswater, Christine having a quick 'smoke' before we rang the doorbell. The door was opened by Stephen – naked except for his socks. Of course we giggled at this – typical Stephen joke we thought. Not at all. Following him into the drawing-room we walked into a full-blown orgy.

All the men were naked, the women naked except for wisps of clothing like suspender belts and stockings. I recognised our host and hostess, Mariella Novotny and her husband Horace Dibbens, and unfortunately I recognised too a fair number of other faces as belonging to people so famous you could not fail to recognise them: a Harley Street gynaecologist, several politicians, including a Cabinet minister of the day, now dead, who, Stephen told us with great glee, had served dinner of roast peacock wearing nothing but a mask and a bow tie instead of a fig leaf, and was presently in the kitchen doing the washing up.

Christine was happy to brazen it out, and thought it a huge joke. I was overcome with embarrassment, for myself and for the guests who, fortunately, were doing nothing more than just sitting around in a desultory fashion – I was not sure if all the action was over or had yet to begin. I was not standing around to find out. Stationing myself beside the buffet table, where a basket of tangerines, still bearing their leaves, was placed, I proceeded to munch my way through these looking only at the food or at my shoes, until I was sufficiently composed to make my excuses and leave.

I was in terrible trouble when I got back home, because although I had opened the windows, Peter could smell pot in the car. I insisted that I had been for a walk up the road but he said, 'You have been with Christine, I can smell that bloody stuff all over your hair.' He knew I would not smoke it.

The orgy amused Stephen. I am not sure he ever went to participate, he went as a *voyeur*. A man of his age, living in London, would be bound to be asked along. All the best people went, like going to the late-night Saturday film. It was a popular social occupation – in Paris and New York you had clubs which fulfilled the same function.

Christine, too, had been to the odd orgy, simply because she had been around more than I had, but she was not into that sort of thing. Neither was I – I do not have the team spirit for it. It was my one and only invitation. I am not averse to sex, but one at a time. I am quite conventional in that way. I have lived all my adult life with a certain reputation, but the men I have met, and certainly those who have been close to me, have never regarded me as a push-over when it comes to bed. I am told I can appear unfriendly, even cold – and in general this discourages men from trying to take advantage. They fear rebuff. Bob Hope's manager, Doc Shurr, summed it up best, talking to his good friend James Bacon of the *Hollywood Reporter*. Doc and I met in London when I was living with Peter. At the height of the trial and world-wide notoriety Doc and James were together, talking of the case, and Doc said: 'And do you know I never did more than kiss her cheek goodnight.'

I need romance: the food, the music, the soft lights, getting to know someone really well. I want to be courted before I will share a bed. Sometimes the courtship is fast, sometimes prolonged. It lasted three months with my present husband.

I realise that this picture of Mandy Rice-Davies going to an orgy and fiddling with the bowl of fruit and staring at her shoes, mentally wriggling with embarrassment, is at variance with the popular image. My discomfort at finding myself there was exacerbated by the knowledge that the other guests were, in the main, famous and elevated people. It added to the indignity, theirs and mine. I was naturally prudish, a trait I have not entirely overcome with age and experience. In fact I have learned that for me there is nothing new in sex except what is in the mind. This is not the memoir for explicit sexual descriptions, endless accounts of couplings bore me.

When Peter and I had our first serious quarrel I decided to teach him a lesson by committing suicide. He had told me he had to go north on business – in fact he dated another girl and I found out. In the middle of the ensuing row, he simply walked out leaving me with the frustration of an unfinished battle. I chose aspirin, because I conveniently had a full bottle to hand. However, I did not intend to kill myself, merely give Peter a fright. What was the safe dose? I swallowed twenty, flushed the rest down the loo and prepared to wait until he came hurrying back, and then tell him what I had done and let him worry about it. Having swallowed the aspirin I started to panic – perhaps twenty was an overdose. Not taking any chances I dialled 999, the ambulance service, and told them I had swallowed a bottle of aspirin.

'Get in a taxi and go at once to the Middlesex Hospital,' they instructed. This was not quite what I had in mind, but I complied. I had expected they would tuck me up in bed and keep me under observation, but not a bit of it.

Before I knew what was happening to me, they proceeded to push a tube down my throat and pump out my stomach. The more I tried to protest that I had not swallowed the full bottle, the more they believed I would say anything to stop them performing this revolting and painful procedure, and they held me down and got on with it. It was a truly horrifying experience, the tube, the vomiting. They let met lie on a bed and recover for a while, and then sent me home. The following day when Peter came round to test the temperature he found me lying in bed and wanted to know what was wrong. I had the humiliation of telling him I had attempted suicide.

Instead of the picture I had hoped to present, wan, reproachful, sad, I was a tearful creature with a bloated face, my skin covered with broken blood vessels caused by the effort of vomiting, marks which, incidentally, have never completely healed. He was kind, brought in flowers and fruit and made me promise never to do such a thing again.

When I discovered I was pregnant I was excited and happy. I had taken no pecautions against conceiving, I always felt instinctively that it would not happen to me. That occasion, and when I conceived my daughter, Danielle, are the only occasions in my life when I have been pregnant. I wanted to have the baby. I rushed out and bought a copy of Dr Spock, and I remember rushing to tell Christine the news. She was back with Michael Lambton and the three of us discussed the baby's future. I even asked Michael about schools and when should I put its name down for Eton.

Peter refused to believe the child was his. He assumed he was sterile – the result of being severely beaten up in one of the prison camps as a seventeen-year-old. As much as I professed he was the father, and there was no way at all he was not since I was completely faithful to him at that time, he would still not accept that he was the father.

He arranged for me to have an abortion, and sent me to see a friend of his, a lovely old Polish doctor. Anything further from the image of a back-street abortionist it would not be possible to imagine.

Doctor C was a cultured and distinguished man with a rich practice in a street full of other emminent specialists. I got to know him rather well and he told me of his life in Poland where he had had a country practice and used to visit his patients in his horse and cart. On the run from the Nazis, he travelled through occupied France, passing along the Jewish network which existed to get people out of the country. One night he was called to attend a woman who was in labour. She was desperately ill when he arrived, and, clasping his hands, she begged him to promise not to leave her baby. He promised, the baby was born and the woman died. Doctor C then continued his escape with his baby girl, brought her up as his own and she now lives in conventional bliss in London, unaware of her origins and of the fact, too, of her adopted father's 'sideline', which at that time was strictly illegal.

He felt that in the old days he was a better doctor, because he spent more time getting to know his patients. Today, people expected a pill to cure everything. He believed that it was more humane to perform an abortion than to refuse to do so. He charged whatever the going rate was at that time, but he also often performed the operation for no fee, if the girl had no money and no one else to turn to.

Doctor C became a prop in my life, which was how I came to know so much about him. After his initial diagnosis confirming my pregnancy, he fixed a time for the abortion to be done and I resigned myself to it. I trusted him to take care of me. The worst part was waiting in the anteroom, a sudden and purely imaginary smell of hot, freshly buttered toast wafted over me, making me think of cosy kitchens and log fires, babies and home.

Because of the necessity not to involve too many people, a full anaesthetic was out of the question and the operation was performed under local anaesthetic. It was extremely painful. I rested for a while, then took a taxi home. Peter had filled the bedroom with flowers. I felt relief that it was all over, and a physical release too from the nausea and general feeling of being unwell. I had eaten only oranges and pickled onions for weeks; now I felt normal again. Yet there was a sadness too, and mainly it was for Peter, as, because of his disbelief, he had missed the only chance in his life of ever having a child.

I remember the day my feelings for Peter changed. It was just before Christmas 1961. Audrey was in America and Peter was spending all his time with me. We went to a film in the King's Road, and during the show Peter complained of feeling ill. I suggested we left at once but he said no, he would be all right in a while. But he got worse.

'I'm sorry, I'll have to leave,' he said suddenly, staggering to his feet. As we got outside I could see he was perspiring very heavily. I drove to the mews, and put him to bed. I sat there watching him as he slept, feverishly. I was overcome with a feeling of utter helplessness, and at that moment I knew I loved him.

10

I DO not scare easily. But I have experienced the fear that paralyses your throat and makes it impossible to cry out. I was about twelve the first time. I was cycling along a country lane with my friend Jill, we had been picking bluebells and our saddle bags were full of the long stems. Ahead of us I was aware of a car parked, and a man standing beside it. Inexplicably it made me uneasy. As we drew level he stepped out, took hold of my handlebars and asked what time it was. We were not wearing watches, so said we did not know the time. 'What colour knickers are you wearing, then?' he asked me. Sooner than attempt to push past him, I turned my bike round and, shouting to my friend Jill, began to pedal furiously back the way we had come. He got into his car, turning it round and drove past us, pulling into crossroads ahead. Jill was faster and zoomed ahead, but I could not avoid him. Grasping the bike, he said, 'Let us go and pick bluebells in the woods.' He had unbuttoned his trousers and was trembling from head to foot and this made the bike shake.

I opened my mouth to scream, but no sound came. A crowd of cyclists came past and I wanted to scream to them for help, but could not make a sound. My open, silent, screaming mouth, and his firm, trembling grip on the cycle, froze into a tableau. Suddenly the scream came, and it broke the tension. I gave him a fierce push that sent him stumbling over the verge, leapt on the bike and pedalled furiously away, moving so fast downhill I could not keep my feet on the pedals.

I made Jill promise to say nothing of the encounter which had made me feel uncomfortable, as if I had done something to be ashamed of. But she could not keep it to herself and later that evening, alerted by her parents, the police called and I was taken through the identification procedure. Picking him up was no problem, he had a record for similar offences, and only the day before had been released from a mental home. I was required to go to court, in case he should plead not guilty, but he did not and I was not needed to give evidence. I was waiting with my father when the police brought him in. I thought Daddy was going to attack him, and at that moment I felt deeply sorry for the man. His face stayed on my conscience as if it were I who had harmed him.

Peter lived in a twilight world. Many of his associates were gangsters, and his employees had unorthodox backgrounds. One of his henchmen was Fred Rondel, an ex-wrestler who worked on and off for Peter as rent collector, club bouncer, general help. He was given to fits of violence – in one fight he bit a man's ear off and swallowed it – and was, at best, irrational. So, when, for some imagined slight, he was temporarily estranged from Peter and put the word around that he was coming to get him, Peter took no chances. He slept that night with the gun under his pillow and Jimmy Houlihan, Peter's bodyguard, keeping watch in the car in the garage below. The following morning Peter said we were moving out for a few days until the coast was clear. We went to stay with a friend of his where we spent the time playing chess. Two days of this was enough for me. Bored and resentful I told him: 'This is ridiculous, hiding out like this. I am going back home.'

He tried to dissuade me, but I meant what I said. I drove home, parked my car in the garage, closed the garage door, walked round to the door of the flat and just as I was about to put my key in the lock, somebody grabbed me from behind. It was pitch darkness, and all I knew was this steel-like grip around me. Again my voice deserted me. I tried to scream but it would not come and that scared me even more. My assailant pushed me from behind into the hallway and up the stairs. The moment he switched on the light and I saw it was Fred, I felt better. He was terrifying enough, but at least I knew him. My voice returned.

'Would you like a drink?' I said.

'Where's Peter?' he asked, and then I saw he had a gun.

I told him I did not know where Peter was, which he frankly disbelieved. But I insisted and began to busy myself with the drinks trolley. I never drank, but this time I poured myself a large whisky. I could see him fiddling with the gun, and I knew that he was capable of going berserk at the best of times.

Then he said, 'I don't want a drink but do you mind if I have some cake?'

'Help yourself, Fred,' I replied.

He put down his gun, went into the kitchen, cut himself a slab of cake and opened a can of Coke, and we sat and had a bizarre conversation about how are you, and I have not seen you lately, what have you been up to? Quite incongruous.

After ten minutes Fred said, 'Thanks for the cake, but I must be getting along,' like a man who has many pressing engagements, and got up to leave. I showed him politely out, belted up the stairs and proceeded to push every piece of furniture down the stars to make sure that the front door remained well and truly barred. Then I phoned Peter who sent Jimmy round to remove me to safety, but I figured that I was already in the one place Fred would not be visiting that night.

Fred's eventual arrest took the combined efforts of thirty policemen and dogs, and he was sent to the psychiatric wing of a top-security prison. From there he wrote Peter a chatty letter, informing him that he did not care for the place, that he had acquired a set of keys and proposed to escape on such and such a date. He added a PS: 'I am bringing a friend with me because he clings to me like stink to a blanket'.

We never saw Fred again, but years later I read of a court case in which he requested to give his evidence standing on his head as that helped his thought process. The judge gave permission and Fred stood on his head.

11

THERE was a restlessness throughout my relationship with Peter that made me do silly, flippant, irresponsible things. He gave me everything I wanted and demanded little in return. I was happy but we were a generation apart and sometimes I suppose I needed to be with people of my own age. Peter was forty-one when we met, but he had missed his youth. What I gave him was the youth he had never known.

The first time I left him we had gone to Bournemouth for the tennis tournament. Peter liked tennis, he booked the best suite in the Carlton Hotel and there we were, all set, for the week. After just one day there was an urgent call for him to return to London to sort out business problems.

'It's a pity to spoil your week,' he said. 'Stay on in the hotel and enjoy yourself.'

He did not specify how. As soon as he was out of town I telephoned Christine to take the first available train and join me.

We headed for the beach, and, as we were sunning ourselves, two young men approached. One, who said he was a photographer, asked if he could take some pictures of us. His name was Brian. I rather liked him, so, when they invited us out that evening, we accepted. They took us to a pub – something I never did with Peter – and we had a pleasant evening chatting and giggling, which was something that had been missing from my life since I had left home. They asked to see us the following day. I gave away Peter's best-seat tickets for the week to a couple staying in the hotel who could not believe their windfall and were overjoyed, and we met the two young men for lunch. Lunch stretched to dinner and it was late when we finally made it back to our room.

I was quite taken with Brian. Christine had fallen madly in love with his friend – the fact that she was also enamoured of

Jack Profumo did not immunise her from other attachments. We were undressing in our room when there was a sharp knock at the door.

'Who is it?' I called.

'Room service,' came the reply.

It was Peter. He strode in, absolutely livid with rage and slapped me hard across the face. I literally saw stars. Then he turned towards Christine, but she, a girl who was capable of rapid thought on occasions, fainted on the spot.

It transpired that Peter had been trying to reach me by telephone all evening. When there continued to be no reply from the room, he asked to speak to the night porter, who told him the two ladies had gone out and were not back yet.

'What two ladies?' asked Peter. When the porter mentioned Miss Keeler, that was all Peter needed. He asked an employee, Peter Rann, to drive him down to Bournemouth to sort things out.

Having hit me, his conscience got the better of him. Now he felt the guilty one. Christine went to bed, and Peter and I sat talking and making it up. When he left, it was understood that Christine and I should return to London the following day.

But during the journey back Christine had other ideas. 'Why go back to London, let's stay in Bournemouth,' she said. She had really fallen for her date, but if I stayed too that would give her the support she needed to make the break from London right then. By the time we were back in town, I was convinced that I wanted to leave Peter.

I packed my bags and told him I had decided to go. He did not question me, but accepted what I said without argument. His emotions were invariably carefully guarded, our greatest love conversations were always over the telephone, rarely face to face.

'What about money?' he asked. 'You'll need money.'

I indicated that I did not want any more from him.

'Look,' he said, 'I'll buy the mink from you.'

I had my mink coat over my arm, ready to leave. As he had given it to me in the first place he knew its worth. He went to the safe and counted out £500 in cash.

That was the beginning of our arrangement. Whenever I wanted to leave he gave me £500 and took the coat. When I returned the coat was mine again. It was a charade enacted frequently during our eighteen months together.

Back in Bournemouth, Christine and I immediately found a flat, unpacked our things and invited the boyfriends to dinner. Their arrival was the biggest anti-climax. I had already cooled off Brian, and was missing Peter desperately, and now I had well and truly cooked my goose. I was surrounded by my possessions from the flat including my expensive record-player and all my records. I did not want to tell Christine how I felt, because she was irritated by my attachment to Peter. I did not dare tell Peter I was sharing with Christine, which in his eyes was the worst thing I could do. Brian was hanging around hopefully and I did not fancy him at all. By ten o'clock I had made up my mind to confess. Making an excuse to leave, I went into the street to find a telephone box and called Peter – who was waiting for my call. I blurted out my dilemma. At the mention of Christine, Peter was furious.

'It's all her fault, she's to blame.'

At this I felt compelled to stick up for her, although, in truth, I knew that I was strongly influenced, that her mad-cap nature brought out the mad-cap in me.

Meanwhile, Christine had come to look for me, and had overheard enough of the conversation to know exactly what was going on. She was angry, but philosophical.

'If you want him, you'd better go back to London,' she said.

And the next morning I returned to London. Peter gave me my mink and we carried on as before.

Peter gave me enough freedom for me initially never to feel tied to him. He encouraged me to work, he was enough of a snob to be impressed when I reported back that I had met this famous person, or lunched with a celebrity. He financed my little jaunts, and was always there to welcome me back.

There was one man I almost left him for. Young, only twenty-two, good-looking, rich, Johnny Casablancas was passing through London on his way to Spain where he was studying international law. We met at La Discotheque and were instantly and strongly attracted to each other. Although Johnny was a sophisticated young jet-setter (his sister, Sylvia, had been tipped to marry the Aga Khan) our romance was a real boy-girl affair. It lasted for just a few weeks, while Peter was away attending to some business up in the Midlands.

I had to be careful to give nothing away of my infatuation for him. I realised I was playing with fire and so as not to give rise to suspicion we contrived to meet accidentally in Harrods. Even so our meetings were fraught for me.

My parents were staying with me in London at the time and I was careful to introduce Johnny to them as a long-established friend of Peter's and mine.

Johnny confided in my young brother, who was about twelve at the time, that he loved me, and for a while young David was the go-between.

Our only times alone together were late at night after my parents had gone to bed, then I would sneak out and meet him in, of all places, the Wimpy Bar near Marble Arch. Even so, I was quite sure somebody who knew us would see us together and report back to Peter.

There was, in fact, a curious twist to this when, after my parents had left, I returned to the flat to find a pane of glass removed from the front door which suggested somebody had put their hand in, opened the door and gone into the flat. I rushed through the flat looking for signs of burglary but nothing had been touched. The next day the German maid I employed at that time (because of his anti-Nazi feelings I pretended to Peter she was Austrian) asked me:

'Did you see the letter?'

'What letter?'

'A letter was delivered by hand. I put it on your dressing-table.'

There was nothing there. I concluded a letter had been delivered, possibly a blackmail demand by somebody who had seen me with Johnny and hoped to earn something out of it. Then they had lost their nerve and broken in to remove the letter before I had time to see it, act on it, perhaps even involve Peter.

When my parents left, and Peter returned, Johnny took a room at the Cumberland Hotel, and there I tried to visit him whenever I could. Deception does not come easily to me, and I was wrestling with making the choice between him and Peter. But his time was up and he had to go on to Spain to continue his studies. Would I go with him? It was not fear of leaving

Peter but of leaving England that stopped me short. Johnny left and I never saw him again. But I did hear from him. Later he sent his love via his friend Jean-Noel Grinda, who was in England to play at Wimbledon.

When the telephone rang Peter was very impressed at such a star calling, and said I should certainly accept his invitation to tea and to watch the trials. During tea I talked about Johnny, and Jean-Noel talked about his sister, Poussy, who was obviously his favourite woman in the world. Then, suddenly, he made a grab in my direction. And I had only just met him. For once my frosty put-down did not seem to work. We struggled indelicately for a while, the more he persisted the more put off I was. Eventually he conceded defeat. He did somewhat better on the courts that year.

I worked hard at my modelling as I cherished ambitions to become famous . . . though, when I did, it turned out to be the kind of fame I could have done without! I wanted to work in Paris, so in November 1961 I went there. Christine came too. We planned to launch ourselves in the *haute couture* world. As I did not want to alarm Peter by telling him I was leaving him, (I imagined I would be away for some time) I could not do the mink-coat routine, but I did have my Jaguar and that seemed a saleable asset. Not so. The garage discovered it was still on hire purchase. With very little money, therefore, compared with our usual affluence we flew to Paris, aiming to find work at once.

We found a small, inexpensive hotel and booked in. Next morning, full of energy, I set off for the salon of Christian Dior and Christine (she and I reckoned she would be a perfect model for Chanel) said she would go to Chanel. At Dior an elderly lady came towards me, and asked if she could help. I said I would like to speak to M. Marc Bohan, (I had made sure I was wearing my Christian Dior clothes) and she asked in what connection did I wish to see him.

'Actually,' I said, 'I would like to see him about becoming a mannequin.'

'Wait a moment, please,' and, ten minutes later, she took me to his workroom and introduced me to M. Bohan.

He looked at me and asked me to walk around and told me they were beginning fittings on 9 February and he would be very pleased if I would come back then. I returned to the hotel terribly pleased with myself. Christine came back and said that there had been nobody at Chanel, I suspect she had not gone but had sat in a café instead.

I had only been gone a day and already I missed Peter, wondering what he was up to. I booked a phone call to the mews in London (in those days there was no STD) and a few minutes later the phone rang. It was Peter saying I love you and come back.

'Dior has asked me to model for him,' which was a total exaggeration.

Peter said, 'No, come back immediately.'

'All right, I will come back tomorrow.'

The next minute the telephone rang again. It was Peter. I thought they had put my call through twice, but he said, 'No, that last one was my call to you.'

'But how did you know where I was?'

'Your sister gave me the number.'

As I had left Pooch with my sister, I had rung her to ask how the dog was and given her my number. Margaret had always liked Peter because he was very good to her, and because he used to tell her how wonderful and clever I was and how he loved me. She felt that we were good for each other. So, when he rang her looking for me, she had given him my number and at exactly the same moment we had put calls through to each other. This seemed so significant, I resolved to return to him at once. Before I could do so we were caught up in the Algerian riots in Paris.

Christine and I were sauntering along the St Germain des Pres when, suddenly, out of nowhere came the sounds of gunfire, banging doors, car doors slamming. Shop doors and shutters were locked in a trice. Within seconds we were engulfed by the surging crowd, thousands strong, and we too were carried along in the tide, as it headed for the Métro and safety. Some people stumbled and fell to be left lying there, others were hit by bullets. It was horrifying and had happened so fast. Down in the Métro we were packed like the proverbial sardines, and many were injured. Surely help would come? Nothing. We were down there for a considerable time, so crowded that movement was impossible.

Eventually, there were rumblings of movement forward and gradually we shuffled our way up the steps and out into the air and the daylight. To be met by the frightening sight of the French Gendarmerie. We were just people off the streets who had run for cover, yet we were treated as criminals. We came up, hands on our heads. One small boy had been badly shot in the leg and they did nothing to help him. Fortunately there was no way we could be mistaken for Algerians. Those who were were greeted with violent blows on the head from a truncheon and thrown, bloody and semi-conscious, into the back of the police van. I was disgusted by the police brutality I saw that day.

There was a funny footnote, though. Later that evening after we had been to the opera, and were walking home we became aware of two men following us. We recognised them as Americans, they were obviously interested in us, and playing it very cool. Suddenly two shots rang out. We looked round – our Americans had disappeared. At the first shot they had dived into a nearby fountain, and there they remained, submerged behind the waterfall, in fear of their lives. Christine and I roared with laughter. It broke the tension.

In early 1962 I received an offer to make a television commercial in the States. The producer had come to England to find a girl with a British accent, typically British-looking. He was very impressed with me and the fact that I looked very much like Vivien Leigh, oddly enough. I was blonde but they planned to do me with dark hair. They did test shots of me and after make up you could not tell who was me and who was Vivien Leigh. It is not apparent in the flesh, but very striking in photographs, for we have similar bone structure and mouth; and, photographed from a certain angle, the bump in my nose is disguised.

Christine was temporarily reunited with Michael Lambton, who was leaving to spend six months with his publishing firm in Philadelphia, and he asked Christine if she wanted to join him there. We planned to travel together, Christine would see Michael, I would do the commercial and possibly get more work in America.

It was my leaving thing again. Peter was very nice about it

and we did the mink-coat act. I had plenty of money, my tickets paid.

We had our smallpox innoculations and, instead of going by plane, we decided to travel by boat and booked on the maiden voyage of the *France*. Peter drove me to Southampton, and had filled my cabin with flowers. Christine too had flowers from somebody, and we set off in a blaze of glory feeling like celebrities.

After one day at sea I started to feel desperately ill. I could not eat, I was sick and feverish. It was the reaction to my smallpox jab. The voyage was a disaster. Christine, true to her habit of getting involved in things, as soon as we were invited to the captain's table, found herself a young officer whilst simultaneously flirting with the captain. By the time the voyage ended, the young officer was confined to quarters and the captain was rushing around like a bluebottle trying to maintain decorum. At the same time she found a very young boy of about fourteen who developed an adolescent crush on her, as well as a musician from the orchestra. So she had four people moon-eyed, each of them so different. She was not having affairs with all of them but somehow she had whipped up the intrigue, passing notes, secret assignations. Sea voyages are the worst because you walk on knowing nobody and by the second day it is like everybody has been best friends for years. The minute you leave the boat you never see them again, you do not even think about them and the petty rivalries and jealousies that flared up on the voyage.

I spent my time feeling ill and talking to a charming man who was something big in Heinz. He had the best or largest suite. He was bored, and so was I.

By the time I arrived in New York I was feeling quite desperate, and as I checked into the hotel on 42nd Street, I eventually collapsed. I called the studio on Long Island and said, 'I've arrived but I am terribly ill.' They sent a doctor around and he diagnosed cowpox.

I had asked for the smallpox injection on my stomach because I did not want it on my arms or anywhere in the bikini line, so when it became inflamed, it was doubly painful. They put me in hospital for two days. By the time I had started to recover I looked so awful that they suggested I go away somewhere for a weekend.

'You are in New York, go over to Fire Island which is just off Long Island,' they said. 'We'll book you into Cherry Grove.'

This was their little joke. Fire Island is a gay resort, and Cherry Grove the gay hotel. We were the only two girls in the place, and the only normal guys were the three Fire Island policemen. Needless to say they made a bee-line for us.

Having arrived in the morning we found we could not check into the hotel until two o'clock and it was then only 10.00 am. We met the three policemen (because the place is so small anyway) and, having assured them we were not lesbians as they suspected, they became friendly. They sorted out our luggage for us, then escorted us to the beach where Christine and I fell fast asleep. When we woke up we were absolutely burnt to a crisp. My lips were all cracked, my eyes were glued together, I could not walk.

Staggering to the hotel, we called the doctor who came hurrying around. We could not bear to be touched, we could not move. The doctor prescribed special lotions, which had to be applied every hour. But we could not apply them as neither of us could move. Fortunately, the policemen came to visit us, so Christine and I, like two mummies covered only by a sheet saturated in some soothing lotion, lay totally naked while our friendly policemen, every hour, would apply the healing lotions. After three days the agony faded and we were left peeling.

I telephoned the studios again and I said, 'I've had this accident – first-degree sunburn. It will take about a month if I am lucky to get my skin back in order.' They were remarkably civilised about it. They had to shoot the commercial, but they also offered to pay me as if I had actually done the whole thing.

I got in touch with Peter and told him as soon as I was over my sunburn I would be heading back. Christine decided to return too, and we flew back together; she had missed her mother.

One of my first friends when I came to London, was screen-writer Earl Felton, who had worked on many major films.

Paralysed by polio, he was nevertheless a bright, witty man whom I enjoyed visiting for a chat. Because of his physical handicap he was permanently at home, always deep into some writing project, although latterly his drinking had begun to create problems with his work. He was the original 'friend to the stars' and through him I met Bob Mitchum and George Hamilton among others.

One day he told me: 'Bob Mitchum is in town. His secretary, who has been with him for years, is pregnant and has had to stay behind in New York. He needs someone to take her place – not exactly secretarial, just be around, take care of things, order his lunch, organise the telephone, keep him supplied with razor blades.'

Keep him supplied with razor blades? Earl explained that Mitchum used only Wilkinson Sword, which at that time were not easy to come by. I figured I could track down his razor blades, it sounded quite an interesting job. What's more, he was Christine's hero, every night before she went to sleep she used to say, 'I am going to dream of Robert Mitchum,' and snuggle down with a blissful expression. I was quite excited at the prospect of introducing the two.

When I told Peter I might be working for Mitchum, he fully approved. This appealed to his love of the famous. I hurried along to the Savoy where Bob Mitchum was staying while preparing a film in which he played an army colonel. A genuine British army colonel had been engaged to work as adviser. Typical colonel-type: white moustache, military bearing, all terribly stiff-upper lip. That was the first day. After three days he was like an adoring puppy dog, just sitting and looking at Bob in rapt admiration. 'I love that man,' he told me. Most of us fell under the spell of the Mitchum charisma.

Bob interviewed me – sort of. He was charming, easygoing, informal. 'That's your room,' he said, indicating one of the rooms in the palatial suite. That Earl had recommended me was good enough for Bob. I went home for my things, signed in at the Savoy, and started work, if you could call it work.

He drank J. and B. Whisky from morning until night, but was never drunk. The days were like one long cocktail party; because of his charm and kindness he collected people. Americans passing in the corridor and recognising him, had only to say, 'Hello, Bob Mitchum,' and Bob would reply, 'Why, hello, boys, why don't you come in for a drink?' By the time I arrived on the scene he had collected a bevy of at least twenty permanent drinking guests, and to keep the J. and B. flowing required considerable organisation. Booking a table for dinner started with two or three and ended up with a dozen as the hangers-on decided to do just that. I saw it as a challenge to dislodge as many as possible.

Mostly it was all part of the friendliness he inspired. Occasionally, through no fault of his own and in perfectly civilised places, he would find himself the target for someone who wanted to punch him on the nose, just because he was tough guy Robert Mitchum. As soon as I grasped this I became adroit at sensing trouble and I would plant myself firmly between Bob and the aggressor and say, 'Kindly disappear, young man!'

Women too made a bee-line, although they had a different reason. Quite famous actresses would turn up, uninvited. Bob was warm and affectionate but I never saw any sign of him showing interest in a woman beyond the sort of brotherly gesture; but women threw themselves at him. One evening I took time off to see Christine (I had meanwhile invited her to meet Bob, but, afraid it might shatter her illusions, she steadfastly refused. She preferred to stick to her dream man) and Bob phoned me there. 'Get your arse over here,' he said in his usual cryptic way. I hurried back to the hotel, and let myself in to the suite. No sign of Bob, his door was open and I crept in. Bob was lying on his bed, fully dressed, fast asleep. In the drawing-room, sitting quite alone and seemingly quite cross at my arrival, was a famous actress. I started to creep out again, but Bob, awake now, told me to come back. His friend looked peeved, Bob was determined not to be left alone with her.

What with protecting him from predatory females, turning out the unwelcome visitors, seeing that food and drink were always available, trying to ensure Bob got enough sleep, keeping check on the bills (he was always paying, it seemed a dreadful extravagance) I was more nursemaid than secretary. In addition I had to listen to him reciting poetry, which he did at the end of a marathon drinking session. It was all quite exhausting and after a month I decided to sneak home to my parents for a break.

Peter had been to America and had brought back a blue Cadillac convertible. A huge thing like a boat. I drove in this to Birmingham, feeling the cat's whiskers and enjoying it. I took Robin for a spin to show off. Then I drove the family to Wales, and found manoeuvring through the country lanes a nightmare, I couldn't wait to hand over the Cadillac and take the Jag instead.

Money had not been mentioned between Bob and me, neither had he known when he would be returning to the States. When I walked into the Savoy and asked at the desk for my key I was told that 'Mr Mitchum has left'. There was a letter waiting for me. 'Thanks for the help, love Bob.' I missed him and the crazy life, and hoped we'd meet again. Little did I suspect just how pleased I would be to see his beaming face when next we met.

12

A HOT June night. An evening swim. A naked girl and a man who suddenly comes upon the scene. The circumstances of that first meeting between Christine Keeler and Jack Profumo have been described and analysed a thousand times. It was an event that was to end the political career of one man, the life of another and rocked a government. It changed the course of our lives, mine and Christine's. And I was not even there at the time!

A great deal that was said and written was not true. Much was left unsaid and unwritten.

Christine, after I left the flat, had gone to stay with Stephen. It was there that I went to see her whenever I could without Peter knowing. There had never been anything sexual between Christine and Stephen. Their friendship was remarkably close, both were eccentric in their way, and it amused them to do outrageous and childish things. They used to pretend, when there were people who did not know them well, that they were brother and sister, and temperamentally they were. When not mixing in high society, they enjoyed to go slumming, Christine wearing a dog collar around her neck and Stephen leading her by a dog's lead. In this fashion they visited seedy London clubs where it was possible to buy pot.

Stephen was not a serious pot-smoker although he sampled it occasionally when the place, the mood, the music was right. Christine smoked it and liked it and needed to go to the places where it could be obtained. In 1961 that meant the black clubs. There was no drug scene in London at that time. I have been amused since to read about drugs and purple hearts being circulated in Peter's La Discotheque. Drugs never. And purple hearts were not around until at least 1963!

What began as something silly became more serious for Christine. Stephen heartily disapproved of her drugging and mixing with the flotsam and jetsam of the black immigrant community. Mixing with West Indians, it was inevitable that Christine should get involved physically, and eventually she formed a liaison with Aloyisius Gordon, known to his friends as Lucky although he did not have much of that, as it turned out. He presumably had something going for him sexually which suited Christine, who returned to him frequently throughout their stormy affair. Christine needed sex. She was not a nymphomaniac, she had full control, but she enjoyed it in a way that if it suited her, she was not too fussy who the other person was.

She was strongly attracted to a daily visitor at Wimpole Mews and Stephen's closest friend at that time, Eugene Ivanov, second naval attaché at the Russian Embassy. And hardly surprisingly, for Eugene was one of the most charming people I have ever met. Very, very handsome in a James Bond sort of way, very easy to talk to, warm, humorous, generous too – his frequent gifts of vodka and caviar always presented with a little joke about 'the luxuries you capitalists appreciate'.

With Eugene, Stephen's usually flippant personality took on a more serious note, and they would discuss important political concepts in great depth. The effect was contagious, I would join in these intense discussions with enthusiasm. I really became interested in Russia and very curious about communism when I met Eugene.

By this time I seemed to be mixing in four different worlds. There was a segment of Peter's life which could only be described as the underworld; my work (modelling and the fringe of acting); the county-society lot, circulating around the Astors and Cliveden; and the political and diplomatic circuit. It was the latter that fascinated me most the more I moved around.

Because I was avid for information and behind-the-scenes snippets, I found this section of society most interesting to talk to. Perhaps too much so. One African head of state told me all about the black panthers that patrolled his palace instead of guard dogs. 'They're not at all vicious,' he said, 'as long as you don't feed them raw meat.' Two weeks later, to prove his point, I had a call to say a black panther was on its way to me and would be landing at Heathrow. Panic stricken I had to divert its destination. A friendly RSPCA inspector helped out, and my gift ended up at Dudley Zoo!

Stephen took Eugene everywhere with him, we used to say he wore Eugene like a mascot, and Eugene, because of his charm, was accepted everywhere. Or almost everywhere. Only once was the welcome less than genial. Arriving at Iain Macleod's for cocktails, Stephen was drawn into a corner by the host, who asked him politely but firmly to please leave at once with his Russian friend.

As young as I was, it struck me that, for a second naval attaché, Eugene had a very special standard of living. He always had money, which he spent freely. He was beautifully dressed. He spoke faultless English. I met many staff when I went to a cocktail party at the Russian Embassy, and Eugene spoke better English than anyone else, including the ambassador, whose English was minimal.

During my years in Israel, I mixed with many United Nations people, and they claimed you could always spot a Russian agent by the money he spent. Russian agents are groomed and trained to mix in society, and you need money for that. Eugene was certainly groomed and he certainly mixed well.

We talked of communism. I had not been the least interested at school – I should not imagine Solihull ever had a branch of the Young Communists and if there had been, I would not have known about it. In my family politics were never discussed because 'it leads to rows,' so I never knew which way my parents voted. I would have earmarked my father as a safe Conservative voter and was recently surprised to find they both regard themselves as Labour. So discussing political ideology was new to me.

Eugene returned my interest by bringing me some pamphlets on Russian cultural and farming policies. He showed no physical interest in me or Christine or any other woman, although he had ample opportunity, for his wife was a teacher at Moscow University and they saw each other infrequently. During one of her summer visits they went down to Cliveden and I met her there. Christine fancied Eugene madly, and he was charming and sweet to her but that was all. I asked Stephen how Eugene managed to remain so impregnable.

'Isn't he interested in women?'

Stephen said, 'He's a Russian, a diplomat, they don't allow that sort of thing.'

Stephen's pride in his friendship with Eugene was almost as if he saw it as his way of doing something special, of rebelling against his true-blue circle. As he waxed on about communism, I used to laugh at him.

'You could never be a communist,' I said on more than one occasion. 'You won't even share a cigarette!'

'That isn't the point at all,' he replied, but laughed and then changed the subject, as he always did if you ever got too close.

But actually, what I know now makes me think Stephen would have been perfect material for a spy – a middle-aged man with no close ties, Establishment background, shabby gentility, no strong family feeling, his lack of interest in objects, his amusement at manipulating people; a character straight out of John le Carré thriller.

It amused me to think of Eugene as a spy.

I asked Stephen once whether Eugene was a spy and he said, 'Everybody at the Russian Embassy is a spy,' and he implied that anyone employed by a government in another country is a spy. (The English came to this conclusion a few years ago when they expelled many of the Russian Embassy staff.)

I remember asking Eugene about spying and what qualifications you needed as a spy. In my childish imagination, I imagined spying meant getting hold of secret documents. His reply has remained in my mind to this day. He said, 'Look, of course I am not a spy, but we all know something about spying. The idea of a spy is not that you have access to secret documents, that's a marvellous find of course, a miracle. The average spy just circulates in certain surroundings and picks up information which perhaps is not important at all, like somebody is going away for a weekend. So the spy reports this and another spy in another country is reporting that this particular weekend something is to happen in Germany, a transference between the Germans and the English. And you have a whole network of people assembling parts of the puzzle. When all the information is gathered back in intelligence headquarters it makes a clear picture. It's a word here and a sentence there.'

I used to ask a lot of questions. Ivanov would tell me to change the subject. He once told me, 'Women – what you've got is more powerful than the atom bomb.'

Once we were talking about secrets, British secrets, what we had and what we did not have, and Stephen turned to me with a smile (this was immediately after Burgess and Maclean) and said, 'Don't worry, little baby, the only secrets the British have is about the latest frogman's suit.' Then turned to Eugene and they exchanged a conspiritorial sort of smile.

I heard the details of that first Saturday in June 1961 from Stephen. Christine was at a loose end in London, and decided to pay Stephen a visit at the cottage. All his friends knew he was always there at weekends and that Sunday was a sort of open house provided, that is, you arrived in party mood and with enough food and drink for your own needs and a little left over for the stock cupboard. Christine found a mutual friend to drive her down, Stephen was delighted to see them and, some time during the evening, they all decided to cool off in the pool.

Lord Astor kept a collection of discarded swimsuits in the changing room for anybody who happened to need one, and, clad in one of these, Christine had a quick dip. As she climbed out it was obvious the swimsuit was ludicrously ill-fitting. Stephen told her it looked dreadful and dared her to take it off. Typically, Christine did just that and was posing, Murray style, on the edge of the pool when the first of Lord Astor's dinner guests, on a post-prandial walk through the grounds, hearing laughter from the pool, headed that way and walked through the gateway to the walled pool.

It was Jack Profumo, closely followed by Bill Astor. The two had a very good look at Christine, who was well worth looking at, before Stephen clambered out of the pool and, as he always maintained, to conceal his embarrassment tried to turn it into a game. He chased Christine round the pool, right into the protecting arms of Jack Profumo.

This was the tableau that greeted the rest of the dinner party, led by Bronwen and Jack Profumo's wife, the actress Valerie Hobson. According to Stephen (for the story was later repeated) Bronwen first asked to be introduced, then handed a towel to Christine saying, 'You will no doubt need this, my dear.' Christine grabbed the towel and scurried away, watched by Profumo, who had, in fact, not taken his eyes off her since that first vision five minutes earlier.

Eugene arrived at the cottage the following morning to help Stephen with some gardening. The conversation was all about Christine's indiscreet behaviour the previous night and they all shared the joke. After lunch the three of them walked across to the pool and there they were joined by Lord Astor, Profumo and several more house guests, including President Ayub Khan of Pakistan.

It was obvious to Christine that Profumo was strongly attracted to her. Stephen noticed it too, and so did Euegene. At the end of the day Eugene took Christine back to London – and to bed.

The following day Profumo telephoned and invited her to lunch. That was the beginning of Christine's affair with Profumo. And it was a full-blown affair. She told me how he took her out to dinner, took her for drives in the country, borrowing a car so that he was not recognised, and took her to his own house when his wife was away. He was a middle-aged married man, and she was a young girl. It is not an unusual situation. She got out of it exactly what he did. He did not give her money or expensive presents. He sent her little notes, and telephoned her all the time. She was very fond of him, he was rich, good-looking, important and Christine was impressionable.

I never met him. Only once, in a cinema, someone pointed him out to me as he was sitting with his wife a few rows behind.

One day when I went to see Christine, I found her in a pensive mood and she said, very seriously, that Eugene had asked her to ask Profumo the date for delivery of nuclear warheads to West Germany. We sat and discussed this in great detail. Not should she or shouldn't she, because there was never any question of this. As Christine said, in all sincerity, 'Anyway, I could never betray my country.' What angered us both was that Eugene should have the gall to ask her in the first place. The whole episode was melodramatic. And naïve too, I thought. Would Eugene really imagine Christine would get into bed with Profumo and say, 'Oh, by the way, tell me about the nuclear warheads going to West Germany'?

It did not add up, but the question had been asked. Eugene never referred to it again. My assessment of the situation now would be different. Now I can see it was the sprat to catch a mackerel. Make a request, see her reaction, decide what use she will be. In the event he saw her reaction and it was no use at all to him.

For Christine's indiscretion at that time she had the dubious distinction of being publicly called a whore and a call girl. In other similar situations, the Cabinet Minister's mistress gets a title. Anthony Blunt, confessed master spy of the decade, received an honour and a job next to the Queen.

Christine's affair with Profumo ended in December. She was not told the real reason, which, as it later turned out, was a warning to Profumo from MI5 that Ivanov was a close friend of Stephen Ward, and Christine was living in Ward's apartment. So he was scared off, withdrew tactfully and sent a brief note saying sorry he would not be around for a while.

Christine felt a little sad, a little hurt, and accepted it as she always accepted a lover's goodbye. As for Ivanov, apart from that one night, after he had seen the effect she had had on Profumo, he never again made love to Christine, or attempted to.

My involvement with Eugene, as a friend, lasted until the end of 1962, and how much I saw of him depended on my commitment to Peter and the free time I had to visit Christine. I was so stimulated by all this political discussion that when the Cuban crisis flared up and it was suggested to me that I could play a part in shaping history, I readily believed this and enthusiastically became involved.

In October 1962 the world was suddenly brought to the brink of war by the confrontation between Russia and America over the siting of Russian missiles in Cuba. We all held our breath waiting for disaster to strike. Better dead than red was the slogan of the day.

Eugene claimed he had a solution. Khruschev, he said, was prepared to come to England if the British Government would set up a summit conference here. This would be a face-saver for Americans and Russians alike, and Britain, with centuries of diplomacy to fall back on, could mastermind this meeting and provide the peace-keeping formula. 'None of us wants war,' he repeated over and over. He seemed to have little idea of how things worked in British politics, believing fervently that the aristocracy ruled and that the only way to get things done was through one of Stephen's titled friends. He was not far out. Through the establishment network, a meeting was set up involving Sir Godfrey Nicholson MP, Lord Arran and Bill Astor to get word through to Mr Macmillan. I was absolutely agog at sitting in on these discussions at the flat, frantically filing my nails and trying to follow the line of argument.

My services were utilised in distributing pamphlets in the Foreign Office. Eugene instructed me to take them in, and the moment I was apprehended to throw them into the air and run out again. But nobody stopped me, I simply walked through the beautiful old building, into various offices, leaving my pamphlets on desks like a messenger distributing memos in the in-tray.

In the event tension was relieved by Mr Khruschev agreeing to dismantle the missiles, and the crisis was mercifully over.

Christine flitted in and out of my life, and in and out of Stephen's with complete unpredictability. She knew that Stephen strongly disapproved of her more wild friends and excesses, so avoided him when she thought she had something to hide. During one long absence she went to live with her latest lover, another West Indian called Johnny Edgecombe, whom she met in July 1962. Her brief and intense involvement with him was to prove even more catastrophic than her brief fling with Profumo.

13

DOMESTIC bliss (and it was domestic) was cracking at the seams. The clubbing, gambling, dining-out lifestyle had changed to cosy evenings *à deux* at home. Peter even rented a television set, for which I signed the agreement, although it stood, blank screened, in the corner of the room most of the time. Neither of us developed the habit.

I didn't object to spending more time at home, in fact I welcomed it, but Peter was becoming more and more morose as he became more dependent on me. 'Would you love me if I didn't have any money?' It was sweet, endearing the first time he said it. But now it became a constant question. He was extremely busy with work problems, I knew about his speculative plans to develop an estate in the Midlands. What I didn't know was that the Rachman empire was beginning to crumble and that he faced financial ruin.

He became a depressing person to live with. He had stopped playing tennis because he said he had pleurisy and mustn't attempt any energetic activity. That sounded convincing. I never suspected there was something wrong with his heart; if I had known that I would never have left him.

There were also his constant diets, aimed at getting his weight down, which made him extremely bad tempered. I needed to escape, occasionally, from this claustrophobic atmosphere but Peter couldn't bear to be away from me. He was convinced he was going to have an accident in the car, and gave me a list of what I had to do if this happened, including removing his rings and his diamond cufflinks, his gold watch and his gold cigarette case, which was a present from Audrey — to decipher the inscription on the case I had bought a Latin dictionary and became fleetingly quite keen to learn Latin. Repeatedly he told me of the importance of the code on his gold bracelet, that I should take it off and give it to his lawyer who would know what to do. When it happened his lawyer was totally mystified. Peter's obsession with not letting the left hand know what the right hand was doing, because he trusted no one, worked against his own interests in the end. So great was the confusion over what property he actually owned that several of his sharp business associates were able to claim ownership of houses, knowing there was nothing on paper to prove the contrary.

Several times he said he wanted to put 1 Bryanston Mews West in my name, and I resisted – I saw it as a tie.

Some time in October 1962 I told him I was leaving, that we just needed a rest from each other for a while, and he agreed, but insisted that we saw each other every day. I took a few essentials, but left my keys and my jewellery because at least it was safe there.

I asked Stephen if I could stay at his flat for a week or two. 'Of course, little baby,' he said. And I moved in.

There was no shortage of company. Christine looked in, Eugene was a daily visitor, always good company whether talking seriously about politics or making light conversation. A young man called David Davies dropped by frequently. At first I thought he was interested in me but came to the conslusion there was somebody else there who interested him more. He was a close friend of Iain Macleod's family, and it was Iain Macleod who had been put out by Stephen taking Eugene uninvited to his party.

I missed Peter. I remember one evening leaving a party to phone the mews, but there was no reply.

I had no reason to feel lonely and every reason to feel I was the social success of the season. I had come to know an amusing and lovable American showbusiness agent called Lou (otherwise known as Doc) Shurr. He was one of the characters of Hollywood, where he had enjoyed an unrivalled reputation for years. As well as handling major clients like Bob Hope and Kim Novak, he also tried to help out the up-and-coming and was famous for the props he provided. When taking out some young starlet who needed to be seen in the right places, he would drape a full-length mink over her shoulders, fasten a rope of diamonds around her neck, and at the end of the evening the mink and diamonds went back to his office. He kept a wardrobe full of minks and a safe full of diamonds! As his guest at dinner I met a host of famous stars – Michael Wilding, George Peppard, as well as Liz Taylor and Richard Burton, both of whom were memorable, she for her strong handshake and he for his readiness to talk to me about Wales. My mother and he came from the same valley.

Doc and I were invited to celebrate Thanksgiving with Bob Hope at the cottage he had taken up the road from Shepperton studios where he was filming *Call Me Bwana*. As I waited at the studios for Bob Hope to finish a scene with Anita Ekberg, I chatted to Susan Hampshire. Always on the lookout for a chance to break into films (I had played a small part in *Hide and Seek* with Ian Carmichael and Janet Munro), when Susan volunteered the name of her voice teacher I made a note; having voice training would be a positive step towards improving my potential. Now that I was away from Peter I was determined not to drift aimlessly.

Back at the cottage the chauffeur had been given the night off while we settled down to enjoy the dinner cooked by a woman friend of Bob's. We had just begun when Doc was taken violently ill. He was haemorrhaging badly, there was blood everywhere. It all happened so fast that we were momentarily incapable of action. Then we all moved in conflicting directions. Bob grabbed the phone.

'Just dial 999 and ask for an ambulance,' I said.

Bob dialled 999 and said: 'This is Bob Hope speaking, send me an ambulance straight away.'

Possibly they thought it was a practical joker. The minutes passed and nothing happened. Doc was unconscious, white as a sheet, cold yet perspiring. I stretched him flat on the carpet and wiped his brow. Bob was sobbing.

'Oh my God, we've been together thirty-five years and now he's dying.'

His friend meanwhile changed into a pair of running shoes and set off at a sprint along the road for help. The nearest village was about four miles away. She raised a doctor and brought him back as the ambulance, which I had summoned with a second 999 call, arrived, and Doc was rushed to the Middlesex Hospital.

Bob and I got to know each other well, sitting on either side of the bed during those visiting hours. Little did he and Doc know they'd be repeating that scene before long.

At a party given by the Lebanese Ambassador, I met a young American called Senta Hitchcock. We immediately had one thing in common – both of us were getting over a love affair. I talked about Peter, he talked about his ex-girlfriend. It was funny in a bleak sort of way. There was to be a grand society wedding, Valerie MacAlpine was marrying a Spanish nobleman and Senta invited me, not just to the wedding, but to accompany him along on the honeymoon – first stop at the Ritz in Paris. It seemed a good idea.

I told Peter the truth, that I was going to Paris as Senta's guest. Oddly, Peter seemed pleased. Was it his snobbism? – glad to see me around with an American millionaire whose family owned their own stable of racehorses. Or did he know he was dying? The night before I left we met at the flat.

He said: 'Maybe when you get back from Paris, you'll move back here again.'

I told him: 'Well – I don't want to promise . . .'

Suddenly he clutched at his chest and fell back in the chair, gasping for breath.

'Please get me my pills, in my jacket pocket,' he said.

I went to his jacket, and found the pills which I gave him. After a few moments, he was composed.

'Promise,' he said, 'you'll put red roses on my grave.'

I was shaken by this. 'Don't be silly, Peter, don't talk like that,' I said. 'I'll be seeing you in a few days.'

'All right,' he said. 'Give me a call and I'll pick you up from Heathrow.'

I left, feeling uneasy. I suspected him of over-dramatising, perhaps trying to make me feel sorry for him. On the other hand there were the pills – he'd never taken pills before in all the time I'd known him. I dismissed it as Peter play-acting, yet I couldn't get his words out of my mind: 'Will you put red roses on my grave?'

Valerie and the count had the most divine suite at the Ritz, with an open fireplace burning logs. I had a suite to myself, next to Senta's. I was determined to enjoy my three days there. The first night found us carousing with Anthony Quinn, outside Ingrid Bergman's front door at three in the morning. The sounds of his guitar playing and our singing woke her, and as she opened the door I was struck by her beauty. How anyone can look that beautiful when they have just been woken from a deep sleep – and be smiling about it – I don't know.

The next day was spent eating, drinking, socialising. We finished up at Régine's. I felt distinctly uncomfortable and unhappy, so when I got back to the hotel I tried calling Peter. There was no reply from the mews, he was nowhere to be found at any of the clubs. I didn't want to call his house in Hampstead because I knew Audrey would be there.

At this point the jaunt turned into a black comedy. Turning on the tap in my magnificent marbled bathroom, the whole thing came off in my hand and scalding water shot upwards. I was drenched, and badly burned. I screamed for help and tried to quell the flood with a towel but this was impossible. Senta rushed in to help – so, a few minutes later, did the concièrge brandishing a stick in Senta's direction; hearing my screams and seeing the two of us he had jumped to the wrong conclusion. By the time the engineers had been able to staunch the flow, the carpets were sodden and water was lapping in the corridors. Both Senta and I were badly hurt. I fell into bed exhausted, tearful and still trying to telephone Peter. I was homesick, unhappy and I wanted him to make it all come right.

First thing next day I phoned the airline for a seat home. There was none. The Paris-London service operated differently then, and it was the following day, 30 November before I was able to get on a flight.

I bought him a stuffed lion as a present, which went everywhere with me for months afterwards. Immediately we landed I phoned him. Still no reply. By this time I was feeling the rising waves of panic. I took a taxi to Stephen's.

He opened the door and came down the steps towards me. 'I've got bad news for you, little baby.'

'Peter's dead.'

'Yes,' said Stephen.

I collapsed in floods of hysterical tears. I wanted to see Peter, I hadn't said goodbye, and I knew I had to. Stephen tried to calm me, I pleaded to be taken to Peter's house. Eugene offered to take me, and the two of us drove to Winnington Avenue. Eugene offered to wait, but I said no, he should leave me there.

The front door was open, in the Jewish custom of sitting *shivas*, with friends calling in to pay their respects to the bereaved. The mirrors were draped in black cloth, the rabbi was chanting prayers, the room was full of peole, many of whom I had been in the habit of dining with over the past eighteen months. Nobody acknowledged me.

Audrey came towards me. I think that was the moment I knew that Audrey was his wife, and not just the woman he had lived with for years.

She said, 'You're Mandy, aren't you? We haven't met but I do know about you, of course. Shall we go into the kitchen and have a cup of tea?'

Brian O'Donnell, her brother, was there, one of Peter's close employees. He didn't speak to me. She gave me tea and I sat at the kitchen table.

She said, 'If you know anything that can be of any help to us we should be grateful. Of course we will look after you.'

I didn't understand the last remark. But I could understand their anxiety for information about Peter's confused business dealings. Audrey had been out of his life for the past two years, and I had been involved with him constantly. Simply to be able to tell them the addresses of his various properties would be invaluable. I told them what I could, which wasn't much.

Audrey told me how he had died. He had spent the night gambling with Jimmy and come home in the early hours, had a heart attack the following morning and been rushed to hospital. There he died.

I got up to leave, and walked outside. There in the drive was the Rolls-Royce. This brought home the sense of loss. Everything about him was still there – his cigar butt in the ashtray, his yellow chamois driving gloves. I took the cigar butt and the gloves, and was lying weeping over the steering wheel when Brian came and dragged me out of the car.

Peter Davies drove me back to Stephen's.

There was a letter waiting for me, from Margaret. She had written to tell me that Laddie had died. Run over. Being a pit pony he had gone blind in one eye. He was on a leading rein when a car approached on his blind side. He died the same day as Peter, 29 November 1962.

14

I WANTED to die. It is the only time in my life I have had that desire. The realisation came gradually as the reality of life grew inexorably worse. Christine was strangely unsympathetic. Stephen almost callous, even repeating with a smile that at the moment of shock I had asked, 'Did he leave a will?' I knew I was stunned, but I also knew what thoughts I had uttered, and anyone with a knowledge of Peter would have known a will was quite out of character.

Some masochistic urge drove me to Somerset House to prove to myself that Peter and Audrey were married. Perhaps it had happened years and years before, I hoped. To discover that they had been married only a short time, their wedding was in March 1960, was salt in the wound. Today I believe his marriage was an attempt to gain British nationality, which had always eluded him. If that was the case, his last try failed.

I had no immediate money problems. I had some jewellery, although Peter's family ensured I was never able to claim any of my property from the flat, including a portrait of myself that graced one wall. I was never even permitted to put my nose inside the door, and I was too down to care.

An overwhelming depression settled on me, I wanted only to sleep away the numbness. Stephen who was very anti pills (he could cure a headache in seconds, by touch) provided the odd sedative but it was not enough to dull my misery. I went to see my old friend, Doctor C. I told him nothing except I was having difficulties sleeping and could he give me something to make me sleep.

'You look dreadful, my dear,' he said. 'You are tense, you need to sit in the park for two hours every day.'

That wasn't what I wanted to hear. I begged him for sleeping pills, which reluctantly he gave me, warning me to be very careful, 'but I know you are a sensible girl.'

All I wanted to do was stay in bed all day in a haze of half sleep, half wakefulness. People called round but I didn't want to see them. My parents asked me to go home but I never want those close to me to see me in my moments of despair. I want those I love to see me in my best moods.

I remember distinctly the moment when I made the decision to kill myself.

I have never been afraid of death. I've always been a person who has thought a great deal about suicide, before and since. It has always struck me that suicide is a good thing, I like the idea that you can take your own life, that the choice is yours. When you don't want to open your eyes and you really don't want to belong to this world it's far more preferable to end it than to endure the feeling of overwhelming despair that used to overcome me from the first moment I opened my eyes. I remember Stephen was going out to dinner with Godfrey Winn. Stephen and Godfrey were friends, although Godfrey denied that afterwards.

I was left on my own. Methodically I went into the kitchen and got a glass of water, took all the pills out of the bottle, wrote a note saying I wanted to be buried next to Peter. How they were to put me in a Jewish cemetery I do not know, but nevertheless at that time I was serious. I swallowed all the pills one after the other, washing them down with water. For the first time in three days since Peter's death I felt really happy. I wasn't afraid. As I got in to bed I felt such a thrill of happiness, I was euphoric. Lying on the bed, very peaceably and contented, I picked up my book *Gone with the Wind*, which I had begun before going to Paris and hadn't looked at since, and I started to read it. There was no panic, I was at peace and I read, and gradually I started to feel more and more sleepy.

My last conscious thought was, 'It's a pity that I will never know the end of *Gone with the Wind*' – which I suppose was a small tendril clinging to life.

A couple of hours later, Christine decided on the spur of the moment to come around to see how I was. She was with her friend Paula Hamilton-Marshall, whom I didn't know. They found me in bed, my head turned towards the wall so that they couldn't see my face. Instead of leaving me in my peaceful sleep for the night, true to form Christine gave me a shake which turned me over and they saw that my face was turning black. Both girls were absolutely shocked and Christine immediately called for an ambulance. Stuffing my goodbye suicide note into her bag, she came with me. In the ambulance they held a mirror up to me to see if I was breathing and there wasn't any breath. They put a machine on me to pump oxygen into me. This time I was not conscious of the dreaded stomach pump.

I had the strangest sensation that I was dead, and was lying in the morgue. I wasn't alone, there were other bodies lying around me. As I lay there I was thinking, If I am lying here I am dead, but because I have the power to think, there must be life after death. Now I have got to go back to tell everybody there is life after death. I was terribly excited about this.

I am alive today because Christine saved my life. According to the Chinese philosophy I owe my life and should devote my life to Christine. I had taken thirty barbiturates, Stephen couldn't have found me in time.

When I recovered consciousness I was blind. The effect of the drug is to detach the retina. Without sight I couldn't co-ordinate my actions, couldn't touch my face or feed myself. The doctors told me my sight would come back, although I would probably suffer migraines all my life.

The police interviewed me because it was a criminal offence to attempt suicide. My case was worsened by the fact that I'd been there before, and I found myself trying to explain that the last time was a pretend suicide and this time it was real. At the same time I had to convince them I was no longer a menace to myself. The police wanted to know where the pills had come from. I didn't want to incriminate Dr C. My evasiveness could have pointed at Stephen. Somehow I had talked my way round it by saying that I had had the pills for years.

The worst part of all was the embarrassment of my parents turning up and sitting on the end of the bed. They were hurt and alarmed and kept saying I should go home to Solihull and start afresh. I didn't want to see them. I didn't want to see anyone. All I wanted was a fresh peach and they were out of season. Christine managed to find me two, and eating them was sheer bliss.

The pain had gone. When I woke up in that hospital bed, I felt neither disappointment nor relief, but a sense of time having passed. Peter's dying was in the past, last year, the year before, a long time ago. I still felt sad, but I didn't *have* to think about him.

Going back to Stephen's flat in Wimpole Mews when they discharged me from hospital had been like waking up after a five-year sleep. Peter was so far back in my past it was almost a dream.

Feelings of grief were intermittent. Instead there was an emptiness that had a numbing effect. I started to drink. I found that half a bottle of whisky kept me in a state of bearable feeling for a whole day, enabling me not to think about anything which could have painful reminders. I made half-hearted attempts to retrieve my belongings from Bryanston Mews – at least books, records, my record player and a portrait were indisputably mine, but my requests were turned down, outright.

Stephen invited my parents to stay at the flat. Once again they asked me to go home with them, but I had grown too far away for that. I preferred to stay with Stephen, at least for the time being. I dreaded being alone. At Stephen's there were always people coming and going and this created a feeling of bonhomie.

To make our arrangement official it was agreed I should contribute towards the rent. Stephen suggested £6 a week, and a half share towards food, electricity and telephone. It was more than fair by any standards (and Stephen was not a generous man) and I had the best of the bargain, since I was at home all day and he was in his consulting room. I have run up vastly expensive telephone bills all my life. It was a straightforward arrangement that was later made to appear sinister. As were two conversations we had at that time.

The lease of Stephen's flat was running out. It was owned by Twentieth-Century Fox, who had indicated on more than one occasion that they would be glad to take possession. Knowing that John Shepridge, Daryl Zanuck's right-hand man, was a friend of mine, Stephen asked if I would 'put in a word' for him about the chances of renewing the lease. I had a good opportunity, as I had been invited to John's Christmas party. So I asked. The request was barely acknowledged. I was not in the frame of mind to ask for a big favour and there the matter dropped – to be dragged up and played out during Stephen's trial as his using me to influence people.

One day Stephen suggested that we might get married. I hardly took him seriously but we chatted around the subject. He made no pretence of being in love with me, but we had grown fond of each other, we respected each other – I am not a difficult person to get along with. Possibly Stephen was getting to like our domestic partnership and found it comfortable having someone to come home to. He was by then in his late forties, a bit of a cynic, basically lonely. Approaching old age, many people in similar circumstances elect for a marriage of convenience.

'We ought to get married some time,' he remarked casually, as if to illustrate the undemanding nature of this proposed liaison. He said he could help me with my career; I wanted to concentrate on modelling and extend my acting, and he said he had influential friends in many walks of life who could help me. It was a conversation that led nowhere – except in the end as evidence against him in court.

It was never repeated. Christine was once more at a loose end and we agreed to turn the clock back and take a flat together. I found a flat at 63 Great Cumberland Place and we arranged to move in, early in the New Year. But first I made Christine promise that she would cut her ties with the black community because I wanted a fresh start.

I was feeling fairly optimistic for the future. Bob Hope and Doc Shurr had been very kind to me after the suicide attempt, and rallied round with great concern after the shooting. 'Things really happen to you!' Bob wise-cracked with feigned nervousness. Doc's interest was more than merely friendly. He viewed me as a possible client – as a new Grace Kelly almost – and was enthusiastically planning to launch me in Hollywood and invest his considerable expertise into building me as a film star.

As the early weeks of depression and drinking which immediately followed Peter's death began to lift I started to organise myself. Finding the flat and planning the move was one step. Fixing up private drama classes with Iris Warren, a retired drama teacher who had been one of the leading lights of RADA, was another. Miss Warren, whose name had been given to me by Susan Hampshire, proved a marvellous pillar of strength. Her eyes sparkled with the challenge when I told her I was shortly to leave for Hollywood and needed a crash course in acting. We fixed on three days a week, at a fee of £25 a week.

My mood fluctuated between lethargy and wild bouts of energy, between black despair and exuberant high spirits. It was in the latter mood, after a particularly boozy session, that Bill Astor called round to say hello. He, Stephen and I sat drinking and joking, and discussing the widest variety of topics. We got on to music. To illustrate a point, I pulled Bill into my bedroom where I now had a new record-player (Stephen never played music) and put a record on the turntable. We sat on the edge of the bed, listening to music, and to my complete surprise Bill started to kiss me. He was warm, affectionate, a true friend. I gave myself over to the feelings which welled up inside me. We made love. Afterwards he dressed and went home and although I saw him many times after that, neither of us ever referred to it, nor had the slighest desire to repeat the experience. To my unutterable regret, I told Christine.

I had the dubious pleasure of meeting Christine's black lover, John Edgecombe, on 14 December 1962. It was not what you would call a formal introduction. I was still fragile from my suicide attempt, he was holding a gun.

I was in any case thoroughly disenchanted with Christine's choice of lovers. A couple of weeks earlier, while I was living with Stephen during that limbo period after leaving Peter and before his death, I had answered a knock at the door to be confronted with a diminutive West Indian asking to see Christine. When I said she was not at home he replied: 'Give her these, with my love,' and put something in my hand. At first I did not recognise the tiny black scraps, and when I did I let out a scream. They were stitches! Souvenirs of a fight between him and Johnny, removed at hospital that day. I thought I should faint with revulsion. Christine agreed it was all very sordid and nasty, and that she was finishing with that side of her life.

And so to events of the fourteenth. I was staying at Stephen's, had washed my hair and was in my bedroom putting it in rollers, when I heard a taxi drive up, sounds of the passenger alighting hastily, doors slamming and a frantic banging on the front door. 'Let me in, hurry.' I recognised Christine and hastily went to open the door. She was terribly agitated. I made her sit down and drink a cup of coffee while she blurted out her latest problem. She had left Johnny, he objected and was now looking for her. And when he found her he intended to kill her.

'Don't be ridiculous,' I said. Even by Christine's standards this was far-fetched. Violence was not commonplace in London. But she insisted the word was out in the circles she moved in, that he had a gun and he meant to use it.

Barely had she told me the broad outline, when a mini cab drew up and stopped at the front door. 'That's him, that's him,' said Christine. I went to the window and looked down. Sure enough the passenger getting out was black.

My first thought was, What on earth will the neighbours think? I had been around Stephen long enough for his snobbery to rub off on me, and a low-class West Indian was definitely out of character in Wimpole Mews.

'It's him all right,' I said.

Christine was rigid with fear. 'Don't tell him I'm here, whatever you do,' she pleaded.

He had started to shout by this time. I went to the window, opened it and leaned out.

'I'm very sorry,' I said. 'Christine isn't here at the moment.'

His reaction was prompt and to the point. 'You bloody liar. I know she's here.' He pulled out a gun from his pocket and pointed it at me.

'Oh my God, he's got a gun,' I said.

Christine was moaning. 'Stephen will never speak to me again. If he hears about this he'll be furious.' She was more nervous of Stephen than of Johnny. 'I'd better talk to Johnny, it's my only chance.'

She went to the window and leaned over the sill, and hadbegun to utter some soothing words when the next moment she was lying flat on the floor as two shots were fired in her direction. One hit the brickwork, the other came through the open window and buried itself in the wall, narrowly missing me.

He now decided to change tactics and was shooting at the lock of the front door. Christine tried to crawl under the bed, which, as it was a low divan, was an impossibility. In her panic she was virtually lifting the bed on top of herself – even in that moment of drama, I could see the funny side.

My first reaction was not to call the police. That would involve a nasty scene with Stephen and I had no wish to upset him. I knew the mini-cab driver was sitting downstairs in his car and assumed, wrongly as it turned out, that he was our ally, that he would summon help on his car radio.

The front door would not withstand much onslaught. A scene from a film flashed into my mind, and, picking up a heavy winter boot, I stationed myself behind the door to hit Johnny in the face as he walked through. Christine could, at the same time, make her escape through the bedroom window.

After a few more shots at the door he gave up and there was silence. Then he decided on another plan, which became obvious as we heard him at the back of the flat. He was planning to climb up to the first floor and break in that way, through Stephen's bedroom window. Now I knew I needed help, but the telephone was in that room. Leaving Christine still trying to hide under the bed, I crawled, Indian style, into Stephen's room, took the telephone and drew it back on its long flex out of the room. Keeping flat on the floor, my voice a mere whisper, I telephoned Stephen's consulting room. 'Christine's black man is here. He's shooting at us.'

'Have you called the police?'

'No, I wanted to ask you.'

'Get the police, for goodness sake!'

We could hear scraping sounds as Johnny tried to crawl up the drainpipe which adjoined the window. I dialled 999 and muttered my cry for help. Help was already on the way, they had been alerted by a neighbour.

Within minutes the police arrived. But no Edgecombe. He had departed in the same mini cab that had been waiting during the whole bizarre episode.

They were high-ranking policemen. Hot on their heels came

two cars with newspaper reporters. These two points seemed significant, and made me uneasy. I was getting into something that wasn't my affair. The last thing I wanted to be involved in was Christine's sordid escapades.

When the policeman in charge asked me my name, I said, 'Mandy Davies.'

'No it isn't,' he answered, 'it's Marilyn Rice-Davies.' From that moment on, there was no way out.

The shooting at Wimpole Mews made front-page news. The degree of interest exhibited by police and, even more so, by the press worried me. It was distinctly ominous. Admittedly shooting was not an everyday occurence but there had been no injury, and Edgecombe was arrested fairly easily. Unknown to me, the press had been interested in Christine since they found out about her involvement with Profumo. Wary of printing anything, even as an item in a gossip column, they had been watching and waiting. Christine's affair lasted only a few months, she certainly never saw Profumo after December 1961, yet in July 1962 *Queen* magazine's satirical writer, Robin Douglas-Home, had made a reference to the liaison. Oblique, admittedly, but to those in the know it was a titillating titbit.

As we left the police station after making our statements, Christine was approached by a reporter from the *Daily Mirror*. He told her his paper knew 'the lot'. They were interested in buying the letters Profumo had written her. He offered her £2,000. We were both horrified, this seemed like very deep water. Christine was even more concerned to know that the existence of the letters was common knowledge. Avoiding the issue, we both hurried off, packed our possessions hastily and left Stephen's flat that evening to move into the as-yet-unready Great Cumberland Place apartment.

The following morning our pictures and the account of the shooting were front-page news. Events moved fast, and were beyond our control. As newspaper pressure built up, I was visited at the flat by two senior policemen, Chief Inspector Herbert and Detective Sergeant Burrows. They questioned me about who I knew and what I knew, and when they said goodbye, Inspector Herbert said: 'Are you planning to leave the country?'

'Yes,' I said, 'I'm going to Hollywood.'

'You're not going anywhere, young lady,' he said. 'There is going to be a trial.'

I assumed he was referring to the Edgecombe trial, and agreed to keep in touch. In the event a few weeks later I received a letter from the American Embassy requesting me to send in my passport. It was duly returned with 'revoked' stamped across the visa.

The saga of my American visa has been what many would call an on-going situation. Continual applications for a visa proved fruitless. When I married and my husband handled my visa application, he was told at the American Embassy: 'Sorry, I can't help. That decision is irrefutable. If it's any consolation, your wife is down with the biggest spies in history!' Six years ago, after Watergate, when the American law was changed to give citizens the right to see their CIA files, my file completely disappeared from the records and to my knowledge has never surfaced.

Nothing if not persistent, I made repeated applications to gain admission to the States, and now have a compatible arrangement with the immigration authorities that I am issued with one visa per visit. I specify exactly where I shall be and the duration of the stay, and am granted a visa specifically for that visit. It does not leave me free to come and go, but it does not shut me out, either.

Christine and I were becoming frantic about a situation which I could see was galloping away with us. We had both been in tight corners before and managed to joke our way through, but this was something different, although just how different had not yet hit us. All we knew was that something unpleasant was building up.

We decided to leave the country for a while. I had not yet had the bombshell from the American Embassy, so regarded myself as free to come and go anywhere. The only thing stopping us was money. Christine decided to try Profumo, telling him she had been offered money by the *Mirror*, which would alert him to the facts.

Typically, Christine mismanaged the whole approach. Her request was seen as a blackmail threat and Profumo, fighting with his back to the wall, was advised by his lawyers that giving her money at this stage would incriminate him – especially as he was vigorously denying to his lawyers that there had ever been anything between them that he needed to hide.

We sat down and made a list of how much we needed to get out. My needs were just the airline ticket. Christine needed to give money to her mother to cover her absence, which we envisaged as lasting at least a year; we pruned our budget down to £1,000.

I decided to ask Douglas Fairbanks. He had remained friendly, he could certainly afford it I turned to him.

'Let me think about it,' said Douglas. 'I'll let you know.'

He then rang Stephen. 'Do you know these girls are really in trouble? They want to leave the country,' he said.

Stephen, who was totally oblivious to all of this, said: 'I think they are exaggerating a bit and I don't think it wise that they should leave the country anyway.'

Fairbanks rang me back and said, 'I've spoken to Stephen and he doesn't know that you are planning to leave the country and he thinks it would be a very unwise thing for you to do because it looks as if you have got something to hide. Of course, I would lend you the money but under the circumstances I don't think it's a very good for you to do it.'

Ironically, Fairbanks, Profumo and Ward had the chance, at that precise moment, to alter events totally. Another dangerous corner, and they took the wrong turn.

Pursued by the press, Christine and I left Great Cumberland Place and moved into Park West. Although we were sharing, Christine used to disappear for days at a time. One evening I had been dining with Bob Hope and Doc Shurr, and invited them up for a drink. I thought I had better check first, so left them in the corridor while I let myself into the flat. At first I thought the place was in darkness, then I saw flickering candlelight. My record-player was on the floor in the middle of the room and grouped around it, rather like natives around a camp fire, were Christine and her West Indian friends.

I went back to Doc and Bob. 'Sorry,' I said. 'Christine is sleeping. It's such a small flat I'm afraid we'll disturb her.'

They said goodnight and left. I went back into the flat, switched the lights on, removed my record-player and said firmly: 'Out.'

I wanted to be left alone. They stood around sheepishly while Christine stonily packed her bags. When she was ready they left together. Nothing was said. That was the last time I saw Christine until the trial of Stephen Ward. She took the *Mirror* offer, and left the country.

On the night of the shooting, while I was packing my things to leave, Eugene telephoned to speak to Stephen. Stephen was not there but I wasted no time in telling Eugene the exciting events of the day. That was the last time I ever spoke to Eugene. He never called back. Stephen never saw him again.

It was later reported that Eugene was recalled to Russia in January 1963. I believe he left London in December. Stephen was as mystified as I was. 'He's probably been sent back to Moscow,' he said to explain the absence of his friend, but he was hurt at not having had the chance to say goodbye.

If Ivanov was a Russian agent, and his masters decided to whisk him away before the Profumo scandal erupted, why not complete the charade and allow him, in the character he portrayed as just a very charming embassy official, to ring his friends and say farewell. Why such a mysterious departure? It was an anomaly that bothered me for many years.

Three years ago I had my answer. I was filming in Israel. I had just announced my engagement to a multi millionaire and been interviewed on the subject. When I was told that two reporters wanted to interview me for *Time* magazine, it seemed reasonable. However, their choice of hotel, and especially their suite, seemed rather extravagant for journalists' expense accounts.

The spokesman of the two immediately came clean. They were not reporters but private investigators from New York, investigating on behalf of a wealthy client one of those messy domestic wrangles involving paternity claims and so forth. The woman in question, to provide an alibi for a period in her life, had named me as a friend in London at a particular time. I did not recognise her name, or her photographs.

'Sorry, I can't help,' I said. 'Incidentally, you don't even look like newspaper reporters. You look more like the CIA.'

They smiled at this. 'Right first time,' said the chatty one. 'I was with the CIA for twenty-five years. I spent a lot of time in

London – I was involved in that George Raft affair at the Colony Club.'

'You'll probably remember the Profumo scandal,' I said. 'What did you make of Eugene Ivanov? What ever happened to him?'

He gave me an odd look. 'Don't you know? We took him.'

'What do you mean, you took him?'

'We. The CIA. We couldn't let him go. We didn't know what he had, and what he didn't have, and we didn't want to take any chances. Let's say he was an involuntary defector.'

15

SUBCONSCIOUSLY, perhaps, I was seeking another Peter in my life which was why I was so receptive to the considerable charms of Emil Savundra.

'Would you like to come along for lunch, little baby?' said Stephen. 'I'm lunching with an Indian doctor friend.'

It was just lunch in the local coffee bar, and there was Emil. Self-styled doctor, con man *par excellence*, Emil had the wit, charm, personality and warmth that added up to sheer magnetism. He was funny and kind and that appealed to me strongly in my mood of feeling lost and alone.

'Well, what do you think of him?' asked Stephen when we had said our goodbyes.

'Very nice,' I replied.

'I can see he was very taken with you,' said Stephen, 'But I warn you he's a real womaniser.'

He sent me red roses the following day. A day or two passed, and Emil telephoned and the three of us went out to the pub for a drink. He was very much in charge of the situation, brimming with confidence. In a way he reminded me of Peter. Left to ourselves, it was inevitable that we two would have got together. Stephen, however, could not resist meddling.

'Emil would like to rent your room,' he told me one day. 'He needs a private place where he can take his girlfriends.'

This was ridiculous, I remonstrated. A man with Savundra's wealth could keep a permanent suite in a hotel. But no, Stephen insisted that because of Emil's fame, and his position as head of a religious sect, he could not risk exposure of this kind. Why not give him the use of the room, then he (Emil) would pay my £6 share of the rent.

I could not see why not. In any case I was planning to move out so I had no strongly possessive feelings about my room there. I agreed, more or less, but the details were unspoken. 'And anyway,' added Stephen, 'if you two get together he won't have to let outsiders in.'

A day or so later Emil invited me for lunch. He called for me in a taxi and when I got in, there on the square seat was a huge Fortnum and Mason picnic hamper.

'What's this?' I wanted to know.

'I asked you for lunch, didn't I?' said Emil. 'Here it is.'

Thereupon he instructed the driver to drive round London, and for the next hour we consumed our lunch of smoked salmon, caviar and cold chicken, washed down with vintage champagne. Our affair began.

Emil was larger than life. Well-born Ceylonese, with a brilliant mind he could have made his fortune in any number of legitimate businesses, but chose instead to give his life that added zest by looking for the dishonest twist in everything he did. When I knew him, he was enjoying the wealth and status of a multi millionaire and on the way to masterminding his greatest swindle of all involving 400,000 British motorists who took out policies with his Fire Auto and Marine Insurance Company. When a mere twenty-five, he had tricked the Chinese Government out of more than one million dollars, then gone on to execute a vast fraud involving the Portuguese. When he was caught and sentenced, he extricated himself from Antwerp prison by producing evidence that he was dying, and later arranged to have his obituary published in Belgium to prove that he had in fact died.

He adored his wife and children, and felt no guilt about his double life. He told me he was head of a religious order in Burma. Initially I took this to mean he was, rather like the Aga Khan, a spiritual leader. The truth was that he owned and financed a Catholic convent, where the main task of the mother superior was to pray for him. When he was about to pull off some particularly disgraceful deal, he would cable the mother superior to ask her, 'Pray for me urgently. And please move documents A to case X.' Back would come her reply. 'Praying for you constantly. Documents attended to.'

He was fun. He was almost mad. He did not send me a bunch of flowers, he had whole cartloads delivered to the door. When I was with him I felt happy and alive, and, most of all, secure. I remained close to him long after I left Wimpole Mews, and what I learned about him convinced me that he was undoubtedly one of the Mr Bigs behind the Great Train Robbery – a drama yet to be played out.

Emil was tactful, discreet and a gentleman. He could have afforded to lavish money on me, certainly he could have provided me with a luxurious apartment had I required or asked. But more as a true friend he volunteered, on inquiring how much my drama lessons cost, to pay for this.

'Twenty-five pounds a week, you must be finding that a bit difficult,' he said. 'Allow me to pay for that.'

And he did. Twenty-five pounds, left discreetly in the flat, proved the most damning piece of evidence the prosecution could muster against Stephen Ward.

16

AROUND the time John Edgecombe made his preliminary appearance before the magistrate at Marlborough Street I felt the need for a few quiet days with my parents. Having no car (my Jaguar had been requisitioned by Audrey along with my other gifts from Peter) I needed to rent one. The regulations required a minimum of four years' driving experience, so when it came to filling in the form I had no choice but to put my age as twenty-one. The sharp-eyed clerk asked how come I had only one sticker on my licence – in those days the licence was sent off each year for a renewal slip. 'Well,' I lied, 'I used to have an Irish driving licence.'

I thought that had satisfied her and I went out with the company's inspector for a test drive to establish my competence. 'A1,' he reported as we came back into the office after a five-minute spin around the block.

Barely had I signed the insurance application than there was a heavy hand on my shoulder. Two policemen had come into the office.

'You'd better come along with us,' said one.

'What for?'.

'For using a forged driving licence.'

The clerk had noticed a disparity in the serial number at the top of the licence, and had telephoned the police to check. We trooped off to the police station, where they asked me how I'd come by the licence, and warned me that by signing the insurance declaration that I was in possession of a full driving licence, I was committing a criminal offence. During the interview we were joined by another officer who wanted to know all about Peter Rachman. In this respect I had nothing to hide. Eventually I was allowed to leave, not knowing what the outcome, if any, was to be. As the months passed I assumed that no news was good news, and pushed the incident

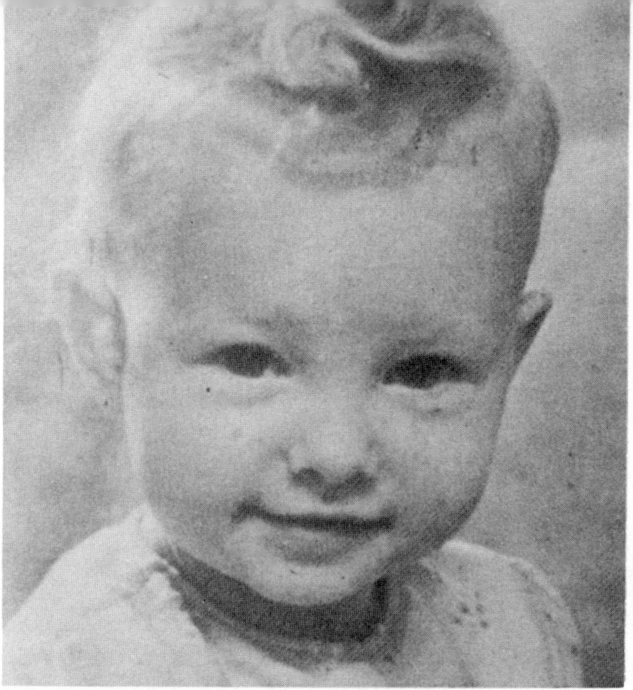
At nineteen months...

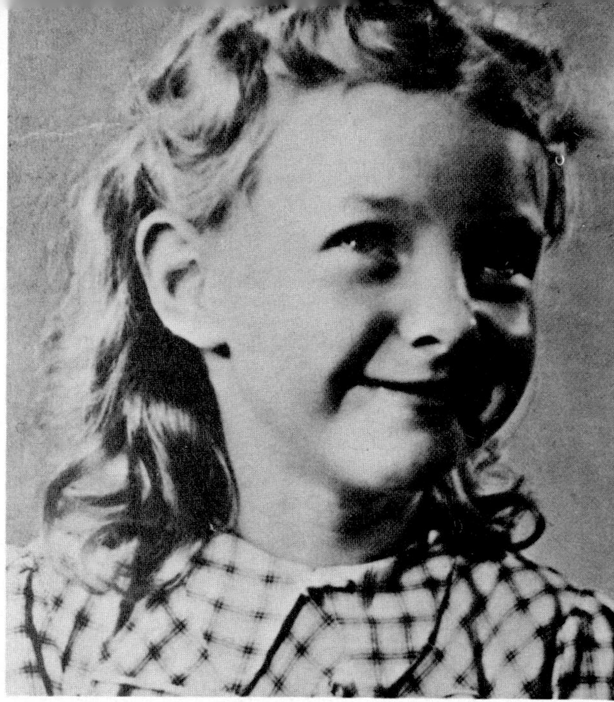
...and again at seven years.

On an early family holiday with my parents and brother David.

A proud moment for me, aged nine, when Princess Margaret, on a visit to Shirley, Birmingham, inspected the Brownie Troop.

ly first modelling picture at
fteen.

Wearing my first evening gown.

Soon afterwards the famous friendship was forged: the first ever picture of me and Christine Keeler, taken in a coin-operated booth at London Airport.

At the beginning of the trial (July 1963), Dr Stephen Ward managed to give the impression of a man not particularly anxious *(Press Association)*.

Deciding to play to the crowd as I left the Old Bailey after giving evidence *(Press Association)*.

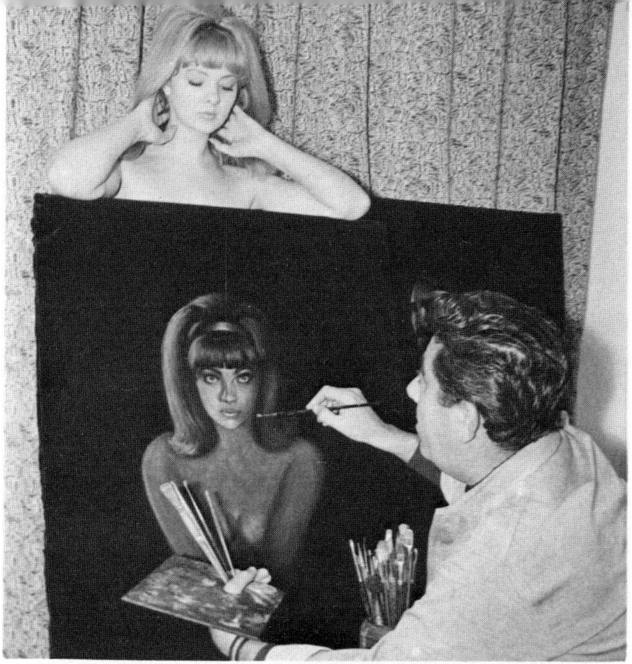
Josef Diftler painting my portrait on velvet, a technique he pioneered.

On the beach in Majorca, 1963.

A wedding-day picture: with my husband Rafael Shaul, September 17, 1966.

With daughter Dana, 1968.

sultry pose.

oing my bit for the war effort in Israel.

A recent promotion picture for Helena Rubinstein cosmetics.

to the back of my mind.

Like a dog with a bone, the press (and by this time Fleet Street journalists had been joined by those from other countries) were refusing to give up on the Profumo story. Unable to print what they believed to be true, for fear of tough libel laws, they ran a series of innuendo stories about high jinks in high places, while they watched and waited.

The break came with Edgecombe's trial at the Old Bailey and the discovery that the chief prosecution witness was missing. A week before, Christine, her path made easy by the considerable payments she was receiving from newspapers, decided she didn't like the scene in London and, true to character, decided to go while she could. I alone was there to describe the incidents of 14 December.

Edgecombe was sentenced to seven years. A separate charge, involving the malicious wounding of Lucky Gordon, was rushed through at indecent haste, and in the absence of the only witness (Christine) he was acquitted.

The mystery of the missing witness made front-page news. It was another excuse to put Christine's picture on the front page and keep the story boiling, and incidentally imply that certain people had very good reason for wanting her out of the way. Where is Christine Keeler? became the battlecry, and I was enlisted by the *Daily Express* to help in the search. We flew to Majorca, where rumour had it Christine had gone. It is a small island, you can comb it through in a day and a half. Had Christine been there we should have known very soon. She wasn't, we stayed on. It was the one light interval in months of apprehension. Squired by top *Daily Express* writer Rodney Hallworth (Rodders to his friends) and the local stringer-cum-photographer, a young Englishman called Terry, I actually had some fun. There was romance too – within days I had fallen in love with a handsome Spanish nobleman, José Francisco de Villalonga. I called him Cisco.

While Cisco and I were murmuring sweet nothings to each other, on 22 March in the House of Commons, John Profumo, acknowledging the rumours that were rife in government and press circles, made a 'personal statement' in which he categorically denied that there was any impropriety in his relationship with Miss Keeler, with whom he had once been on friendly terms. His address ended: 'I shall not hesitate to issue writs for libel and slander if scandalous allegations are made or repeated outside the House.'

It could be said that up until then, Profumo had done nothing terribly wrong. He had played around with a young girl, he had cheated on his wife – minor indiscretions, surely. And he had backed away from the situation the moment he was made aware, in late summer of 1961 by M15, that Ivanov was a frequent visitor to Wimpole Mews. According to Christine he tried then to persuade her to move out and leave Stephen and it was when she refused that he ended the affair, as gently as possible and in the most charming way, but nevertheless firmly.

Possibly if he had owned up at that point that he was no more 'guilty' than all the thousands of married men who spice up their life with a little extra-marital sex it might have ended there. But on 22 March he overstepped the mark. He lied to his colleagues, and sufficient of them were aware that he was lying to set up a chain reaction. Wheels within wheels within wheels began turning. Stephen, who had so far endorsed Profumo's account of events, now felt justifiably concerned at finding his name and Ivanov's bandied about the media and started to look for allies in high places. He was now living at my old address, Bryanston Mews West, which he was renting from Audrey. Christine and I began to enjoy a type of celebrity. The effect of the scandal on Stephen was disastrous for his practice. He felt aggrieved and began writing to newspapers to clear his name.

Christine, returning from Spain, was mobbed when she changed planes at Paris and arrived at Heathrow like a superstar. On 17 April, used by now to her celebrity status, she was somewhat put out to be confronted with a snarling Lucky, who leaped at her, knocked her to the ground, then kicked and punched her as she lay there. It was only the intervention of a passer-by that saved her from being murdered, Christine claimed. Lucky was arrested and his trial subsequently fixed for 5 June.

I was, meantime, engrossed in my own affair of the heart. Back in London Cisco and I spoke every day on the telephone and wrote constantly to each other. Impetuous with love, he had proposed marriage – he'd face the consequences from his family later. On 23 April, en route for Palma, I was stopped on my way through Customs at Heathrow. 'Would you mind stepping this way, please?'

Two policemen took me into a small room where I was formally charged with 'possessing a document so closely resembling a driving licence as to be calculated to deceive' and arrested. They took me in a police car back to London, where I was locked in a cell overnight and appeared before the magistrates the following morning. The police asked for remand while they prepared their charge, and the magistrate fixed bail at £2,000 – not only did I not have that much money, but the policeman in charge made it very clear to me that I would be wasting my energy trying to rustle it up. They had numerous other potential charges, and would introduce them one at a time if necessary, which would escalate the bail out of all feasibility. I was remanded in custody, which, as the court was going into recess, meant nine days in Holloway Jail before my case could be heard.

First there was the depersonalising process of being removed from freedom and locked away. Then came the indignity of the search, the body search (what was I supposed to be smuggling in?) and submitting to the strange ritual of the shaving of pubic hairs. This was the ultimate violation. 'Touch me and I'll scream bloody murder.' I said I would do my own shaving, thank you very much. They did not insist, and later I discovered that they had not even the right to inflict this on remand prisoners.

As if the fact of imprisonment wasn't bad enough, Holloway is a disgustingly depressing building. Dirty, falling to pieces, the immediate impression is that it really is like the inside of a prison as seen in films: floors stacked one above the other with safety nets to catch the people who are hurled or hurl themselves over the railings.

I was locked in my cell for twenty out of every twenty-four hours, allowed out to change my library book and once to go to the Warden's office. Earl Felton had sent me in a gift. Chocolates, oranges and a packet of 200 Peter Stuyvesant. He'd forgotten I didn't smoke. The rule was ten cigarettes a day. I took them back to my cell and within a few minutes there was a strange face at the door.

'You've cigarettes, then?'

'Yes, but no matches.'

'Give me a cigarette, I'll give you a match,' she said. The deal was done. I had never smoked before. I disliked being in the company of people who smoke, and Christine's smoking when we shared drove me wild with exasperation. By the time I left Holloway I was addicted to cigarettes and I have never been able to give them up.

I began my remand, fired by indignation at the unfairness of my own plight but also at what I saw as the dreadful indignity of prison life. My righteous anger was fuelled by Oscar Wilde's *The Ballad of Reading Gaol*, and Upton Sinclair's *The Jungle* conveniently provided by the prison library. I was ready to kick the system any way I could. But ten days of being locked in alters the perspective. Anger was replaced by fear.

Lesbianism was the prevailing force. Mannish women in trousers with butch haircuts were in charge: in the kitchen, in the garden, eyeing me in a way that made me nervous.

'When's your case coming up?' one authoritative female asked me. I told her.

'You'll be back, Davies,' she said ominously. 'We'll look forward to having you among us for a while.'

To keep out of their way I sought the help of the prison doctor and pleaded to be excused the regulation walk in the yard. He wrote a note to say I had a cold and wasn't to go out and at the same time gave me a priority milk allowance to compensate for the lack of food. Prison meals were so revolting to me, I couldn't eat.

As contact with the outside world weakened, I was more susceptible. The repeated remarks, 'We'll soon have you in here for sentence,' began to make an impression, and though logically I could see the idea was ridiculous, I started to believe that perhaps I would be sent to prison.

A solicitor came in to see me, and to prepare my case for court. I wasn't sure who had sent him, and oddly, I suppose, I didn't ask. I was so relieved. I told him everything I could and he said he would plead mitigating circumstances, that because of my being so young when the car and licence were given to me, I behaved foolishly rather than criminally.

The following day, as I was beginning to feel some degree of hope, I was visited by the two senior policemen – Detective Chief Inspector Herbert and Detective Sergeant Burrows.

Chief Inspector Herbert's first words were: 'Mandy, you don't like it in here very much, do you?'

'No.'

'Then you help us, and we'll help you.'

All they wanted of me was a little chat. I was to answer their questions and everything would be all right. The questions were of a general nature; who I knew in London, where I went, what I did, who paid for what. Then every so often a question about Dr Ward. Although I was certain nothing I could say about Stephen could damage him in any way – he was peculiar, certainly, but that doesn't mean criminally so – I felt I was being coerced into something, being pointed in a predetermined direction. Rumours that the police were investigating a call-girl racket for VIPs had been reported, but by no stretch of the imagination could this involve Stephen. Certainly he made introductions, he enjoyed manipulating people, and possibly his motives weren't entirely pure, but financial gain never came into it.

Whenever I hesitated, Chief Inspector Herbert would say reassuringly: 'Well, Christine says . . . ' He told me they had interviewed Christine numerous times, and Christine had been most co-operative. All I had to do was confirm what Christine had said.

My case came up on 1 May, my solicitor pleading that I 'had been thrown into the high life of London and lived at a fanastic rate'. I was fined £42 with £16.12s. costs. Such a trivial offence to rate hundreds of column inches in the national press.

The first thing I wanted was to take the plane to Majorca and Cisco. He, meanwhile, had read the papers. The English scandal was making news all over the world and in Majorca his strict Catholic family with centuries of breeding and impeccable morals behind them were extremely put out to learn that their intended daughter-in-law was, according to garbled reports, in Holloway being questioned on vice charges. Escorted by the ever-staunch Rodders, I arrived in Majorca to be met by Terry with instructions that now Cisco and I would have to meet secretly.

The reunion was like the lovers' tryst from *Romeo and Juliet*. The more I confided in Cisco, the more I realised he had grown up in another century. There were things he didn't wish to know about. He would even have been shocked to know I wore false eyelashes.

Inspector Herbert telephoned me. They would be sending out my ticket, they wanted me back in London, and if I didn't go voluntarily they would issue a warrant for extradition. I had befriended the village policeman, so I asked him about this and he insisted emphatically that there was no extradition arrangement between the two countries. Nevertheless, I couldn't stay away indefinitely, so I returned to face whatever music awaited me.

It was a veritable cacophany. I was met off the plane by two uniformed policemen who, whisking me through the formalities at impressive speed, took me in the waiting car to Marylebone Police Station. Oh no, I thought, not again.

This time the charges against me were stealing a television set. That same set Peter had rented for our fireside evenings together. I had signed the hire papers, and after he'd died I had never been allowed to remove the set. It was cut and dried. I had an answer, a good answer, to the accusation. I was given bail of £1,000, which I managed to muster, and my passport was confiscated. The hearing of my case was fixed for 28 June.

During my absence events had moved fast. The continuing saga of 'Is there a top-level call-girl racket?' and 'Is there a security risk?' continued to dominate the news, fuelled by revelations from Christine and various anonymous witnesses. At the same time the Duke of Argyll's divorce action against his wife, reported to have initially contained no less than 200 named co-respondents, jostled for the front pages. The uninformed reader might easily have believed it was all part and parcel of the same huge society orgy.

This was all background to the two major stories of the day.

At the end of May, seven months after his death, Peter Rachman became famous. The housing problem, slum property, racketeering landlords, became a crusading issue. Rachman, whose name had been mentioned in my case, was found to be the most villainous slum landlord of them all. It was not difficult to make him out to be a gangster, responsible for organised crime and vice as well as a monster who used thugs with vicious dogs to do his rent-collecting.

The Labour Party, in opposition, saw it as another nail in the coffin of a government already discredited by the Profumo allegations. The decisive nail soon followed.

On 4 June Profumo issued a statement, in the form of a letter he had written to the Prime Minister, the Rt. Hon. Harold Macmillan.

Dear Prime Minister,

You will recollect that on 22 March following certain allegations made in Parliament I made a personal statement.

At that time rumour had charged me with assisting in the disappearance of a witness and with being involved in some possible breach of security.

So serious were these charges that I allowed myself to think that my personal associations with that witness, which had also been the subject of rumour, was by comparison of minor importance only.

In my statement I said there had been no impropriety in this association. To my very deep regret I have to admit that this was not true, and that I misled you, and my colleagues, and the House.

I ask you to understand that I did this to protect, as I thought, my wife and family who were equally misled, as were my professional advisers.

I have come to realise that, by this deception, I have been guilty of a gross misdemeanour and despite the fact that there is no truth whatever in the other charges, I cannot remain a member of your administration, nor of the House of Commons.

I cannot tell you of my deep remorse for the embarrassment I have caused to you, to my colleagues in the government, to my constituents and to the Party which I have served for the past twenty-five years.

Yours sincerely,

Jack Profumo.

On 5 June Lucky Gordon, with thirteen convictions behind him, went for trial, was convicted and sentenced to three years. On 8 June, just as Lucky Gordon was beginning his prison sentence (later squashed on appeal) Chief Inspector Herbert and Detective Sergeant Burrows arrested Stephen Ward on charges under the Sexual Offences Act. He was taken into custody, bail was refused. The magistrates' hearing was set for 28 June, significantly the same day and the same court as my own appearance.

Everything I did made news. I was connected with the Christine Keeler-Jack Profumo scandal; I was the former mistress of Rachman, whose name was on everyone's lips. My theft charge and, more importantant, the fact that I now had no passport were the subject of a question in the House of Commons. Had I been charged or not? If not, by what right were the police holding my passport? I now realise, of course, that the trumped-up theft charge justified the police in holding my passport to ensure I would appear at the court to give evidence against Stephen.

A few days before the magistrates' hearing, I was contacted by a firm of solicitors who had been asked by Emil Savundra to help me. I made an appointment and went to their offices in 21 Quebec Street, W.1. The lawyer I met was John Dennis Wheater, and his clerk was Brian Field. It was suggested to me that because of Emil's religious position it was essential his name be kept out of Stephen's proceedings, and for this favour I would receive a substantial sum of money, an offer which I declined.

It was unethical of Wheater to ask this, but I sympathised with Emil's religious responsibilities because I was heavily into a religious period, drawn to Catholicism by Cisco and actually going through a conversion as preparation for our marriage. I wore a Santa Maria round my neck. I liked the atmosphere, the superficial ambience of religion. The theatrical flavour of Catholicism was attractive to me. I've tried various religions since, I am still searching for my spiritual awakening. Although I am not religious, I am not anti-religious.

I had no reason for wanting to mention Emil, or anyone else, and throughout the magistrates' hearing I was never asked to name him. He was known only as the Indian doctor.

All along I was convinced that the case against Stephen would come to nothing. Stephen might have lacked conventional morals where sex was concerned, but in no way was he a criminal. The fact that I was being put forward as a prosecution witness and I knew nothing incriminating about Stephen confirmed how weak the case must surely be. Although I had had no direct contact with Stephen, the word on the grapevine was that he was confident of the outcome. The worst that could happen had already happened, his name and character had been blackened his practice was in ruins. Common sense told me that this would all prove a storm in a teacup. Intuition suggested that it had been blown out of proportion and beyond control. I determined not to look dejected.

I wore a grey wool dress and white gloves to go to Marylebone Magistrates Court. Christine had gone ahead of me, and over the radio in the *Express* car I heard that as she arrived somebody in the large crowd outside threw eggs at her.

I felt a sharp contraction of fear, but I knew I wasn't going to run, cringing, into the court. As the car arrived I got out like the Queen of Sheba. Flashing a wide smile I waved to the crowd. It worked like magic. People smiled back. 'Hello, Mandy,' they shouted. That smile became my camouflage.

My own case was settled out of court as a representative of the television rental firm accepted the price of the missing set and the charge was dropped.

I was unprepared for the shock of seeing Stephen in the dock. After twenty-six days in prison he was carefully composed, listening intently to the proceedings, busily sketching in a pad; I could only guess at the inner turmoil.

It was my turn to stand in the dock. The prosecution questioned me on the men I knew, whether or not I had had sex with them. Read out in court it sounded like a catalogue I had prepared with pride, rather than information that had been coerced out of me. When Stephen's counsel, Mr James Burge, challenged my account of sex with Lord Astor by saying that Lord Astor himself had categorically denied this ever took place, it struck me as the height of silliness.

'Well, he would, wouldn't he?' I said. It now reads as a

cheeky remark, but I said it in all seriousness. The court, however, burst into laughter, even the magistrate had difficulty keeping a straight face.

When I had completed my evidence and was about to step down from the box I had a brainwave. 'Excuse me, may I ask something?' I said to the magistrate.

'What is it?'

I said: 'Would it be possible for you to ask the police to give me back my passport.'

Having inquired of the policeman present that indeed they were holding my passport and that there were now no charges against me, he instructed them to return it to me at once.

'And if they do not do so, I want you to come and see me,' he said.

I left the court with my passport.

Stephen had denied all of the nine vice charges and reserved his defence. He was committed for trial and, despite police objection, granted bail.

I left the courtroom knowing that the trap was closing, not only on Stephen. I had heard evidence given by a succession of young women which I knew to be completely false, and I had heard evidence which I knew to be a distortion.

References had been made to Stephen's two-way mirror in Bryanston Mews West. This was the same two-way mirror I had broken two years earlier. How could a broken mirror have any relevance at all to what was supposed to go on in that flat? How, indeed, could any of the perversions and immoral sexual practices have gone on at all in Bryanston Mews when Stephen didn't move in there until March and the police, by their own admission, had not begun their investigations until April? In any case, from the beginning of the year Stephen's every move was dogged by reporters, and there were always at least one or two journalists camped out, using the phone, discussing the Profumo affair. The case against him didn't hold water.

I couldn't believe the police case hung on such a slender thread as my and Christine's evidence. I kept thinking the police must have something else up their sleeves. Stephen was never a blue-and-white diamond, but a pimp? Ridiculous. And taking money off us! I've already described my finances. As for Christine, she was always borrowing. Every time she arrived in a taxi she would say, 'Stephen, lend me the taxi money,' and, very unwillingly, his hand would creep out with a fiver or a couple of pounds. This would all come out, and he would be vindicated.

For my own self-preservation I was also very worried. A string of girls had stood up in the box and, asked their occupation, had stated, 'Prostitute, sir.' Where did that leave us, Christine and me? Whatever we were, we weren't prostitutes or whores, but this was the company we were now linked with. I contacted Christine.

'Before this whole business is over,' I said, 'we are going to be tarred with the same brush. As far as the court is concerned we're all in the same mould.'

I flew out to Palma, hoping to find consolation with Cisco. My fiancé could not cope with the shock of my court appearance, richly reported in Spain, and the invincible disapproval of his family.

'My father has a heart ailment and I have promised him never to see you again,' he told me at our last tearful meeting. 'But I love you, and all my life where ever you go you will carry a piece of my heart with you.'

Tears were streaming down my face as he said, 'I must go now.' I remember seeing *Duel in the Sun* when Gregory Peck goes out of the door and Jennifer Jones throws herself at his legs. As Cisco was going through the door I threw myself at him, clinging to his ankles. He picked me up, kissed me passionately on the lips and left.

I went back in floods of tears to the hotel and Rodders, packed my bags and left for the airport, and the midnight plane. I was still in tears when we arrived back in London.

Years later, when it was all too late, I learned from Cisco that in a fit of passion he had defied his father, leapt on to his motor bike and driven to the airport in time to see my plane taking off. Isn't fate peculiar? Minutes sooner and today I could have been living in Spain, a countess with a couple of children. An hour in one's life, and it can make all the difference in the world.

Everybody it seemed wanted to meet me. I was sent an invitation on behalf of Mr and Mrs Harold Wilson, asking me to have tea with them at their house in Hampstead. Somehow I never quite got around to it.

When MI6 decided they wished to interview me, it was an offer I couldn't refuse. All rather James Bondish, I was driven to a faceless building somewhere in central London. I wasn't allowed to know where we were going or who we were to meet. I was taken into a room, no windows, a man behind the desk, another beside him, two more men standing behind me.

'Before we proceed,' said the man behind the desk, 'I have to remind you that espionage is a very serious offence and carries a penalty of up to twenty years.'

'Why me?' I wanted to ask. 'What have I done?' It was frightening, at the same time it had its funny side. They just asked me the same questions that the police had. Exactly like a spy thriller, with the bad guy asking the questions, worrying me, making me anxious, and the good guy chipping in to say, 'Would you like a cup of tea?' to make me feel that he was really a friend.

On my way through Heathrow, for what turned out to be *my final* meeting with Cisco, I was stopped by an authoritative female delivering a letter from Lord Denning which she thrust in my hand. He was to conduct an inquiry into the security aspects of the Profumo Affair, and the letter was a request for me to go to his offices and answer questions. Cisco was a great deal more important to me than Lord Denning, and I told his secretary (privately and in confidence I believed) that regrettably I had no time for Lord Denning right now, and would contact him on my return. My remark was widely quoted to show how disrespectful I was.

An American tourist, seeing me the centre of a crowd, came up to me.

'Hello, my dear, may I have your autograph. And would you mind telling me who you are?'

I hated having to say my name. For years Mandy Rice-Davies was such an embarrassment to me. It is only in recent times I've been able to say my name without a quiver of discomfort.

'Call me Lady Hamilton,' I said.

Silly, I suppose. And what repercussions. People wrote to *The Times* demanding to know how dare I compare myself with the great lover of Lord Nelson. I gave up trying to explain, but my foolish quip hung around to haunt me.

'Tell me,' asked a TV interviewer some years later, 'do you still think of yourself as Lady Hamilton?'

'No,' I replied. 'Nell Gwynne!'

A meeting was set up between myself and Lord Denning after I returned from Spain. First I needed to get my hair done at Vidal Sassoon's in Bond Street. In those days you made a nine o'clock appointment and were lucky to be out by noon. It wasn't unusual to see irate clients marching out of the salon, their hair dripping wet. Inevitably I was late: 'Mandy holds up Lord Denning for her hair-do'.

I loved his room, the walls covered with shelves of old law books; he was courteous but I found him intimidating. I answered his questions, the same old questions, but could sense my replies were superfluous. His ideas were already formed.

People queued from midnight to buy the first copies of the White Paper when it was published in September. It contained many inaccuracies and was quickly dubbed the Whitewash Paper.

17

STEPHEN Ward's trial began on 22 July at the Old Bailey. On the same day an exhibition of Stephen's drawings was held to raise money for his legal costs. He asked me to go along, and create interest. It was the least I could do; as it happened it was the last thing I ever did for him. Stephen's royal portraits were highly priced, and remained unsold for several days until one morning, as the exhibition opened, an elderly man in a bowler hat turned up, paid £5,000 in five-pound notes for the lot and took them away wrapped up in brown paper. I believe they were purchased on behalf of the royal family.

Morris Krevatz made me a grey gabardine dress for the trial, and I wore it with a hat of pale pink petals. One wore something different every day, of course, but that was my most special outfit. I bought it to boost my confidence.

It was a trial in which the accused was guilty until proved innocent. Several of the charges made at the magistrates' court had now been dropped, namely brothel-keeping and two charges relating to procuring abortions.

It is difficult today to imagine the emotiveness in 1963 of the word 'abortion', the mere association of ideas provided a black mark against him. Now he was charged with living on the immoral earnings of Christine, myself and a prostitute known as Ronna Ricardo, and of procuring two girls under twenty-one to have illicit sexual intercourse.

Nothing you have ever read or heard can prepare you for the experience of going on to the stand and giving evidence. The diminutive judge, Sir Archie Marshall, was, despite his lack of inches, quite terrifying in his billowing red robes. The press joked about his self-importance; it was his first High Court case and he deliberately walked in all his finery from his chambers so that the photographers could take pictures. I had thought of a judge as a benign, impartial listener, a collator of facts, sifting the truth from the lies and passing fair judgment. Now I saw Sir Archie Marshall as a wrathful figure from another century. I felt he actually disliked Stephen.

The prosecuting counsel, Mr Mervyn Griffith-Jones, was thin-lipped and pale and looked as if he had been carved out of church wax. He conducted the examination of witnesses as if he had been appointed custodian of public morals. His most famous appearance had been as prosecutor in the trial of *Lady Chatterley's Lover*, the D. H. Lawrence novel selected as a test case by opponents of the 1959 obscene publications law. During this case, he asked the jury: 'Would you allow your servants to read this book?' That he should assume all members of the jury employed servants, and that he should also assume they would exercise control over their servants' or anybody else's choice of reading matter, completely summed up the thought process of Mr Griffith-Jones. He referred to Stephen as 'This filthy fellow' and suggested that a liaison between an old man (Stephen was nearly fifty) and a young girl (anyone under twenty-one) was in itself an act of depravity.

When told by me that on the one occasion I went to bed with Lord Astor, Stephen was in the flat – in fact in the *next room* – he confessed himself appalled and disgusted. I was amazed that a man who played such a prominent role in the judgment of others should be so divorced from the reality of everyday life. 'Don't you know, you silly old fool,' I wanted to shout out, 'that most people make love with their children in the next room.' But I didn't shout out or say anything; I kept quiet because I was helpless.

My courage had been ebbing steadily as the Old Bailey trial approached. It left me completely at my first sight of Stephen in the dock. Neatly dressed, outwardly composed, considerably thinner, he gave the impression of concentrating intently on the proceedings, while sketching on a large pad the faces of the people around him, for the most part his accusers. Once or twice, towards the end of the trial, his control snapped and he shouted angrily. But always he apologised. The thing that really cut me up was the fact that he had broken his glasses. They were mended with a piece of string, tied at the side. The sight of it affected me deeply and the memory still moves me.

It was said that the police had interviewed 147 people in preparing the case against Stephen. Christine had been interviewed twenty-eight times (and was promised that she would not be prosecuted). The young girls paraded through court admitted that their sex with Stephen was voluntary; the damning comment Stephen was alleged to have made to one – referring to his two-way mirror – that he didn't want her to watch but to perform, was another example of Stephen's humour. He said outrageous things for effect. In any case that mirror had been broken two years before, although in court it was consistently referred to as if it still existed, despite my evidence that it was I who had broken the mirror.

Two prostitutes were the main witnesses against him. One of them I knew, Ronna Ricardo. It was no secret that Stephen liked prostitutes, he felt superior to them and this was necessary to him, certainly in his sex life. There were many examples in his past life of girls he had met when they were young and new to London, and went to bed with. Like me, I suppose. But once they gained confidence and moved in his circle as an equal, he had no sexual interest in them, although he retained their friendship for years.

When Ronna Ricardo, who had provided strong evidence against him at the early hearing, came into court she swore under oath that her earlier evidence had been false. She had lied to satisfy the police, that they had threatened her, if she refused, with taking her baby and her young sister into care. Despite the most aggressive attack from Mr Griffith-Jones, and barely concealed hostility from the judge, she stuck to her story, that this was the truth and the earlier story she had told was lies.

The other prostitutes, Vickie Barrett (she had not been produced at the earlier hearing, and Mr Burge, Stephen's counsel, protested but was over-ruled), gave evidence of being picked up by Stephen and taken back to Bryanston Mews, where she had intercourse with men waiting there. She gave explicit details about being required also to 'whip' with 'canes' and 'horse whips'. Much of what she said was discredited. It was obvious to anyone that Stephen, with the police breathing down his neck and the press on his doorstep, would hardly have the opportunity or the inclination for this sort of thing.

She was completely suspect to the majority of people in the court, except presumably Judge Marshall who, in his summing up, appeared to give weight and credence to her evidence. (In the event, after the trial she retracted, and said that she too had been pressurised by the police who threatened her with nine months inside for soliciting if she didn't co-operate. Perhaps she didn't need much persuasion. To be involved in this society scandal was a step up the ladder – like a pavement artist being linked with Picasso!)

None of this helped Stephen. I had an overwhelming desire to stand up and scream for what they were doing to him. I had to clench my teeth to stop myself shouting out. I was afraid. I couldn't believe what was happening, as if some malevolent force was taking over and we were powerless. Somebody like me had no hope of fighting back. My only hope was to stay calm, get through it somehow, have it all behind me.

I could see now that before the trial began I had underestimated the seriousness of events. I'd told myself that the magistrates' hearing was one thing, rather amateur really, but once we got to the Old Bailey the real wheels of justice would be set in motion and they don't roll over the innocent, do they? Not that we claimed to be innocent in a strictly moral sense. It is extraordinary to think back to how easily shocked most people were in 1963. Before the page 3 nude and sex on TV right there in your living-room, people were sheltered, I suppose. When Christine said in court that she had had an abortion, there was a gasp from the court. People didn't hear that word too often.

I hated Griffith-Jones. If ever anyone deserved a custard pie in his face, he did. I thought he was a hypocrite. If he practised what he preached, then he was undoubtedly too good for this world. He belonged in a Victorian melodrama, was cold and cutting.

'Did you have intercourse with Lord Astor?'

'Yes.'

'Did he give you £200?'

'Yes – but – '

'No buts. Answer the question, yes or no.'

By the time the defence, Mr Burge, could extract the information that there was a two-year interval between my receiving £200 from Bill Astor and my going to bed with him, which by any standards alters the emphasis entirely, the damage had been done.

I lunched with Christine one day during the trial at a pub near the Old Bailey. It was the first time we had spoken deeply. We were both appalled at what was happening; Christine in a way blamed herself for telling the police so much, but I could understand how it happened. When the police want something they usually get it. What was so frustrating was that the press, the lawyers, everyone was saying the trial was a farce, and yet here it was, taking its course. It was almost a joke in the media. Like the Osbert Lancaster cartoon in the *Daily Express*. One man saying to the other: 'If I give my wife's lover the winner of the 4.30 would I be living off her immoral earnings?'

I still cannot understand why I was ever called a 'call girl'. Promiscuous, perhaps, but not a call girl. I was Rachman's mistress, that doesn't make me a call girl. I had men friends I went to bed with, but they were friends. A call girl goes to bed with strangers. If I had been passionately, madly in love with every man in my life, would that have altered things? If a woman goes to bed with her husband, not because she passionately fancies him but rather than upset the *status quo*, does that impugn her morality? I tried to express myself to the judge, but every time I went to open my mouth he would say: 'Stick to the questions, or I'll have you for contempt of court.'

At one point the judge, trying to establish whether or not I had sex in return for money asked me, 'What was the *quid pro quo*?' I stood there speechless with indignation that he should be so supercilious as to address a witness in Latin. It so happened I knew what he was asking. He mistook my silence.

'That means what did you give in return,' he said testily.

It is my lasting regret that I didn't reply, 'Amora, you silly old fool. Amora. That's Latin for love, don't you know?'

Sex for money. Love for money? Where do you draw the thin red line? Where are the borders? I've asked myself this question a thousand times, and I don't know the answer. I believe I am fairly honest, and I deserved some of the mud thrown at me. I went through life superficially, guided on two levels – one by the comforts I came to enjoy, and the other by feeling I might be missing something. Maybe I sacrificed moral integrity for comfort.

The trial lasted over a week. On Tuesday of the second week, 30 July, the judge began his summing up. We knew there was no hope. Much was made of the fact that in his hour of need none of Stephen's good friends came forward as a character witness. They didn't because Stephen asked them not to. He was embarrassed at involving them needlessly, he believed. When the investigations began he couldn't believe they would lead anywhere, and he insisted his friends stay out of it. Bill Astor certainly volunteered, and probably others did, too. By the time he knew he needed help, the fat was in the fire. My father always said he regretted not coming forward. That would have made news – Daddy appearing for the defence, his daughter for the prosecution.

That evening Stephen went back to the flat in Chelsea where he was a guest during the trial. He wrote several letters – including one to Vickie Barrett – to be delivered 'only if I am convicted and sent to prison'. He cooked a meal for himself and his girlfriend, Julie Gulliver, then drove her home. He drove around for a while, possibly thinking things over, then, his mind made up, went back to the flat. He wrote another letter, to his friend and host Noel Howard-Jones, and swallowed an overdose of nembutal.

When Howard-Jones found him the following morning on the mattresses, piled on the floor, which were his bed, Stephen was unconscious. His letter read:

> Dear Noel,
>
> I am sorry I had to do this here! It is really more than I can stand – the horror, day after day, at the court and in the streets.
>
> It is not only fear, it is a wish not to let them get me. I would rather get myself. I do hope I have not let people down too much. I tried to do my stuff but after Marshall's summing-up, I've given up all hope. The car needs oil in the gear-box, by the way. Be happy in it.
>
> Incidentally, it was surprisingly easy and required no guts.
>
> I am sorry to disappoint the vultures. I only hope this has done the job. Delay resuscitation as long as possible.

Stephen was rushed to St Stephens Hospital where he hovered between life and death. We were not officially told details of Stephen's condition, but I was better informed than most. Rodders told me that whatever the outcome, Stephen's brain was damaged beyond any hope of recovery. If he lived, he would be a vegetable. When I heard that, I wanted him to die. It was inconceivable to think of Stephen without the intellect, the jokes and biting wit.

The machinery of the trial proceeded. The judge finished his summing up. The jury retired to consider their verdict, during which they sought guidance from the judge on the definition of prostitution, and delivered it after four and a half hours. He was found not guilty on all counts except the two involving Christine and myself. The law said that he had lived off our immoral earnings. The jury, by reaching their conclusion, had decided that in their view Christine and I were prostitutes.

The judge never delivered sentence. On 3 August Stephen died. I was stricken with anger and remorse and sorrow. Christine was hysterical with grief. He was her closest friend. She had never experienced death before.

18

NOTORIETY is an unreliable companion. Twentieth-Century Fox invited me to the première of *Cleopatra*. They needed all the publicity they could get. The movie was the most costly ever made. Elizabeth Taylor was the star but her attendance at this great occasion was highly doubtful, whilst I guaranteed to make the front page. So there I was, dressed up in all the finery I could muster, escorted by Christopher Courtenay, photographed leaving my flat as well as arriving at the cinema. During the interval Christopher and I walked into the private reception. Assembled was the London crowd at that time, and I knew, personally, most people in that room.

Christopher went to the bar to fetch my drink and I stood there, alone. Not just alone but surrounded by space as people seemed to melt away. There was a terrible silence. I was embarrassed for myself, and embarrassed for them because I knew they were feeling very uncomfortable, wondering, presumably, if someone was going to break the ice. It was all I could do not to burst into tears. I tried desperately to look unconcerned as I waited for Christopher to return with the drinks.

'Hello, Mands!' A loud voice, a flurry at the door and Bob Mitchum was striding towards me. He gave me a big hug and a kiss. 'This is Dorothy.' His wife smiled and said hello, and turning to the other woman he introduced me to his secretary, whom I had understudied while she was having a baby.

'This is Mandy,' he said to her. 'I've told you all about her, how well she took care of me last year.'

Had he been the Queen his spontaneous display of friendship could not have been more cataclysmic. People started to crowd around and join in the chat. They had been afraid before, now they knew it was all right. When you are a big star, and as big a man as Mitchum, you do not have to think about going along with the crowd.

After the film, there was a formal dinner. I was just about to take my seat when one of the organisers said there had been a slight mix-up and would I mind sitting at another table; in fact I was then placed on the top table with the real VIPs. The truth was that John Bloom had objected to my sitting at his table. I cannot say I was sorry a couple of years later when his washing-machine business collapsed. Pompous little man.

When Ivor Spencer, the famous toastmaster, wrote his memoirs, he gave a different version of events. According to him, I had gatecrashed the première and embarrassed officials had been given the tricky problem of finding me a seat, and the only one was at the top table!

One loses count of the hundreds of inaccuracies written and told. Daddy kept press cuttings for a while and many of the stories were complete fiction. Of course, it is intensely irritating, because it is impossible to hit back. I never sue, I do not write threatening letters demanding retractions and apologies. Over the years masses of rubbish has been printed about me. Had I decided to complain about every inaccuracy that came to my notice, it would have been a full-time job. All that is pointless.

Like royalty, I simply do not complain.

It is nevertheless, a weird experience to see yourself as others see you. In Germany once, I passed a cinema where they were showing *The Christine Keeler Story*. Originally Christine and I had been approached to play ourselves in this film. Because Equity would not give approval for Christine to work and had refused her membership, the producers went ahead and made the film anyway. I declined to appear and my part was played by a German. Persuaded by my companion that it would be amusing, I went into the cinema. The scene purported to represent Cliveden. There was the pool, surrounded by twenty or thirty people, some black, some very hippy with freaked-out hair, some lying around smoking dope. This was supposed to be Cliveden, that peaceful English spot where Nancy Astor had said, incredulously, 'Is that a bikini I see?' Peter was portrayed as a grotesque character, enormously fat, bald with a black shirt and a white tie, like a hit man from an old gangster film. Watching somebody playing me was one of the all-time horrible experiences of my life.

In New York I picked up a book on a newsstand entitled *Whatever Happened To?*, and there was a graphic description of Mandy and Christine 'entertaining their Johnnies at whipping parties, £1 a stroke, in a room with a two-way mirror,' which was followed by an account of every known sexual deviation attributed to us. All totally untrue, of course.

My family came in for the same treatment. My sister, Margaret, sitting on a bus with her fourteen-year-old daughter, heard two women swapping Mandy stories. One told the other, 'Did you know she bought her sister a house in Bentley Heath, and the two of them hold orgies there every night?'

I received mail by the sackful. Friendly, compassionate letters from people like vicars and their wives inviting me to come and stay for a week or two. Hundreds of letters from lesbians all seemingly in the WAAFs. Many letters were obscene – I came to the conclusion that at least one man in a thousand must be mentally deranged. Daddy used to sort them out before making a bonfire at the end of the garden, but with experience we developed a speeded-up sorting process. All typed letters, we decided, were either official or from maniacs. I belive that the psychopath without treatment progresses – or rather regresses – from the overt gesture (like writing an obscene letter) to violence and I suspect that the Yorkshire Ripper may have been among my early fans. I was the ideal target.

I seemed to have become part of folklore. I would feature somewhere in any topical TV play, satirical programmes like *That Was the Week That Was* had a field day with me. The Archbishop of Birmingham said I was in danger of becoming Birmingham's patron saint. The French referred to me in their anti-Common Market propaganda, concluding 'the British have demonstrated by their attitude to the Profumo affair that they are not yet mature enough to join the Common Market'. Germans, Spaniards, Americans, Swedes, even the Japanese had some cogent comment about me.

When a publisher approached me with an offer to publish my memoirs in the form of *The Mandy Report*, to come out on the heels of the Denning Report, it seemed reasonable. My profit would be threepence on each copy sold, and in a fit of altruistic generosity, prompted by some recent world catastrophe, I volunteered a percentage of my royalties to Oxfam. Their response came soon after, in the form of a publicly announced letter saying they would decline the offer. People were starving in the Third World, and at Oxfam headquarters they were turning away good money. After their announcement I received a communication from the Sunshine Homes for the Blind saying they would welcome my donation. Sadly there was not one. The book was published, I threw a party to launch it, and the publishers disappeared. My memoirs sold round the world, and I never succeeded in extricating a penny. It taught me a little more about human nature. It also left me with an unfavourable impression of Oxfam. I have never set foot in an Oxfam shop.

Life was absurd to extremes. I was banned by the New Zealand Government from entering that country; but, on the other hand, I was sought out by the media for some extraordinary reasons. On the night of 22 November 1963 a dozen reporters turned up on the doorstep of my parents' home to ask me what I thought of the assassination of President Kennedy! Mothers' Unions and church committees were particularly interested in my activities. A northern vicar, whose parish I was to visit, logged my every movement and whereabouts, and even telephoned my agent to harangue him for being associated with me. 'He that casteth the first stone . . . ' said my agent, and the telephone clicked dead. When I made the highly publicised visit I was somewhat apprehensive, and so was my father who was with me. The personal appearance passed off without mishap. I kept wondering where the vigilantes were – I knew they had been mobilising like mad in readiness for my visit. We were walking to our car when a crowd of old ladies appeared round the corner, waving umbrellas in a most menacing way. My father, on the basis of discretion being the better part of valour, said, 'Run for it.' But I preferred to brave it out, and stood my ground waiting for the first blow. I suddenly realised they were not threatening but greeting us.

'Mandy, Mandy, cooee,' they called. They weren't after my blood, they were after my autograph.

Visiting my home town for a TV documentary, the director wanted me photographed outside the gates of my old school. Sherman's Cross had not changed, after all it was only four years since I was a pupil there. School turned out and several girls on their way home stopped to say hello. That was all – but the local education authority was incensed. 'We cannot,' said the town clerk, 'have the girls thinking that the Mandy Rice-Davies way of life is the thing to do.'

Scandal followed me around. When I became engaged to Baron Pierre de Cervello, his wife cited me as the other woman in her divorce despite having left him for another man two and a half years before I had even appeared on the scene. They were so incompatible, Pierre used to chew gorgonzola cheese before going to bed, to deter her amorous advances.

When I was invited to hunt with the Weston Harriers during a weekend in Somerset, I little expected *that* to make headlines. The press turned out to watch me, so, with a crowd around, it seemed only polite and considerate to the other riders and their horses to wait some way off on the green at Webbington until the start. This was interpreted by the press as my being snubbed by the hunt.

On balance, for all the people who preferred not to know me, there must be hundreds who claimed acquaintanceship. For a long time there were accounts of my doing a strip show. When I looked into this, the strippers were girls who had adopted my name. Anyone tall and blonde called herself Mandy Rice-Davies and was in business as a stage act in places where there was no Equity to step in, I am continually meeting people who say, 'Jack sends his regards,' and go on to remind me of somebody who claims close friendship with me, and whom I have never met.

I used to travel in disguise, which meant that I went as myself: quiet clothes, no make-up, and glasses with clear lenses. In this way I blend into the background. Travelling home to Birmingham one day the train was crowded and I found one corner seat in the first-class carriage. There were five men, typical business types. One kept looking over his newspaper at me, and eventually he said, 'You look like Mandy Rice-Davies.'

'Really?' I said in my most hoity-toity manner, which always worked like a charm, sounding insulted to be called Mandy Rice-Davies. Usually they then dropped the subject, but he kept repeating 'Really you *do* look a lot like her.' Then he said, 'And actually I know her very well.'

By now I was interested.

'I met her a few years ago. I have had dinner with her on many occasions. She is a very nice girl despite what you read.'

I have an exceptional memory for faces, and I knew I had never set eyes on him. He warmed to his subject, the conversation growing more detailed, the innuendoes as to how well he knew me creeping in. The other men were riveted. I was fuming, and determined on revenge.

As the train arrived at Birmingham, I stepped from the compartment and said loudly for the benefit of his fellow passengers, 'Well, I *am* Mandy Rice-Davies and I am happy to say that I have never met you in my life.' I shut the door with a bang and stalked off, leaving him absolutely red-faced.

People used to send me good-luck charms, key rings, odds and ends like that, and in this way I acquired a rabbit's foot. It figured in a weird experience.

Travelling from Birmingham to London, once again in my nondescript disguise, this time with my nose buried deep in a book on psychology, which was then my current obsession, I was disturbed by the arrival of another passenger. I had been dimly aware he had passed by a few times, looking in at me. Now he came in, clutching a cardboard suitcase, tied round with string, and sat in the corner, staring.

Ten minutes later the ticket collector came in and asked the little man (he was barely five feet tall) for his ticket. He admitted that he had only a second-class ticket but would pay the difference. Now I felt guilty – he was paying the difference because he wanted to be in the carriage with me and obviously could not afford it or he would not be carrying a paper suitcase. I felt overwhelmed with pity. Suddenly he said, indicating my book *Sense and Nonsense of Psychology*, 'I've been through all that, you know.'

Being interested in psychology, we struck up a conversation. He told me he had been in Broadmoor or some similar institution. He said things like, 'My wife is a dwarf' (he was very small himself), 'and all the boys laugh at me in the pub.' It was a weird monologue of his problems. He said he had been terribly unhappy and had tried to commit suicide many times. He was so pitiful.

As I was searching in my bag for cigarettes, I came across my lucky rabbit's foot. On impulse I gave it to him. 'You have tried to commit suicide,' I said. 'Take this for luck.'

He thanked me, took the rabbit's foot, the train journey ended and we parted. He was a sad creature, and I forgot about him.

Months later, after a show, the telephone rang for me back-stage. I answered it. A voice said, 'Hello.'

I answered, 'Hello.'

Then he said, 'Mandy, I've still got the rabbit's foot,' and put down the telephone.

This was more than a little frightening – was he there by coincidence or was he following me? I felt most peculiar, began to be careful where I went and took to constantly looking behind me.

Months passed. I had been riding. It was late, I left the horse at the stable and had to walk the long drive up to the clubhouse I was staying in. Tall trees lined the drive, there was no moon and thick cloud. As I was walking completely alone, somebody came running, softly, from behind. It was the little man from the train. He stood smiling at me, and dangling from a string the rabbit's foot, swinging it in front of my face. It is not easy to run in riding boots, but I belted up the drive for all I was worth, leaving him standing there not saying a word, just staring with that glazed look and dangling the rabbit's foot.

The men in the country club rushed out into the grounds to find him, but without success. I never heard from him again although it was many months before I overcame the fear that he was somewhere, a few footsteps behind me.

One of the searchers that night was an ex-police detective who had been Prince Charles's bodyguard for many years. In fact, he had been dismissed after Prince Charles's much-publicised tipple of cherry brandy when still a fourteen-year-old schoolboy. He said that he was still missing Charles, having been with him since infancy, that it was a close personal friendship and they still wrote to each other. He had worked closely with many famous people and, realising my admiration for Sir Winston Churchill, told me this marvellous anecdote, concerning an episode when he was on duty.

Churchill and Anthony Eden were involved in a top-level conference at No. 10 Downing Street, and sitting on opposite sides of the table. During the conference, the detective who was recalling this noticed Eden pick up his pen, write a note and pass it over the table to Sir Winston. Churchill read it, screwed it up, put it in the ashtray, wrote a note and passed it to Eden. Eden read the reply, screwed it up and threw it in the fire, where it smouldered but fell out of reach of the flames. When the meeting was over, the detective unscrewed the note in the ashtray. Eden had written: 'Sir, your fly buttons are undone.' He then retrieved the note from the fireplace to read Churchill's reply: 'A dead bird cannot fall out of its nest.'

For some months after the trial I continued to see a great deal of John Wheater, my solicitor. For one thing he was handling the purchase of a mews house in Cornwall Mews West, the first property I had owned. It took all the cash I had (£1,500 for a twelve-year lease and £6 a week rent) but was worth it for the security of actually having a home of my own. I spent a fortune painting, decorating, re-fitting the kitchen and bathroom. Just as the carpet layers (Harrods, of course!) had completed and were packing their tools, I received a visit from two men with official-looking briefcases who informed me the flat was the property of the Sun Life Insurance Company (coincidentally Fairbanks's company) and whatever deeds I might have to the contrary, it looked as if I had been conned. They were absolutely right. When I tried calling John, he had disappeared. In fact, he had just been arrested in connection with the Great Train Robbery.

That could perhaps account for those furtive meetings and conferences with Emil and the other man, when I had read magazines and listened to music instead of their conversation. The other man was a close friend of mine at the time, a suave Irishman who is still very much around. He had had several rich wives and moved with ease in society as well as the twilight criminal world. He had an eccentric sense of humour and collected weird objects. His authority was obvious. Everyone listened to him. I have no doubt that he and Emil were the brains behind the Great Train Robbery and that he, Mr X, was the Mr Big.

My father, when the story of the robbery broke, said: 'Thank goodness something has come along to push you off the front pages for a while.'

19

THE career of Mandy Rice-Davies, cabaret artiste, began by accident, with a visit from a stranger with a proposition, as I lay in a hospital bed coming round from an anaesthetic.

I have to go back a little. I had acquired a contract with man-about-town Tim Bryant – frightfully well connected, and into a variety of successful projects. He put me on the books of his 'stable', as he called it, though as far as I could make out there was only me. He had plans to film *Fanny Hill*, with me in the title role. Martine Carol was to play the madame, and the script was being written by French lawyer-writer, Monique Drier, who had worked on *Le Verité* with Brigitte Bardot. Monique invited me to spend a weekend at her house in the South of France while we discussed the film. In the early sixties nudity was not part of the scene, so there was no question of my being expected to break my self-imposed rule of not stripping off completely, semi-nudity only in silhouette, nothing full-frontal or risqué. I have always worked on that principle – it has been my insurance in life. You never know – you might one day be Prime Minister!

It was a pleasant houseparty, a scattering of the super rich who felt competely at ease in her house where Renoirs hung like wallpaper on the walls. Woolworth's heir, Tony Hubbard, was one of the guests, and there were several French people present. I was still at the stage of trying to live down events of earlier that year, and it was refreshing to be among people who saw me as a rather glamorous character: Americans are interested in anyone with a claim to fame, whilst the French have a more polished, sophisticated attitude to scandal.

However, the ambience was wasted on me, due to a violent case of toothache. I dosed myself with aspirin and flew back to England. The deal had been done, I was to receive £25 a week while the production was set up, and could not fail to earn money from what was sure to be the box-office hit of 1964. (Actually, the closest the public ever came to seeing me as Fanny was a magazine feature which had me dressed in costume. The film itself was never made.)

Believing I was on the brink of cinema stardom, I flew into Heathrow and went immediately to hospital. The consultant dentist took one look at my teeth and said I had several serious and highly poisonous abscesses and the condition was critical. If they did not remove my teeth, I might die!

'You're not taking my teeth out,' I declared. 'Anything but that. I'd sooner die than be toothless.'

They rushed me into the operating theatre and performed a brilliant (how much I owe to that surgeon) operation which cut open the gums, removed those sections of infected root, stitched me up again and left my teeth intact. Painful but effective.

Lying on my bed, still dizzy from anaesthetic, I heard the nurse say: 'You have a visitor. Do you want to see him?'

It was Christmas Day. I thought this must be my Italian lover, Pierre Cervello. Instead it was a dapper German, who introduced himself – Herr Peter Tauber.

'I am an agent,' he said. 'I have come at the request of Herr Max Muller, owner of Eve's Bar in Munich. He would like you to come along and do something.'

'Do something? Like what?' Speaking was difficult.

'Anything,' said Herr Tauber. 'Can you sing?'

'I was in the choir,' I replied.

'Excellent. And perhaps you can dance?'

'Yes, I can dance. It isn't striptease by any chance?'

'Oh no,' Herr Tauber assured me. 'Definitely not striptease.'

'I'm not sure,' I said. 'I'll think about it.'

'We will pay you $250 a night,' said Herr Tauber. That was a fortune. Close to £150 a night. Shirley Bassey was getting £1,000 a week in those days, the Beatles were not making much more.

'I accept,' I said.

I lay in bed unable to sleep thinking about what I had let myself in for. I had about two weeks to prepare for my début,

I had always enjoyed singing but I did not deceive myself that what was right for the choir was right for a nightclub. What to do next. Fortunately I had a good friend, the bandleader beloved of so many debs dances, Confrey Phillips.

Confrey agreed to coach me. He hired a rehearsal room with a piano, and I arrived for my first session, prepared with the sort of music I felt I should sing, inspired by Eartha Kitt and Marlene Dietrich, whose records I had been playing non-stop.

For a week we struggled on. I affected not to notice the pained looks which Confrey and Pierre exchanged. My voice was wrong. 'It might be a lovely soprano, darling, but . . . ' Confrey tried to be kind. It was not just my voice. My gestures were like Action Man – I simply could not get in the mood. I needed the dress, the lights, the applause, I was later to discover, before I could perform with any degree of enthusiasm. I have never mastered the technique of acting to a table and pretending it is the leading man, and in that respect at least I am in good company. Many top actors have the same blind spot. Confrey kept saying he wanted to find my voice range, as if this would help me stand up on a stage and sing. At every opportunity Pierre would grab the mike and take over – he had a good voice actually, but this was not the time or the place to demonstrate. As the coaching dragged on, Pierre looked increasingly worried and eventually produced a pressing business engagement that would unfortunately prevent him from being present at my début.

Confrey and I decided to concentrate on songs which required talking rather than singing, and I put together a repertoire including 'An Englishman Needs Times', 'It's So Nice To Have A Man About The House', 'Let's Do It' – where would I have been but for Cole Porter, who wrote such memorable tunes, yet provided songs which could be spoken and not sung with devastating effect? For good value, I learned a few lines of German to throw in, although I had been told that this was a top international club and all clients spoke English. (By the end of my cabaret career I had learned to speak four languages using Linguaphone records – Hebrew I picked up off the streets – so that I could throw in remarks in the relevant tongue.)

Dispirited by Pierre's distinctly patronising air, armed with my music arranged by Confrey in the key appropriate to my voice, and my stage dress – full-length black velvet, halter-necked, bare arms, slinky all the way down to a fishtail effect around the hem – I set off for Germany. The press had been alerted. My employer knew how to get his money's worth and my every move from Heathrow to Düsseldorf (where the plane was diverted because of fog) then by train to Munich was chronicled as if I was Olivier playing in rep. At Munich station, a red carpet had been laid and I was greeted by a reception party, including a bevy of handmaidens in national dress and our Max with a bunch of red roses. Unfortunately, because of the delay in arriving, I had lost my rehearsal day and was to open that night.

Fear has a rationalising effect. I have always been a trier, I have not always won, but I have tried. I decided at that moment, and it has been my philosophy since, that there is no dishonour in failure. After a perfunctory rehearsal – well, I went through my songs with the band – I retired to my hotel room to prepare for the evening. I had equipped myself with a sun lamp; white limbs, I decided, looked inelegant with black. I knew nothing about lighting, or how marvellously the lights can enhance the skin. By the time I arrived at my dressing-room I had two arms of hideous lobster pink, not evenly matched I might add, which I attempted to disguise with make-up. I had read somewhere that the great Caruso used to drink champagne before he went on. I drank two glasses, and instinct told me this was enough. Any more and I would be insensible.

The efficiency of the Germans was my salvation. I could not fail. Max had built the show around me, the microphone was absolutely right, there was a technician to balance the sound, there was a cheering audience, a sea of press bulbs, everything to convince the crowd that here was a star. I started off shakily. Half-way into 'An Englishman Needs Time', my second song, something happened to me and I began to enjoy it. The feeling grew stronger. By the time I had finished I was swamped with elation. I was Samantha Showbiz, as one of the critics wrote.

Of the many reviews, this one from *Time* sums it all up.

In Munich's Eve's Bar, where the B-girls are affluent and fat businessmen roar like jungle cats, there is always something special for the sex-exotic eye. Maybe a dark-tressed Parisian stripper, full-bodied and beautiful, mounted on a prancing white horse. Or a trainer, three tigers and one notable nude, all together in a cage.

Last week the main attraction was just a singer, without props, and reasonably dressed. But the place was full. Mandy Rice-Davies of London was making her showbiz début.

She came onstage trembling, spoke in a whisper, and apologised that in her nineteen years she had never used a microphone or appeared before a crowd. Facing the wigged high judges of Britain had failed to dent her brassbound confidence, but facing this crowd was something else. 'Because my name is Mandy Rice-Davies,' she had told avid reporters a few hours earlier, 'I have to start at the top. It's twice as hard.'

Her face had a pouting innocence, but seemed too small for her long body. Her small blue eyes were cold and sandbagged with mascara. The spotlight glare was hard on her, emphasising the coarse redness of her plump arms.

Almost inaudibly she began to sing

A kiss on the hand may be quite continental,
But diamonds are a girl's best friend.
A kiss may be grand, but it won't pay the rental . . .

Flashbulbs gunned at her, two tablesful of old British businessmen bellowed raucous chauvinistic cheers, and Mandy clutched the mike so tight her knuckles lit up. If by nothing else, she was held on her feet by the converging leers of Central Europe's richer playboys, who were there in packs.

By the time she got into her second number ('An Englishman Needs Time'), she wasn't trembling any more. She did slow, undulous bumps and highly negotiable grinds, a smile spread round her ice-blue eyes, and she gave quite enough of a hint of the carnal power and consuming ambition that had made her famous. "*Ein richtiger Teufelsbraten*," shouted a bull-necked German. A veritable devil's dish.

Flip, relieved, and sassy as ever after it was all over,

randy Mandy Teufelsbraten was suddenly Samantha Showbiz.

I was well into the swing of the celebration party when Pierre called me. 'How did it go?'

'Marvellously.'

'Really!' he sounded surprised. He could hear the party, and it was not a wake. He had planned to be on business three days but now he found he could be with me tomorrow after all.

If somebody had told me at that moment it was the start of a career which would last until I married and went to live in Israel, I would frankly have disbelieved them. I knew I had got by, that I had not made a fool of myself. I also knew that people had not come to hear me sing, they had come to look. I thought of it as a one-off, but it was not. As my career progressed and I travelled England and Europe I was frequently invited back, time and time again, to do the same spot.

I even made records – and I could not sing. Although, as I very soon discovered, not everybody who walks into a music-recording studio is a tip-top professional. One of the drummers in a session reassured me. 'Don't worry, love, I was playing Ringo Starr's drums for his record last week.' And I found that with double tracking and echoes and a whole coterie of tricks, I would come out sounding like Maria Callas if that was required. One of my records actually won The Golden Juke Box Award of Italy, although I have my suspicions about this. When they presented me with the award, I asked one of the judges what he thought of it; he looked blank and admitted he had never actually heard it. Pierre had very good contacts in Italy.

It was impossible, it seemed, for my life to proceed smoothly, I walked into trouble. When two rival club owners in Istanbul requested my services, I elected to appear at a club called the Cordon Blue for an astronomical fee of close to £2,000 a week. Pierre by this time had decided to accompany me everywhere and to act as my business manager, which could possibly have something to do with the ensuing trouble.

Oblivious to what was in store, I flew out to Turkey, arriving to a waiting crowd of about 3,000 and, I might add, minus all my shoes which were lost in transit and never recovered. (From that day I have made it a rule always to carry my music and stage clothes for at least the first night as hand baggage.) The police escorted us to the hotel, giving a demonstration of their effectiveness in crowd control by actually driving the car at the crowd. I then had to register for my work permit, a mere formality obviously, as I had meanwhile eaten lunch with the Chief of Police. I was used to crowds by this time, but the hysteria in Istanbul was beyond belief. No blonde of any consequence had visited the city since Carrol Baker publicised *Baby Doll* in 1956. The owner of the Cordon Blue was delighted at such publicity, but the rival club owner had taken to telephoning and uttering rasping threats into my ear. It would all blow over, I persuaded myself, it is just the Middle-Eastern temperament.

When it came to the shoe-buying expedition, we made a secretive exit from the hotel and drove without incident to the street where the shops were, and it was literally five steps from the car into the shop. Choosing my shoes, and enjoying a cup of coffee with the proprietor, I could hear a fantastic racket coming from the street. The owner asked me if I would mind going to the window and waving to the people. Otherwise he said he was afraid they would smash the glass. When I looked into the street it was so jammed with men it was a seething mass. I was terrified – how was I to get out? The back of the shop backed onto other buildings, there was only one way out. The police were called and came in a car with attendant motor bikes, literally scattering the people before them.

'When we say the word, just run,' said the policeman in charge. What a joke! I stepped out of the front door, Pierre in front of me giving fisticuffs to everyone in sight. As fast as he got one out of the way, another came up. The last I saw of Pierre for about two hours was him being sucked into the crowd, gradually disappearing. Now I was in the middle of that crowd of people, grabbing at my clothes and hair. One wore suspender belts in those days, and I had on a woollen skirt; when I got into the car I had no skirt, and my suspender belt, which everybody had been grabbing at, had left bruises on my legs. My top was practically torn off, my bra was in pieces, I had no shoes. Whole chunks of my hair had been pulled out. The police revved up the engine and took off, people banging on the car all the way along the street. It had been a perfectly decent-looking police car when it arrived for me, but when it dropped me back at the hotel it was a wreck. My next worry was how to make it to the club that night, but the police were prepared, and cordoned off the whole area.

The show was a great success. So great I did not get the chance to do many more nights. Returning to the hotel after a delightful day sailing on the Bosporus and lunching with some of Turkey's social *crème de la crème*, I was met by the owner of the Cordon Blue. He was distraught.

'No more work, it is finished,' he said.

I demanded to be told more. He said the police were looking for me, I was in big trouble. I had hardly had time to check this out when the police arrived, telling me I was to accompany them to headquarters. I looked out of my hotel window, fifteen storeys up, and there below, on each balcony, were stationed uniformed police. Did they think I was going to jump? This must be serious.

Later I discovered that the owner of the rival club, angered by missing out on all the business and publicity, had complained to some relevant ministry that I was singing obscene songs. The foundation for his complaint was not that important, as he happened to be related to the minister concerned.

I telephoned the British Embassy and left a message. Half an hour later the British Consul rang and I told him the police were arresting me.

He said, 'Miss Rice-Davies, we can be of no help to you whatsoever in this country. The only thing I can advise is for you to be as nice as possible, be agreeable, and see exactly what they have on their minds. I can bring you an unlimited amount of things to prison.'

This was the opposite of reassuring. He said he would keep in touch with the situation and I was led off with Pierre staunchly behind me. Pierre was very good at things like this, always behind me. He was just a moral coward.

When I saw *Midnight Express*, it brought it all back to me. Police headquarters was an old, old building of stone, iron bars everywhere. Just to put one foot in was frightening. The same police chief whom I had lunched with now had an unpleasant duty and he was terribly embarrassed. I had no idea what I had done, there had been no actual charges, and I thought perhaps I was causing too many problems, which seemed logical because they literally had to shut off Istanbul for me. The worst indignity was being fingerprinted and photographed. Pierre had disappeared by this time because they would not let him come with me, and I was physically afraid. The rooms were eerie, big, stone floors and walls. It was night and there were naked light bulbs staring from the ceiling. Compared with this, Holloway looked like Buckingham Palace.

Eventually, it was explained to me that I was in danger of being imprisoned because I had sung an obscene song (Cole Porter's 'Let's Do It') and they were discussing if they should slap me in prison while they sorted it out. There was obviously an argument going on, because I could hear a lot of shouting, and the telephones were ringing frantically. Finally the police chief came in and told me: 'You can go back to your hotel tonight but you must leave Turkey on the first plane tomorrow morning.'

Imagine the relief – I had been held in custody for seven hours.

Next morning with full police escort I was put on a Pan American flight to freedom. My favourite cartoon was Lancaster's, which had a large Turkish policeman sitting at his big desk with a picture of Mandy Rice-Davies on it, and a telephone in his hand: 'Yes, yes, Abdul, I remember also the days with the soft plop in the Bosporus.' In other words, in those days you did not deport them you just threw them in the Bosporus and did not have to bother with all the paperwork.

Meanwhile Tim Byrant had sold my agency contract to a marvellous theatrical agent called Phillip Hindon, which was a stroke of luck for me. Phillip worked with Maurice Winnick Associates, and looked after the professional lives of top celebrities of the chat-show circuit. When people rang to inquire who he had available for a certain venue, he would reply, 'Lady Isobel Barnett, Lord Boothby, Mandy Rice-Davies!'

Thanks to Phillip Hindon I began doing the Working Men's Clubs circuit. That is where the money was. My first engagement in the north prepared me for that particular type of business. I arrived the night before to have a look around (it was the first time that I had ever seen this sort of set-up). A huge hall with hundreds of people sitting at long tables drinking beer. Alma Cogan was appearing. It was the last night of her run. The MC (also club secretary) was trying to quieten the audience before she came on. They were all chatting and shouting, exactly like being at a football match, and it was the same sort of atmosphere. She came on to perform but they just carried on talking, so he picked up the microphone and said, 'Give the poor cow a chance!' I nearly died.

Next night it was my turn. By now I had put a little act together which was really quite smart for somebody like me, quite untrained. I had learned to walk on very very slowly, whilst the music kept repeating the opening four bars. I had figured that the only way to get an audience was just to be so full of confidence that nobody dared say a word, and I have proved many times you have an absolutely captive audience if you show you do not give a tuppeny ha'penny damn what they do anyway. Then they are like sweet little choirboys sitting there.

So I walked on with my hand on my hip, walked around the audience, took them in with my glances, so that everybody had the feeling that I was looking at them. Then I started the song and frightened them to death actually, because the whole audience seemed to jump in the air. They were so engrossed by my walking around and my silly smile that when I sang my first word, they all jumped out of their seats, especially as the first word was 'If' – with a sharp f.

The first night I walked on stage there was a peculiar sound. It resembled the sea. Throughout the show this puzzled me, a continuous slurping sound like waves on the shore. It was not until the second night that I realised it was the sound of a thousand men supping their beer! At the end of my first night's act I heard a lot of shouting from the audience. It sounded like 'Get her off'. I was terribly worried, I could not understand it, surely I was not that bad? There was great applause, I could not understand why people were shouting 'Get her off'. The secretary explained that they were actually shouting 'Get 'em off!' A compliment of course!

One-night stands were particularly well paid. A night here and a night there meant £250 a time. One club in Wales had allowed its members once a year to have *the* artiste of their choice. They voted for me, their most popular act.

During all my working life I have never (if it has been up to me) been late. I have never not turned up for a booking. Phillip Hindon used to say I was paid on the dot and I was there on the dot, and I was the only artiste in his life that he had never worried about professionally. But once, for the first and only time in my life, I went down with a lightning attack of laryngitis and lost my voice.

What happened next is history! Phillip rang to say, 'Mandy can't make it.' They had to fill in with an unknown called Tom Jones. At the same time a bus conductor from Tonypandy on a night out to see Mandy Rice-Davies was in the audience. He was a young man with a burning desire to get into showbusiness. His name was Gordon Mills. Gordon did not find me there, but he listened to Tom Jones, went backstage afterwards and that famous partnership was formed.

I was making a good living. I worked a lot in Spain (to avoid the risk of problems over performing material they simply inspected your repertoire when you arrived and stamped it to give it the OK for Spanish musicians) and I rented an apartment in Torremolinos, which in those days was a small village, and used it as a base.

My periods away from Pierre were becoming more frequent and extended. As a business manager he was not that hot. There was the fiasco in Italy when, during an extensive tour, Pierre persuaded me to ignore Equity's advice ('Cash in advance, just before the performance. No cash, no show.') and insisted he would take charge. After all, he said, he was half Sicilian and this made for a certain understanding between people.

It certainly did.

Somebody called Sacha, who was the agent in charge of the whole tour, took us around. Each time I told Pierre that I thought we should ask for my money, he said, 'No, I am Italian. We are best friends.' It was a strenuous tour, and got off to an inauspicious start. During my week in Milan, in a club called El Morocco, somebody shot the owner while I was on the stage! Towards the end of the tour we arrived in Florence. At the beginning of my act I came on, just looked, then suddenly burst into song. There was a very old man sitting in the front row of the club called the Open Gates in Florence. I walked on, looked – he was staring at me. Suddenly I sang 'If . . . ' and he had a heart attack! They had to stop my act to carry him out.

Finally we reached Rome, the last stop on a six-week tour, so by now I was owed something like 8,000 dollars. 'Pierre,' I said, 'we are on the last gig now, so take the money.'

First thing in the morning he went off the agent's office and did not return until eight at night. 'Here,' he said, 'I have the cheque.'

'What do you mean – cheque,' I said. 'I want cash not a cheque.'

Next morning we presented the cheque made out for millions of lire to the bank and, of course, there was no money in the account.

Sacha had packed his bags and disappeared. I had lost the lot. Trying to bring a court case in Italy is tantamount to throwing a bottle in the ocean and hoping that one day it will arrive at its destination.

So what with his hazy business sense, his intense jealousy and his numerous dramatised suicide attempts, Pierre was becoming rather bothersome. I thought of making a complete break.

By then I had money to invest and was about to exchange contracts on a pig farm, and I negotiated a deal with Walls to sell them all my pork. I am fond of pigs, and have always been attracted to the idea of farming to a very high standard, eradicating the foot and mouth disease. Rather like Marie Antoinette, I fancied running a model farm. But my plans fizzled out when another tour came along, and so the months passed.

When I was invited to play Australia, a whole new area opened up for me. My agent got busy and booked New Zealand, Hong Kong, Singapore. I made plans to ride a horse across the Australian outback after my work was finished.

'We've hit a spot of bother,' said Phillip Hindon. 'A complaint from the New Zealand Brownies and Girl Guides.'

Those busy little do-gooders in New Zealand had apparently lodged a formal objection with the government not to allow 'this home destroyer' to set foot on their beloved soil. It was not clear whose home I had destroyed – in fact I know of a few I have helped build. The New Zealand agents were keen to get me in and engaged a lawyer to speak in the New Zealand Parliament. There followed a three-day debate when MPs discussed nothing but me. Supporters stood up and said 'Elizabeth Taylor has been here, and she destroyed three or four marriages, and here is this girl who only wants to come over here to sing . . .' It became a moral issue, and the moralists won. After New Zealand refused entry the Australian management cancelled my booking and I was left with Hong Kong and Singapore, delightful spots no doubt but just not viable.

Worse was to come. The Sands Hotel, Las Vegas, offered me a spot, but the American authorities were refusing to grant a visa. Not only was the deal worth a small fortune, it would have provided me with the one thing I really needed – prestige. They would have built a show for me, not only establishing me as a top-bracket entertainer – but during the eight-week rehearsal period I would have gained so much from their expertise.

But – no visa, no job. I could have pursued it – there is always somebody you can appeal to, and the Sands might have backed me, but I felt it was not worth it. Now and again I feel a bottled-up rage, but more often than not I let matters slide away and let time pass and the feeling of anger goes.

Meanwhile, I had Mexico City to look forward to and a club called El Patio. Or did I?

Things were proceeding beautifully until someone with a highly developed sense of diplomacy discovered that Prince Philip, on a royal tour, would be calling in at Mexico City around the same time as Mandy Rice-Davies. Negotiations took place between the Mexican Government and the owners of El Patio. I still have the telegram cancelling my show.

> Due royal visit to Mexico, début Mandy has to be postponed until he has left. Advise if you agree. We are still willing to fulfil contract. Sorry this means great loss to us too. El Patio. 15 October 1965.'

I had to laugh. In any case I still had a contract for Israel, Greece and Cyprus. I set off for Tel Aviv, little realising it would be a journey of no return. Almost.

20

ON my first night in Israel, after the show, I was taken to one of Tel Aviv's two night spots, a disco called Whisky-A-Go-Go, and introduced to the owner, Rafael Shaul. I knew at once that this was the man I would marry. With this insight came a second thought that I did not especially like him, to be followed by a third, how ridiculous that I should be thinking any of this. We hardly spoke. The following day he telephoned to ask me out. 'I'm in the bath, call me back in five minutes,' I said, which has always been my ploy for stalling, either to think out a decision or just avoid the issue altogether. I arranged to be out when he called back – I made it a policy never to get involved emotionally while I was working.

A couple of days later he called at the club where I was appearing, and found me fishing around with a piece of Kleenex trying to extricate some grit from my eye. He took over, fished around in my eye and found the offending object. The romance was on.

I was falling in love, too, with Israel, particularly Tel Aviv. It really is an ugly city, totally new, thrown together really to cope with the swarms of people who have thronged in. It has been a haphazard development which, in presenting a challenge to the various architects, has somehow inspired them to try to be cleverer than each other, with the result that nothing has form. For all this, the city had then and still has a vibrancy which is seductive, and an earthy response to life that appealed to me. I have seen many changes there – today it is amusing to recall that when I first arrived I was not permitted to sing any of the German songs in my repertoire, as feeling was so strongly anti-German, and today the city swarms with Volkswagens.

Doing my show in Tel Aviv was a mixed pleasure. Israel was technologically way down the line, the baby echoes and sound effects I relied upon to bolster my rather weak voice simply did not exist. Left to make out on my own, I could hardly have sounded the best singer in Israel, yet the audience apparently liked me and the club did good business during my three weeks. Unlike today, the audience was comparatively unsophisticated, and performers started off with the great advantage of being appreciated for the simple fact of even going there in the first place.

I was invited along to spend a few days at Elat, on the Red Sea, with Rafi and a group of friends. There was a busty blonde in the group, I rather resented her and the interest she showed in Rafi. When they proceeded to go off snorkling, including Busty Blonde who was wiggling her bum in all directions, I decided to join in.

'Can you snorkel?'

'Of course,' I said, making a grab at the various pipes and tubes. You only live once.

Bravely I headed out into the deep water and took the plunge. Water came in through every conceivable orifice, bursting into my throat and lungs. I flailed about in the water, praying someone would help me.

Fortunately Rafi guessed what had happened, took me back to the beach and spent the rest of the day by my side.

When the time came for me to leave for Greece and Cyprus on my tour, I knew I should return to Israel, and took the precaution of leaving at least half of my luggage in Rafi's apartment.

The strangest thing happened in Athens. Walking along the main avenue I saw coming towards me a man in full airforce uniform, complete with gold ceremonial sword. He was a very handsome guy and, as we passed, we looked at each other and realised that we recognised one another. But who was he? Simultaneously we both turned to take another look and he said, recognition dawning, 'Mandy?'

'Good God – it's Aziz', I said. 'What are you doing here?'

He told me the Jordanian airforce had an exchange system with the Greeks. He had served in the Jordanian airforce, now he had been sent to Greece for two years' training. He had just attended an important funeral, hence the ceremonial dress.

We went into a nearby coffee shop and talked about old

times and what we were doing now. When I said I had just come from Israel, and that I planned to go back there, he was horrified.

'Don't go', he said. 'One day we will come and destroy the country and I wouldn't want to think of you there while I am dropping bombs over Tel Aviv.'

'Nonsense,' I said. He asked where I was to live in Tel Aviv and, jokingly, I told him a spot right in the centre, near Chen Boulevard and Frishman Street, which seemed a good place to be. He made me describe exactly where this was, and said, 'Well, I wish you luck, and try not to worry. If something happens and we take over, just mention my name and I will see you are all right.'

Back in Tel Aviv, Rafi and I talked of marriage. I was nearly twenty-two, he was twenty-seven, we were both old enough to know our own minds, or were we? I was globe-trotting most of the time, and Rafi was a steward with El Al Airlines (the club, which he owned with his brother and a close friend Avi Abromovitch, was a sideline) and this hardly struck me as the most sensible foundation for marriage.

His parents welcomed the idea. Marriage between Jew and non-Jew, which is so controversial in England, is accepted in Israel. People who fight for survival have a different perspective about priorities. If anything, the only mixed marriages viewed with concern are those between western and eastern Jew, where the basic culture is at variance.

By the same token, Israelis seldom make moral judgments. There, the only important issue is: Are you pro-Israel or not? If you are a patriot, that is all that matters. Your past is unimportant – a factor often used to advantage by people escaping from problems elsewhere, and for this reason sometimes misinterpreted.

Putting several oceans between us, I returned to England to think things over. I was suffering dreadful identity problems within myself, added to which I realised I was terrified of marriage. Philip Hindon obligingly fixed me up with plenty of work to keep me occupied, and it was while I was appearing in Wales that Rafi turned up (he had unlimited travel scope) with Avi, and informed me that marriage was on. Avi had come along to be best man. I gave no resistance.

I had experienced first hand what happens when the press turn up *en masse*, and wanted to avoid this at all costs. Rafi, too, had been told categorically by the airline that they would not take kindly to their staff being plastered all over the front pages. Rodders by now was running his own news agency, so I offered him exclusive pictures of Rafi and me together after the wedding. All was arranged, but we had overlooked one small item. The old-style marriage licence required you to fill in your name and also there was a space for 'otherwise known as'. With Marilyn and Mandy down in black and white, it was inevitable the news would leak.

It was 17 September 1966. Rafi made the usual mistake substituting awful for lawful. 'I, Rafael Shaul, take Mandy Rice-Davies to be my awful wedded wife.' I laughed but the registrar was poker-faced.

To avoid the press photographers at the front door, Rafi took his jacket off and walked through carrying two chairs. I left with Avi, whose picture appeared world-wide as the man who married Mandy Rice-Davies.

Rafi and I spent our wedding evening at the Leicester Square Odeon watching a strange film which starred Oliver Reed dressed as primitive man. Next night we were home in Tel Aviv.

I settled down to married life, though not exactly to domesticity. Almost at once I moved into the club business. Rafi had for some time been eyeing a nearby property, owned and run as a type of club, and had been making overtures to the owners for some sort of merger. Hitherto, they had resisted. Now he was married to a potential publicity attraction – the obvious benefits did not escape them. Overnight we formed a partnership and Mandy's Club was launched.

Not surprisingly it was an immediate success. Tel Aviv was ready for it. It was so far behind Europe in many ways, only one coffee shop and not a single boutique in the main street. Men wore shorts and a shirt, or black trousers and a white shirt. Coloured shirts were always a present from a visiting American. Jeans had not arrived, many people wore army uniform (still do, but now it is from choice, then there was no alternative); the general impression was austere. Imagine me, a blonde, with a wardrobe full of minis, and imagine the Israeli interest in any new face, especially a visiting celebrity, and it is obvious that a chic club had to do well. The top 5 per cent of the population are very wealthy, travel extensively, have cosmopolitan tastes, Tel Aviv has many diplomats, correspondents, top business people, so undoubtedly the clientèle was there. Mandy's was a membership club, 500 official members and a waiting list which reached several thousands. Membership implied such cache that people carried their membership cards and used them to prove identity.

Running a club keeps you informed on everything. People talk. You hear when there is going to be a devaluation; you know where they have just found oil because you are serving the same geologist on his trips home from the Sinai, and one night he comes in elated, and he has struck oil. I was intimately concerned with every detail, from the décor (all art nouveau, I made the lampstands out of polystyrene, and painted black they looked the real thing. The club has changed hands many times since, and the Tiffany-style lampshades I painted are still as good as new), to choosing the staff, supervising the cooks, and training the pretty girls who worked as waitresses and go-go dancers.

The club was the first of several. Our brand of expertise became extremely marketable. What we did not own we sold in franchise form – like the club opened in a former Turkish bath-house in Jerusalem after the Six Day War. So many people objected that it seemed we were to be discussed at the United Nations. The fuss blew over – I said nothing. I have had years of practice at not answering back.

All our business ventures were successful, but for sheer excitement nothing competes with that first opening night. Once you have climbed the hill, it loses its challenge. This was Mount Everest – it is only the first time you do it, the bells ring.

At the start Rafi still had his airline job, but was running into trouble as the company frowned on employees having such a full-time 'sideline'. He had to choose, and left El Al. His brother lived with us, and in fact, I found I had married the whole family, the brother's girlfriend and whoever else happened to come along. Israel is very much like that. It does not suit my temperament to have a stranger knocking on my door. I began to get annoyed when people popped in, but I grew used to it. Or rather I got used to it enough not to pull a face.

I was happy, despite not having a real friend there at first. I was very disoriented because I did not have time to make friends, and because I did not speak the language at all, could not read and had no time to take lessons. But I picked up Hebrew where I could. I spoke German to the grocer, French to the Moroccan taxi driver, and had my real conversations with visiting businessmen from England and America.

After the Six Day War, Israel took on a totally new aspect. In the early part of 1967, Israel was going through an economic depression. The Six Day War in June altered all that, drawing hundreds of thousands of tourists and earning millions of dollars with the powerful surge of pro-Israel feeling, and Mandy's rode on the crest of that wave, despite members taking a slight risk. Our neighbour upstairs had been in a German concentration camp and consequently suffered from insomnia and fits of midnight madness, when he would sit in his pyjamas on the balcony, directly over the entrance to the club, and bomb anybody who came in or out with potatoes. We provided umbrellas for customers who had to run under his balcony.

The club had great scope. I saw it as a present-day version of a nineteenth-century salon – a Nobel Prize winner, artists, actors, they all came. The club was on two levels: upstairs was Paradise, glassed in, and from there you could look down on the Inferno. Paradise was where we could see it all, but did not have to participate – there was the chance to talk. This was my little salon, the part of club life I enjoyed because it was just like my own house, only I did not have to wash the dishes afterwards as it was all organised for me. I went there in the evening and met everybody: Sean Connery, Stanley Baker, Charles Clore, diplomats, musicians, writers – it was a wonderful period, really one of the best times of my life.

Not content with that we decided to open a Chinese restaurant. Chinese food was popular among Israelis, although there was only one restaurant in Israel that sold Chinese food and that was in Jerusalem. But finding a Chinese cook was not easy. The Chinese are peculiar, you can get a Chinaman to go anywhere if there is another Chinaman, but to get one or two to go where there are no others is exceedingly difficult. I scoured London going from restaurant to restaurant in Soho. I found above every Chinese restaurant (which looks normal downstairs) an upstairs room behind a beaded curtain, where about ten Chinamen are always sitting around with long grey beards and wearing Chinese robes, just like the mysterious China of the old films. There everybody is deferential, bowing, and you feel like bowing back – although it is quite frightening. Each time I explained that I wanted a cook, they would all chat in Chinese. My efforts paid off and I returned to Tel Aviv with a woman whose name was Polsan – she immigrated from Singapore, was thirty-six, not married, a spinster and a virgin. She had been engaged in her youth, something happened to prevent the marriage and she had not found another man she wanted. She agreed to come to Israel and start the restaurant. Back in Tel Aviv I ran around organising an order of Chinese food to be shipped out to Israel. Polsan was not a great cook but she knew how it should be done, and the idea was that she would train Israelis. Then we found another Chinese – Sunny, who was a wonderful cook. His problem was drink, but when he was not on drink he was all right. So we were in business.

A Chinese came to Tel Aviv University for one year on a sabbatical to teach the Chinese language. He came to the restaurant, met Polsan and they fell in love. They left Tel Aviv at once to get married. I thought that was an extraordinary example of fate. Happily for us, Sunny had a cousin, and his cousin had a cousin. Today in Israel we have a community of a thousand Chinese. When we opened the Chinese restaurant there was not one, except for the Chinese wife of the Israeli who had opened the Jerusalem restaurant.

War is good for marriage. The man goes to war, and the wife he hates suddenly becomes the most precious thing in life. Women who could not find a good word to say about a man begin writing ten-page love letters. War ends and there is the inevitable population explosion to celebrate the new-found optimism in their relationship.

Rafi and I were no exception. The war crystallised our feelings, too, and whatever maternal instincts I had were stimulated in the desire to have a child, at once. It did not happen quite like that. Dana arrived in October 1968, wanted, planned and loved. In those days I wanted a large family, I cannot think why, for now the prospect would appall me. I had a vision of a rambling house, children running all over it. It was a romantic image, silly, unpractical and not me at all. With motherhood came the realisation that my marriage was over.

Almost from the beginning there had been another woman in Rafi's life. At first I barely acknowledged this threat, except for an uncomfortable feeling I had the first time I saw her, when she applied for a job as a waitress. A beautiful leggy Australian (most of our female staff were). I took one look and knew this spelled trouble. She was walking down the stairs, Rafi was meeting her for the first time. I sensed something electric.

'I don't think we'll take that one,' I said afterwards.

'Why not?' said Rafi. 'I think she's OK.'

I watched them. I am not the sort of woman to ask where are you going. I knew fidelity was not Rafi's strongest point. Over the months my suspicion grew into certainty. I remained friendly towards her, I even brought her little gifts when I went away. Once it was a bottle of my perfume, 'So there won't be any problems,' I said as a joke, knowing that she knew exactly what I meant.

Rafi and I got on as we had always done. The business was our baby, that brought us together. The girl was frequently away herself, typical Aussie with itchy feet. What is more, she had started modelling and was moderately successful. But, because she and Rafi had many mutual friends, I knew they had a perfect cover for seeing each other. When I knew I was pregnant Rafi was as thrilled as I was. But it did not affect his double life. So far I had no actual proof and I could, at moments, kid myself I was imagining things. My proof came in a way any woman will immediately recognise as conclusive.

Rafi had been out of the country for several weeks. She was in Tel Aviv, and called into the club most nights. She came in without make-up, unpressed clothes, hair scraped back. The day he arrived back, she turned up dressed like the proverbial dog's dinner. It was a real giveaway. She had made a play for him, and Rafi was not the type to run too hard in the opposite direction.

When I was about three months pregnant there was a Convention of Gynaecologists in Israel, attended by world-famous gynaecologists who normally charged $1,000 a consultation. They would gather at Mandy's every night, so I had something like thirty of the best gynaecologists in the world all giving me advice – and all different. Being in Israel I decided to opt for natural childbirth. I did not stop any activity, I swam daily and carried on a normal life until, perhaps, the last few weeks when my legs swelled painfully.

When the first contraction came I was in the club. I hurried off to have my hair done because I knew I would not get another chance and I knew the minute I had my baby the press would want a photograph.

By now the contractions were coming every half-hour and my hairdresser was absolutely petrified – I have never had such a quick hair-do in my whole life. He could not wait to see the end of me, he was convinced I was going to drop the baby on the spot. I thought it was still too early to go to hospital, as I did not want to go until the pains were every two or three minutes, so I visited a girlfriend and we sat playing cards.

As I lay in the ward, waiting for something to happen, a woman came running in moaning, a doctor hurrying behind her with a cigarette in his mouth, and another little chap behind him carrying her suitcase. They all hurried past me into the delivery room. Two minutes later the baby had been born; the doctor hurried by and still had the same cigarette in his mouth. I remember asking my doctor, 'Why can't I have my baby as quick as that?' He said, 'The next one you will.' I smoked all during labour. What could they say? 'You are not supposed to smoke in here!' 'OK, what do you want me to do, leave?'

She came to see me twice in hospital. Once I broached the subject of her friendship with Rafi.

'People are talking about you,' I said.

'Yes, I suppose they are,' she replied. I think she was rather embarrassed.

It was the most vulnerable time in my life. Possibly that is what put me off having more babies, as much as I enjoyed motherhood and having Dana.

All the time I was being pushed in the direction of taking charge of my own life once again. Had I needed a boost to my morale it came when the Israeli Government Tourist Office asked to use me for promotion. Why not? They brought out a poster with a picture of me and the slogan 'Everything in Israel is not an old ruin'.

Now I was officially sanctioned as a national asset. Every reporter who came to write a piece about Israel was sent to interview Moshe Dayan, then Mandy Rice-Davies, and later Golda Meir then Mandy Rice-Davies again. I was giving an interview a week.

I decided that the club was one thing but I should do something else as well – if only for financial reasons, as I was not seeing much money from it. I had started modelling, but, together with a fellow model and her brother, decided to open a dress factory aimed at the younger market, the sixteen to twenty-five year olds for whom there was no ready-to-wear boutique fashion available. During the Six Day War I had become friendly with Monty Marks (a London-based fashion manufacturer), so, cashing in on his pro-Israel feelings, did a deal which gave us his patterns at a very cheap price. We started off with six machinists. By the time I left Israel, it was a very big factory with a huge turnover, and still has. I was stimulated by the excitement of launching a new project, often working through the night to have fabric cut for the machinists to sew in the morning. Dashing home to be with Dana, going to the club at night, then back to the factory. Frantic activity combined with hard work and little rest is a pattern that has often reappeared in my life. I thrive on work.

My stage career took on a new lease. First, in a quiet way, travelling around the lecture halls and universities with Israeli poet David Avidan, giving bi-lingual poetry readings. And then acting. I had worked on a film several months before Dana was born, and that was the impetus for a new phase in my working life. I was not Israel's greatest actress, but I played in a series of plays and films that could boast a certain success. (Very much later, in a play which toured for many months, I had to act the entire part in Hebrew! The critics were reasonably kind – I figured if I could get through that I could do anything.)

In the early days I had begun preparation for converting to Judaism, and was warned this could take about seven years. I should have liked this mainly for the sake of my parents-in-law, and also for our child. Rafi was discouraging. When I told him that I must promise to keep a kosher kitchen, it upset him, he did not want to eat kosher food at home. There was the stipulation, too, that I must change my name and take a Jewish one. The theory is not that your past must be wiped out, but that you should convince the community you are going into a new life.

'Rafi, we will have to change the name of the club,' I said.

'Damn it, how dare they,' said Rafi, furious.

That was the end of that. Having always been interested in religion, and believing implicitly in God, I continued my studies alone and unofficially, with no particular end in sight. Dana, according to the Christian church, takes the faith of her father, which means she is a Jew. But the Jews say religion proceeds through the mother, which makes her a Christian. She will sort it out some day, for herself.

The busier I became, the more Rafi and I grew apart. It had its advantages, it eased the pressure on a relationship that was already cracking, enabling us to live harmoniously at least. My image of myself as the Jewish housewife and mother was fast receding. I was too busy to brood over my marriage, at the same time I knew it was not what a marriage should be. I am too much of a romantic, there is a side of me that thinks marriage should be everlasting love and holding hands. Rafi's strong point was not fidelity, perhaps if it had just been her I might have compromised, but he seemed to spread himself around quite generously and no woman likes to feel demoralised. We were growing apart in many other ways, our attitudes were at variance.

I suppose I should have said to Rafi that we must save our marriage and at least try to talk things over. Some people you can talk to and some people you cannot. We were not fighting or arguing but it had gone too far, too many things had happened. One night, the girlfriend, who had been abroad, returned and, as she walked in the club, there was something in her attitude, a patronising air which was, suddenly, too much.

I walked up to her and I said, 'Get out.'

'What?' she said.

'Just get out,' I replied quite calmly.

That was it.

I am not sure if she left. I marched out, went home, said everything to Rafi that there was to say. To this day he is convinced that somebody shopped him, he never believed I had known for so long.

Our marriage was over. We remained friends and business partners. Long after that I helped him to decorate new restaurants and worked for him as editor when he launched his magazine *Moniter*. I still regard him as family and his mother is very close to me. Rafi loved me but he was not ready to settle. We finally divorced in 1977.

The first time we went to the lawyer I said, 'You've got to sign this document.'

He was cursing and did not want to sign.

He said, 'Maybe I don't like my right arm but I don't want to cut it off.'

Rafi liked me around. He was not unhappily married, it suited him, but it was not romantic enough for me. I must be loved, intensely, to be able to return it.

Many of our friends might have seen it as a gradual parting, but for me the moment of break-up happened four days after I had confronted him with what I knew.

Telling him I needed time to sort myself out and think things over we parted in January 1971. A few days later going to the factory, I heard over the taxi radio a newsflash that Mandy's had burned down.

This seemed unbelievable. 'Quick, take me there,' I said to the driver. We rushed to the scene and, sure enough, Mandy's was a smouldering ruin, victim of a grudge from two men who had been turned away for membership.

It was almost symbolic. Rafi was there, surveying the damage. 'That's it, isn't it?' I said, and turned away.

21

IN June 1967 I returned to my parents after spending a few days with relatives in Wales, where there had been neither TV nor telephone, and was greeted at the door by worried faces.

'There's something brewing in Israel,' said Daddy.

I was mystified. Brewing? Like what?

'Nasser has thrown the United Nations troops out of the Gaza Strip. It looks like war,' he said.

'Then I'd better get back, fast,' I said, already hastening up the stairs to start packing. They thought I was crazy and said so – in Birmingham I was safe, yet I wanted to head straight back to danger. But I am one of those people who feel better in the middle of the action than on the outside worrying about it, so my mind was made up.

My only problem was actually getting there, no airlines were flying in and El Al were carrying no civil passengers, only men with military connections. However, I headed straight for the London office of El Al and the manager Morris Natomi, whom I knew, and, bursting into tears, begged him to fly me to Tel Aviv. Who could resist? He promised to send a telegram asking for security clearance: 'If they clear you, I'll put you on a plane. Don't ask what we're carrying, just get on it.'

As I walked out of his office there was a queue of people trying to arrange passage out of Israel for close relatives and friends.

'You see,' he said, addressing the crowd, one arm around my shoulders, 'here's one who wants to go back. And she isn't even Jewish!'

Now I knew I was definitely on the way, and I didn't want to waste the opportunity. Nobody would charge me excess baggage on a trip like this. I zoomed through Harrods like the last of the big-time spenders, stocking up on make-up, undies, Harrods' own sausages and all the things I'd been missing. I boarded the plane clutching my grandmother's antique secretaire under my arm.

'What's that?' I was asked.

'A barricade,' I replied.

The plane had flown in from America, stopping at Heathrow for a consignment of gas masks, which apparently the British Government still had in plentiful supply from the Second World War. There were fifteen passengers, and I sat next to a Chinese, which intrigued me. Why should a Chinese be given preferential treatment to go to Israel? He explained that he was eighth-generation Jewish, had volunteered his services and was being flown out as part of a scheme to release men working on the kibbutzim who had military training. He would take their place and work on a kibbutz. We parted and I gave him my card, saying as I often did, 'When you come to Tel Aviv, call in at the club.'

The funny thing was that months later he did. He presented the card and was shown in. I asked him how he was enjoying life on the kibbutz.

'Great,' he said, with an expression of distaste. He looked me in the eye. 'The kibbutz is all right, it's what I'm doing there. They've put me in the laundry!' How ironic that a Chinaman, albeit an American one, should be put in the laundry.

When I had left Tel Aviv a few weeks before it had been a regular airport. I returned to a completely different picture, nothing but bombers and anti-aircraft guns.

It was another ten days before the war erupted. During this period many of us thought and hoped nothing would happen, but, at the same time, we were busy. Everybody had to buy blue paint for car headlights and windows, and as it was in short supply invariably you ran out when you still had half a window left unpainted. Sandbags cost nothing, as there is no shortage of sand. The government issued sacks, and schoolchildren had time off for sack-filling. The sandbags were to place around the basement of your building and against your windows, to stop things falling in. Most buildings have a type of shelter, but Israeli buildings are fragile – one whiff and they fall down. In any case, I hate closed-in spaces, so air-raid shelters were out for me. The club was in the basement, so I regarded that as the most luxurious air-raid shelter in the whole of Israel, and many took advantage of it.

There was a feeling of apprehension, a feeling of war which is difficult to describe to anybody who has not been through it. Moments of fear, but mostly people think nothing will happen to them. You think the whole city could be flattened but *you* will be all right.

Within days half of the world's press turned up and Mandy's became their headquarters. This was good because it kept us well informed. Marvellous people, war correspondents – Don Wise, Robin Stafford, Winston Churchill, Auberon Waugh, and a lovely man, Sean Flynn, Errol Flynn's son, to whom I became very attached. Sadly, years later, he disappeared on an assignment in Vietnam. He looked like his father, very, very handsome and very courageous. He and an Italian correspondent brought a cannon half-way across the Sinai to give me as a present. (I got some very odd gifts, I might add.) Sean was a photographer, and always went into the thick of everything. He was doing in real life what his father had done in films. He was mad-cap. I adored him – he didn't give two hoots about anything except doing his job. He always said there was only one way to die and that was under cannon.

Amazing people turned up. One was the son of a well-known Nazi, who came over to help. He had become a priest and often quoted the Bible: 'The sins of the father falleth on the son.' He of all people knew how true that is.

I remember Winston Churchill, a super guy, having to go back urgently to London (his wife was pregnant, I believe) and he reached the airport to find he had forgotten his passport. He told them his name was Winston Churchill and they all fell about laughing.

The army needed a substantial blood bank, and I thought it would be a very good idea to persuade members to give some. The time to persuade them was while they were enjoying themselves dancing and drinking, for I've discovered that with anything charitable you have to catch the person on the spot and make him do it. If you leave them to think about it they never will. We arranged for the Magin Davi, the Jewish Red Cross, to come in with ambulance and equipment, accompanied by a CBS television crew. Some members were dancing whilst others were laid out on benches donating blood. Whoever got their blood that night received a high percentage of alcohol in it. The CBS commentator actually had tears in his eyes, he was so moved by the occasion. We thought it all great fun.

Something very unpleasant had been going on. The other side had a radio station called Radio Cairo. People forget how primitive Egypt was – there is no comparison between the way they manage things today and at the time of the Six Day War. For example, when you switched on Radio Cairo it went like this: 'All you Zionists, you get out, if you don't get out we are coming for you, and we will chop open your bellies and chop off your hands, we will take the living babies from your stomach!' You could giggle about it when there were two or three of you, but when you were alone it was horrific. Yet you had to listen, like looking at a road accident, or listening to an obscene phone call.

One evening over Radio Cairo I heard, 'And what about your Moyshe Dayan, you think he is going to handle this war for you? He is with Mandy Rice-Davies in the bed. And we all know how she ruined the other war minister in England.' The whole of Israel laughed with me over that, including Moyshe Dayan (and Ruth, his wife, whom I knew through my work with WIZO – Women's International Zionist Organisation).

But I didn't like the sound of this. Using my name officially meant they had me slotted for something in the future. If they caught me, then they were going to reserve something special for me, I could see that.

I prepared myself by making a box for my Siamese cat, but the cat didn't like the box so I carried her around under my arm. I made up a parcel of gold, and little diamonds. This was to bribe my way out – from watching too many films again, but it is not as stupid as it sounds. Bribery is no use when the soldiers come, but is useful if you are in a prison camp which is run under conventional rules and where you are allowed certain privileges if you can buy them. On this premise I sewed my parcel in the hem of my coat.

Apart from that, life went on as normal: mothers took children to school, you went shopping except you didn't buy more than six eggs or one bottle of milk per family. There was no hoarding. Even today, when sugar prices are going up, people would look askance if a woman bought ten bags of sugar. It is just something you don't do in Israel.

The night before the war broke out Rafi was called up. I said to Auberon and Winston, 'They have called up Rafi, so tomorrow it's war.'

I believed I knew what to expect from seeing war films, but was unprepared for the worst feeling – the helplessness when imagining a bomb is falling on you. I was upset to see Rafi go but tried to put on a brave face and hide my feelings when the Civil Defence knocked at the door and gave him his papers. He went off in good humour. In the Israeli army everybody knows everybody. Groups are picked and trained from the same area and it is like a club, you go for one month every year. (There is only one other country that trains one month every year and that is Switzerland.) This sort of cameraderie works very well. But instead of training, this time it was for real.

The men had kit but they looked like a bunch of ragamuffins because everybody used their army kit for cleaning the car. Non-enlisted officers in old army trousers with grease on them, and a few holes; stripes put on with safety pins; all done on the spur of the moment.

Rafi had been gone five minutes when the air-raid siren went. We had heard this before during practice, but this time we knew it was war, it had real feeling behind it, it was quite the most chilling sound. Suddenly all the things you should do which you carry in your head desert you. I decided to telephone my mother-in-law in Haifa.

'Hello, Ima,' I said, 'have you got the air-raid siren on?'

'No. But I can hear it your end. Why don't you go down the shelter?'

'No,' I said, 'I don't want to. I'd rather die.'

'Well, unplug all the electric plugs for safety,' which I did.

I put Pusspuss under my arm and went to look in the shelter. It wasn't very pleasant, full of old people from the ghettoes, a few religious ones wailing, others praying. I left and returned to the apartment. After the All Clear, I decided to head for the club. There had been some long-range shooting – all missed their targets, except one. That had fallen on the corner of Frishman Street and Chen Boulevard – the very place I'd told Aziz that he'd find me. So much for his promise!

At the club I found an air of excitement. The rumour was that the Israelis had destroyed all the enemy planes in one go. They had been simply sitting on their airfield when our air force flew over: plop, plop, plop and that was that. It seemed too far-fetched to be true – but of course that was exactly what happened. It was not immediately made official; they still had their long-range missiles, which could certainly reach us in Tel Aviv (twenty kilometres from the border), and there was heavy fighting on the Golan Heights, where the Syrians had the benefit of Russian tanks (and presumably Russian expertise). The war was not over.

I had no idea where Rafi was. I soon heard, for he had managed to get a call put through to the club.

'Hello,' he said, 'don't get hysterical – I'm all right.'

Could any remark be more designed to engender anxiety? He had been injured, it seemed, trying to prevent a prisoner escaping, and had been hit by a rifle-butt which had cut his arm and required stitches. As Rafi's main military occupation was physical-training instructor, he temporarily became redundant, having only one arm, and was soon back in the bosom of his family.

People took up residence in the club. It was so convenient, and also very chummy. Every soldier passing through with any claim to membership, or having even known a member, stopped to say hello. They drank us out in a week, it was great for business but dreadful for profit! The journalists used it as a headquarters, going into the press club just to pick up messages and use the telex. War correspondents are undoubtedly the world's best drinkers – I didn't meet one who couldn't drink any ten men under the table. Don Wise, of the *Mirror*, polished off a whole crate of Guinness in a night.

The Pope had appealed to the combatants to respect the precious monuments, so, since the Jews have the same attitude to Jerusalem anyway as do the Moslems, by unwritten agreement they all decided to fight hand-to-hand. Mandy's was packed with men on their way to battle. Everybody wanted a last dance. I learned then the smell of death, a smell not like any other smell. It is not a smell of decay, or sweat, but a peculiar sweet-sour smell. It's the smell of fear that has emanated from people, has dried on them. It was magnified a hundredfold in the club, and it transmitted fear to us as we danced and drank together.

Prompted by fear people tell things about themselves they would hesitate to tell a psychiatrist – or a priest. And within five minutes of meeting. One soldier told me how his wife had died in a road accident. He couldn't believe she was dead and when they left him alone in the room with her he made love to her because he wanted to bring her back to life again. He had never been able to look at a woman since. He couldn't forget what he had done to his dead wife, who was dead even though her body was still warm. What does one say when you have just listened to somebody pouring out their heart like that? The guy is going off to war, he doesn't want to die with this on his conscience, and in two minutes out comes this story. You can spend years with someone and know very little, but in five minutes, with death close at hand, you can know that person's life story.

One night an officer came in, an extremely good-looking man, on his way to Jerusalem. I was sitting out between dancing, he sat down and we started to talk. Odd things happen during war, the senses are heightened, everything is at a highly dramatic level. I was drawn to this man, and he to me. By the time he left, an hour later, he said, 'I've fallen in love with you. I'm married and have children and I will never lay a finger on you. I love you, you will stay with me until I die.' In the cold light, this perhaps sounds corny. But, at the time and in that place, it was sincere, and moving. When he stood up to go, he said, 'If I live through Jerusalem, I will see you on my way back.' His face and voice stayed in my mind. Many nights I watched the door, half waiting to see him again. It was one of those strange affinities that happen only in wartime.

Meanwhile the government press department had decided I was good pro-Israeli propaganda material and asked me to co-operate with Auberon Waugh, who was writing about the auxiliary services. I volunteered at the Red Cross offices run by the Swiss, who had set up a small hospital intended for officers. They said, 'We can probably use you for typing up prisoners' names,' because they had already started to take prisoners. Unfortunately we never managed to get any officers as prisoners; officers weren't captured, they were the first to run!

My services weren't required for long; I tried typing for an hour and remember to this day how to spell Arab names in English letters. It was a salutary lesson typing those names and imagining all those poor people, primitive and scared to death and their families waiting for news. One becomes terribly conscientious not to miss a name out. I desperately wanted to do nursing, but the hospitals didn't want me because I couldn't speak Hebrew and in any case they weren't that short of help. I had a white jacket which they had given me in the Red Cross to wear, and, accompanied by Auberon, we visited hospitals as a sort of morale-boosting mission, to cheer the men up. Which doesn't leave one very cheerful. A broken arm, or a hand blown off – that wasn't too bad. But it was hard not to cry, not to burst into tears, hard to maintain the bonhomie when you see a man lying in a tent absolutely burnt to a cinder – his skin is so black, it is coming away from his body, one leg blown off, one arm blown off, and blind. You struggle not to cry or to show revulsion, to bend down and say hello, whilst the medical staff explain to him who you are. What does one do when such a man smiles at you?

The sense of being in a fantasy was never far away. I remember being caught in a hail of snipers' bullets in Jerusalem during a propaganda visit. Everybody dived for cover, and, as I ran, I passed a mirror, a Coca-Cola advertisement. I actually paused to check my appearance before jumping round the corner. Sometimes I felt I was acting in a film – or perhaps that is the easiest defence mechanism.

Had I been in any doubt about my loyalty to my new country, the war put an end to it. I became involved in working for charities, helping the soldiers, raising money. One idea involved providing basic equipment for pseudo-Mandy discos on every army base. People gave money for record-players, and Radio Caroline, Decca, as well as other companies, gave thousands of records. In the end we had so much that we extended it to include forty record-players in the hospitals and twenty-five television sets and refrigerators.

The army decided to give me a special tour of the discotheques, so I was taken off by army plane to the Sinai, on a day when one of the tank corps was giving a display. Travelling across the Sinai after the fighting we saw an incredible amount of military litter, including thousands of boots. The Egyptians are not used to wearing boots, so the minute they saw the Israelis coming they would take off their boots in order to run faster. We were shown an underground station built by the Egyptians with Russian help, a labyrinth of passages beneath the desert. I found out during that tour that I was on the list of people, if captured, to be kept alive and brought to headquarters. And in one of the officer's desks, in the underground, they even had a copy of *The Mandy Report*. I don't know what they had planned for me, but it would not have been very nice.

Weeks after the war my officer came back. I was still half watching the door for him, and one day there he was. He brought me some Arab beads, and we spent four or five hours talking together until well into the dawn. It was as if we had known each other all our lives. He never touched me, not even when we said goodbye.

'I'll never see you again,' he said. And left.

22

WAR came again. In October 1973 I was once more in England, this time with my child and a carload of furniture for the new home I was building in Israel, after a long affair which had kept me in Europe.

My only chance was to reach Venice in time for a boat sailing to Israel. The drive took three days. I refused to listen to the radio for fear of hearing the worst. Already we knew this war was different from the last. The Six Day War had been exhilarating, victory for Israel a foregone conclusion. The Yom Kippur war showed a new, and different, and frightening change in power. Not that I feared Israel would disappear off the map before I could get there, but I was deeply afraid for my friends and family.

I reached Venice. No ships – try Trieste. I drove to Trieste, and Marseilles. No ships, go back to Venice. For several days I drove backwards and forwards between ports. By this time I would willingly have left the car and taken a chance on getting a flight, but there was no way I could safeguard my roof-rack full of furniture and household effects.

I was phoning my father-in-law every day, and, as he was a director of the Israeli Zin Line, he was well informed. Eventually he told me the *Dan* would be sailing from Trieste.

It was the most terrible, terrible journey. I have made that voyage many times, on three occasions in force 11 gales. That was one of them. The *Dan* lost a propeller en route and had to be retired afterwards. My fellow passengers were in the main simple people who had been on holiday touring Europe when the news broke. Now they were anxious to get home as soon as possible, and all of course had their cars with them. A car in Israel is too expensive an item to consider abandoning. A street full of Minis in Tel Aviv is the same, moneywise, as streets full of Rolls-Royces and Porsches in Europe. There was an atmosphere of tension on the boat, unrelieved by the edge of excitement that had percolated through the Six Day War.

The Arabs had attacked at night, during Yom Kippur, the most holy festival in the Jewish year, and caught most Israelis sitting in the synagogues. The attack was totally unexpected, out of the blue. We had a line of defence which they cracked in two minutes. And because it was Yom Kippur most soldiers had been given leave. Only small pockets of men remained and they were quickly liquidated. The generals had been caught with their pants down. It takes forty-eight hours to mobilise the Israeli army, and that is quick. It also takes forty-eight hours to de-grease a tank and to get it ready for use.

The other side were not so inept this time. They had got themselves together, and everybody knew the day would come when the Arabs would be practically equal. The main difference between Israeli and Arab is the difference in attitude. The Arabs are invaders and the Israelis are defenders. The minute you have nowhere to run, you have to fight. That's why Israel will defend itself to the last man. So this was a very worrying war.

When we arrived the ceasefire had been declared, the sort of ceasefire where you keep fighting.

I drove at once to Rafi's apartment in Tel Aviv. Dana was only five. I was worried how she would react to the conditions but I think she was too young to be afraid. She had vague ideas, but I kept a lot from her. On our first day, she was sitting on the balcony looking up at a plane overhead, and said, 'Mummy, is that one of theirs or one of ours?'

I said, 'No, no, it's one of ours, darling. If it was one of theirs it wouldn't be up there.'

I immediately volunteered my services with the colonels who were in charge of entertainment for the troops. They asked me if I minded going to the front line, but I told them I'd be annoyed if I did not. *Chanucah* was coming round, and I felt it essential that this was celebrated.

I'd heard that the Israeli Philharmonic Orchestra had been out there, and one of the men told me how amusing it had been. In the orchestra there were a hundred men and one woman, a 25-year-old violinist. While the whole orchestra was playing Mozart every single soldier had his eye on this girl.

They simply didn't see any girls, and it was what they needed. We suggested fashion shows, and persuaded several boutiques to make some specials – sexy stuff, but not too sexy.

There were five of us – each different. There was Pnina. She had one of those very slim bodies but huge breasts and a nice bum – really very sexy. (In fact when she later got to the age for national service they demobbed her after three weeks. The Israeli army couldn't handle the problem. Wherever she went she attracted a crowd of soldiers. She was a natural bum wriggler!) Another girl looked very much like Candice Bergen. Another was very dark haired and vivacious, the fourth looked like a young princess out of a fairy tale. We started off at the Golan Heights. It was there that I really knew what war was all about.

During the Six Day War when I first went into Jerusalem I had been shocked to see bodies lying in the streets. The Israelis had dealt with their dead quickly. But sometimes the dead Arabs were left there with a sheet over them, and a red cross, in various stages of decomposition. This had horrified me, but not in the way that the real futility of war now hit home. I sometimes wondered what would happen if I were shot on duty, as I had been drafted into the army for the tour. Would I get a military funeral? If so, how would they manage it? There are only Jews in the army, and I'm not a Jew. As we drove closer to the front line I saw a big shed, and, scrawled in red paint, I saw the name 'Mandy's' and some Hebrew words.

'What's written there?' I asked.

One of the girls said, 'It says "Mandy's discotheque of the dead".'

It was the place where they put the dead soldiers until they could arrange burial.

We stayed in huts of corrugated iron. It was now well into December and bitterly cold, with snow in the mountains. We wore our ski clothes. The conditions were appalling. The men were sometimes knee-deep in mud, and frozen. I kept thinking of the trenches during the First World War. Everyone in the country had knitted hats and scarves, uniforms were anything the right shade of khaki. A Mr Cohen, vest manufacturer from New York, had sent 10,000 vests with Cohen printed on them. Morale was very low. The men had been stopped mid battle by the ceasefire, and the soldiers were very bitter about this. They were in the mood to fight. They didn't enjoy the feeling of helplessness. Killing is contagious.

As it was the time of *Chanucah* (for eight days you light candles) the general of the one camp said: 'These girls have come to share *Chanucah* with us. They are like the *Chanucah* candles. You can look at them but you must not touch.'

After the fashion shows we went in to the huts, which had sometimes a hundred men, and each one of us would sit at the head of a table and play Mother for the evening. The soldiers hadn't bathed for two months, they had no showers out there in that freezing cold, there was no running water. They were well fed but they were homesick and demoralised.

The thing that really shocked many of the Israelis was the amount of armoury the Egyptians and the Syrians had. Every Israeli soldier knows the cost of it for he is constantly told, this missile cost $20,000, make sure you are aiming on target, make sure you hit a target. In other words, don't shoot three with the hope that one will go. They are literally brainwashed into that. Now they saw what was being wasted by the other side.

The girls provided an oasis in the desert. The men reacted with cheering and dancing. We always had photographers with us and this prompted the men to play around and act a little, so what was an ordinary fashion show would end up as a two-hour entertainment with everybody taking part.

We left the Golan, drove back to Tel Aviv and flew in an army transport plane to Suez, the city on the other side of the Canal, which was now split in two, one half held by the Egyptians and the other half by the Israelis. The Israeli army was based in what had been a British army camp, and still seemed like one despite having been held by the Egyptians and then Israelis.

Hitting the sun and the real desert with the palm trees was a peculiar change of atmosphere after the place we'd left. We were all excited about the trip, none of us had flown into enemy territory before. It was a dangerous trip, too, there were still snipers and mines. We were met at the airport and were being taken by a small army bus to our first camp. En route I had a curious premonition. The face of the officer, my officer of six years before, flashed into my mind. Simultaneously, I looked out at a jeep driving past us and, sitting in the back of the jeep, was this guy. I banged on the window to attract his attention. Our driver said, 'He's in charge of the camp we are going to – you'll see him later.' As our bus drew alongside his jeep he looked at me and our eyes met. We arrived at the camp and sure enough he was there, in charge.

'Everywhere you go, I'll go,' he said.

I went through the next few days in a dream. Suez had been ransacked. The Israelis had taken everything that would be of any use: telegraph poles, iron railings, anything metal. There wasn't a building intact. We did a show in the casino but the swimming pool had been blown up. You had to sidestep great big holes.

The idea was to give parties, we were there to cheer up the soldiers, but they went to such trouble to do things for us. One buffet consisted entirely of tinned food, all beautifully decorated. I had taken a stock of French perfume, and I made sure each of us girls reeked of it. So whenever we walked in, you knew you'd been there. The men loved it, clouds of perfume wherever we went, a sample of civilisation.

The UN commanders came along to see us and were given front seats.

In retrospect it seems absurd. So much was. We were in Suez, standing near what had been the swimming pool of the casino. The pool was the line of demarcation, the bit in between was no man's land. Across from the hotel grounds the Egyptian soldiers wandered around. So long as we stayed our side we were all right, walk across and you would be shot. The Israelis and the Egyptians chatted to each other across the pool. The Egyptians called all Israelis, 'Moshe'. The Israelis called all Egyptians 'Mohammed'.

Seeing us standing there, five girls and several soldiers, a cheeky Egyptian shouted, 'Hey, Moshe, you don't know how lucky you are. Why doesn't that sonofabitch send us some things like that from Cairo!' They waved and we waved back.

My officer never left my side. We never touched each other in a physical sense, it was like something I'd read about – almost biblical. Him looking in my eyes, taking my hand and giving a little squeeze – an overwhelming look of love and affection.

Once I saw him on the army bus carrying my make-up bag, which had my heavy sweater on top. He was holding the bag very tightly, and bending his head lower and lower until it touched the sweater, smoothing it against his cheek. It was one of those situations in life, rather like death, that defies description. I cannot adequately describe what it was we felt for each other. It wasn't love in the normal sense of the word. It wasn't love that would have compelled me to go off with him somewhere alone. But it had an intensity and excitement that was generated by the war. I felt pure with him. I understood that men in battle need to hang on to something pure to balance the degrading things they go through. He found this with me. And I had fallen in with it, and played along. I was caught up in a feeling of overwhelming pity which was akin to love. It was exciting. There was no tomorrow, no worries about whether we liked or suited each other, or whether we should go our own ways. There was none of that.

I never mentioned it to the others, but they all felt it, the sheer electricity between us. He came close to a mental breakdown out there and had believed he couldn't hold out much longer.

'You came along at exactly the right moment,' he told me. I provided the escape – however brief.

Our feelings were never consummated physically. If it had been consummated it would have lost its excitement; this was much deeper. We were so incredibly close, spiritually and mentally, that I understood him, totally.

On our last night we girls were supposed to sleep at the UN building, but we decided instead to stay in sleeping bags in one of the empty apartments.

We slept in one room. It was very eerie, no electricity, no furniture, but there was a fitted wardrobe. I opened it and there was a long red evening dress, just one dress on a hanger. There were pot-marks and bullet-holes on the wall, and this red dress in the wardrobe. It frightened me, it was untouched. Nobody undressed, except to take off our coats. We tried to wash and take off our make-up, but the water supply had gone.

I had to leave early in the morning. My officer drove me to the airport. I was taking a different plane from the other girls, so was given clearance to take a flight that left at 6 am. He came to pick me up in the jeep, and as I came downstairs the sun was rising. It was an hour's drive to the airfield. In the desert early in the morning the silence is deafening, you get a ringing in your ears, and as the sun rises over the desert it is quite beautiful. We were completely alone out there in the silence. He was holding my hand. I could see he was deeply moved. When we arrived at the airfield, there was a lone plane standing there and a few soldiers aboard. He drove me up in the jeep, had a word with the soldier in charge. Then he looked me straight in the eye and said, 'See you next war.' He watched the plane take off. I saw him standing there.

The desire to help in some way persisted and back home I became involved with guys who, because of the shock of the war, were kept as much as possible on the army camps. They couldn't be discharged because there was no place to discharge them to. They were damaged but couldn't be put in mental homes because, in some cases, they were so shocked they were paralysed. There were about thirty of them and they were placed in special huts and kept on the army base and visited continually by psychiatrists. Visiting one of them one day I was shocked to recognise José, our club disc jockey. A disc jockey is always full of chat and gaiety. When I saw him I thought I was going to faint. He just sat there, silent and withdrawn.

With a few girlfriends I arranged to devote one evening a week to a social with this group. The idea was to interest them in *something* – it didn't matter what. They had lost interest in everything. They never read, they wouldn't go for a walk, they just sat for hours looking at the floor. Somewhere along the line there must be something to stimulate the brain.

We organised fashion shows using Gotex swimsuits. The first couple of times it was horrible because there was absolute silence. No wolf whistles, nothing. Afterwards we put on records of dance music – my idea was to get José interested so that eventually he could take over the music for us. I tried to speak to him, but he could only stutter in reply. Most of the men had lost the power of speech. They either didn't want to say anything or they'd pretend you weren't there.

José had a very bad stutter. On the first night I said to him:

'Look, we're going to do some dancing and you're the best dancer.' He used to be a fantastic dancer.

He replied: 'No, ccccc . . . ' He didn't want to do it – I didn't want to push it.

'Well,' I said, 'just show me how to work this.'

He fiddled around with the player, and then started to cry.

By the third session there was interest and they looked forward to us coming. Some of them even started to shave. Then one day, after several weeks, José got to his feet and started to dance. 'These Boots Are Made For Walking,' was the song.

There's one sure way of knowing when life is back to normal in Israel. During war or states of emergency you won't see a hitch-hiker on the Haifa road because people stop and give lifts. It's an unwritten law in Israel. But in peacetime everybody leaves everyone behind and goes off on their own. The minute you start to see more hitch-hikers, or the minute you see the pretty girls picked up and the plain ones left behind, life's back to normal.

So life was more or less back to normal. Rafi had opened a piano bar, which was always crowded, invariably with a few men in raincoats. The pianist sang songs and everyone joined in, and when you looked down there would be pyjama bottoms and slippers poking out of the raincoats. Hospital escapees made tracks for us.

At this point I got involved in something that was too heavy for me. I'd always kept my welfare work on a totally impersonal level – this was very important. Now a man called Amity started to come to the club, an extremely good-looking guy, tall, blond with blue eyes. A professional soldier and lieutenant, he was married with a daughter and perfectly happy when the Yom Kippur war came. He had had the most horrific experience. He had been parachuted, with his group of about a hundred men, in to the Golan. When they landed they found themselves in a trap, and were overwhelmed by the Syrians. All the men were killed except Amity, who to escape had pretended to be dead. The Syrians then threw all the dead bodies into a pile, and he was buried under the whole mound of them and couldn't move. There he lay, paralysed with shock, under dead rotting bodies for a couple of days, hardly able to breathe, face to face with his dead friend, in a state of shellshock. After three days, the Israelis came. As they started to take off the bodies, they found him alive. His injuries were slight and as often happens, when he was sent to a hospital for observation he appeared to be all right. They wanted to keep him under supervision, so sent him to work in a prisoner-of-war camp. One night he and another man went berserk, and machine-gunned the prisoners. From that minute he went into himself and was like a vegetable, kept in a mental home and pumped with pills. Months passed before he had been considered well enough to be moved to a more open mental home near Tel Aviv. Then he was demobbed.

He moved straight into the best hotel in Tel Aviv, and proceeded to spend all his money and run up bills. He became quite friendly with Rafi, who knew something of his background. When Amity tried to commit suicide, Rafi decided he should come and work at the club – it would give him an interest and Rafi could maintain watch over him.

Part of Amity's problem and his suicidal tendencies was caused by his not wanting to remember what had happened. Trying to hide it, to cover it up, created a terrible strain and pressure. Somebody always had to accompany him on his sessions with the psychiatrist and I had to take my turn. The psychiatrist would administer some sort of drug, then when Amity was suitably prepared he would play tapes of the sounds of gunfire. The effect of this was to trigger him off. It all sounds rather silly, but the point was to force into his conscious mind what was buried in the subconscious. Amity would be sobbing and crying, then I would take him home and sit with him while he slept it off.

In the meantime he was becoming extremely reliant on me. His apartment was filthy, he never washed dishes, so I would clean up while he was sleeping, generally tidy up and I suppose take on the role of wife and mother. When he felt suicidal again, I had to sit holding his hand every night. I began to feel that I was the guardian angel, and the responsibility was horrific. I was weighed down by it. Once when I wasn't around he tried to commit suicide, and called me ten minutes after he'd taken the pills. I had to whisk him off to hospital.

I think we fell a bit in love with each other. People with mental problems don't really fall in love, they feel a heavy dependence and this is where many people are fooled – it's not real love. I became quite involved. In a way it was almost a crystallisation of everything I had felt for all the boys I had seen injured.

One had this feeling that if you went to bed with them all – it sounds awful but it wasn't just me, it was all the others as well – by having affairs, by making love to them, you could somehow help to make it right, to give something. You felt that you had to fall in love, give everything. You thought of all the people made impotent by war and you felt sure you could cure them. Women always feel that, where others have failed, they can succeed. It was not easy to break away from Amity. Whenever I said I was cutting away, I felt guilty.

23

I FINALLY made it to America. Had I been tackling the Himalayas solo, I could not have been more delighted to be told I'd finally won the right to enter the USA. Winning is the wrong word, for it suggests I set the pace. All that happened was the American Embassy in Tel Aviv had a new consul, a woman I had met socially at the club a few times. When I visited her to discuss, yet again, my desire to visit the States, she said with female logic: 'I can't see why we are preventing you. Let me look into it.'

Two weeks later they issued a visa. My past was still haunting me. A writer, Vernon Cassill, had written a novel called *Dr Cobb's Game*, based loosely on the Stephen Ward-Profumo affair. The American publishers invited me to 'come over' and chat about the book. Since I hadn't read it I preferred to reserve judgment, so a copy was duly posted to me. What I read infuriated me – it included us all. I was cast as the dumb blonde, and what was worse was that its style could only encourage people to believe this was the truth behind the scandal, whereas it was only fiction. It even had Stephen (Doctor Cobb) working for the Russians with a plan to blow up the world.

My intention to set the record straight turned out to be a great promotional tour for the book with the author. But I wasn't complaining if it gave me two feet over the US threshold.

I was thrown into the deep end immediately. On my first day I was booked to appear on the Dick Cavett show. 'He'll tear you to pieces,' friends warned me with morbid concern. My nerves weren't helped by having worn too tight boots on the plane; my legs were swollen and a small scratch on my foot had become painfully infected. I limped to the TV studios. I was prepared for the fact that the show was coast to coast, the biggest chat show in the States, resigned to be asked the inevitable questions about Profumo (which I was, predictably), but nobody had told me who the other guest was.

'My next guest,' said Dick Cavett, after I had completed the preliminary hurdles and was concentrating on mind over matter regarding my painful leg, 'my next guest needs no introduction, folks. Billy Graham.'

Oh boy, here's where they make mincemeat of me, I thought. At least I had the advantage of having read his books – hundreds of copies of the works of Billy Graham, along with the Bible, were sent to me in my most public hour. He turned out to be quite dishy. Handsome, virile-looking, dynamic and nice as pie. Straight away, one look into those cornflower-blue eyes, and I knew he was a friend.

Dick Cavett tried to provoke a little *frisson*. 'Billy, if you were alone with Mandy, what would you want to talk about.'

Snigger, snigger from the tame audience.

'Why, Israel, of course,' said Billy. His son-in-law had studied in Jerusalem and he was passionately interested in the country. (After the show I told him an amusing story concerning a friend of mine, daughter of a rabbi in America, who had fallen in love with a non-Jew and wanted to marry him. To break the relationship, the rabbi, who was completely horrified at the prospect of a mixed marriage in the family, despatched his daughter to study theology at Jerusalem University. There she fell in love with a Greek Orthodox priest, and married him.)

Inevitably the conversation came round to the type of fame that had dogged me for the past seven years. And Billy had this to say on that subject: 'Ladies and gentlemen, the greatest sin in the world is lack of charity.' Turning to me he said, 'If you have any trouble here, you can call me any time. The symbol of Christianity is charity.'

They proceeded then to talk lustily about whores. I interrupted.

'Excuse me, but why as soon as I am around do you start discussing whores?'

'That's a good point,' said Billy. 'They are all over the place, they are part of our life, they are outside the studio door now.'

It was unreal. The conversation turned to the book, *Dr*

Cobb's Game and I was asked what I thought of the author. 'A sort of Jacqueline Susann in trousers,' I said. For some reason this not very witty remark brought gusts of laughter from the studio audience and Dick Cavett, and became widely quoted afterwards in the States. Miss Susann was less than pleased. Later in the Beverly Hills Hotel, the publicity executive who was looking after me spotted her out of the corner of his eye and, grabbing my arm, steered me away. He had seen Miss Susann steaming across ready to do battle – but literally. It isn't every day one is bashed in the foyer of the Beverly Hills Hotel. I was very sorry I had missed it at the time.

Americans, when they are charming, are delightful. But when they are brash they are incredibly brash. I found this out when I appeared on the Chicago Cup Show. One of the other guests, a studio head, asked me to describe Christine. 'Christine', I said, 'had the possibility to do anything, she was extremely photogenic, she was very much wanted by modelling agencies, but it never really appealed to her.'

'Yes,' he replied, 'she is more of a whore than you are.'

What can you answer to that – apart from getting up and walking off the show. I felt my face burn scarlet – thank goodness I had a fellow Brit on the show, Sir John Mills, no less. I overestimated his chivalry. He sat, wooden-faced, aloof, cool to the point of being glacial.

Then he started talking about Valerie Hobson, Profumo's wife – what a lovely woman she was, and what a great actress. What could I say? I couldn't join in, I'd never met her, I couldn't say I admired her acting – I'd never seen her. It was a subject which I wanted to leave. It was one of my all-time embarrassing moments. I consoled myself later with the thought that if this was the price I had to pay to be allowed into America it was worth it.

I was taken along to meet Hugh Hefner at his palatial Playboy HQ – everybody gets invited there, it is the ultimate in open-house hospitality. There was a meeting of black legislators going on at the time, and the house was swarming with black men in business suits, women carrying babies, and bunnies of every description, though mainly blondes, running around.

Hefner and his live-in girlfriend Barbie greeted me. She

really looked like Barbie Doll, very small with enormous breasts, her skirt so short it looked as if she was wearing a box. I imagined she had American Prime stamped on her, she was just like a piece of meat. She is Jewish and had spent a year on a kibbutz, so we had Israel in common.

One house guest was a fascinating character, a professor of Latin who had been writing serious books for years until his publishers said, 'We keep publishing your wonderful masterpieces but nobody buys them, how about jazzing them up a little!' So he sat down and, between correcting the Latin homework, wrote two utterly pornographic novels, which, of course, made a mint. He has allegedly earned even more millions since, a sort of Harold Robbins, four steps up or down, whichever way you look at it.

Earlier on, the publicists organising the tour had inquired my choice of hotel.

'Take your pick,' they said. 'In Chicago we have this very old hotel, English-style, then we have the Astor Towers, a highly unusual type of hotel.'

When I hear the word unusual I'm sold, so still limping with my infected foot, I checked into the Astor Towers. My suite was brilliant red. Everything – walls, carpets, furniture, drapes – all shiny, satiny, plasticky red. It had its own kitchen, complete with automatic pre-set oven in which, each night, croissants baked in Maxim's and flown in from Paris were placed to emerge piping hot for breakfast.

Then on to Hollywood to do the Tempo Show and, of course, the sights.

Instead of the Universal Tour, the 'in' experience of the time was to get to look at the underground press – not to seem too unkind I could see why they needed to go underground. The entire editorial and production team was made up of junkies, homosexuals, transvestites and assorted weirdos. No wonder they felt a persecuted minority, it was so depressing. They were busily engaged at that time publishing a list of private addresses and telephone numbers of the police force, which didn't make the most fascinating reading.

An interview had been arranged with one of the most, if not the most, influential of the Hollywood columnists. He remembered Doc Shurr (who had since died) talking about me and saying I was the next Grace Kelly, so it was almost like meeting a friend.

We settled down to dinner in the restaurant of the Beverly Wiltshire, except that before the first course was served, my host had quite a lot to drink and the ensuing dialogue (which I assume was the liquor talking) sounded like an old Hollywood script. A very old Hollywood script.

'You're so beautiful, kid. Stick with me, baby, I'll make you a star.' Vernon Cassill sat, open-mouthed, listening.

The ensuing column, which was complimentary, ended with the line, 'After dining with the girl who shook the government, I kiss her hand goodnight.'

What actually happened was that he fell, drunk, face-first into his soup, and two waiters carried him out.

I loved those interviews. When American journalists enthuse they really go overboard. As one reporter wrote: 'Here I am sitting next to Mandy Rice-Davies in a restaurant in the flesh. What would you do if you got on a plane and found yourself sitting next to Jackie Onassis? This is how how I feel.'

The Americans didn't judge me, I had no stigma to overcome. They welcomed me as a celebrity, and I enjoyed the spree.

Now that I had been given entry into the States I was able to take up the invitations that came my way. Flying in to Vegas, the pilot was laying odds on how many times the wheels would bump before he landed.

I hadn't been interested in gambling since, working in the north of England, I had gambled and lost a week's earnings in a casino in Manchester. But as a study in people, Vegas provides a fascinating insight. The Vegas airport has the moving-pavements system – arrivals and departures passing each other in transit, demonstrating in their expressions their hopes and disappointments.

My suite in Caesar's Palace was the biggest and best in a town that is larger than life. Not a bunch of flowers, a roomful of flowers. Not a bowl of fruit, ten baskets of fruit.

Not being a gambler, I could go to bed early and get up early and spend the day by the pool. First thing in the morning the only sound was a jungle call and a loud splash. Johnny Weismuller was the resident Tarzan.

'Do you play tennis?' I was asked one evening. 'Well, not since school.'

'Get yourself some tennis gear, and I'll give you your first lesson tomorrow.' That was Pancho Gonzales. His son was the resident pro, and Pancho was there on a visit. After that lesson I became hooked on the game.

When I was invited to visit La Costa, the health spa near San Diego, knowing that a top pro was resident there was a big attraction. My friends, Evelyn and Alard Rowen, were the managers of La Costa. Evelyn was once the darling of the Copacabana and still had the body of a showgirl although well into her fifties. I'd spent many amusing days with them, once in Monte Carlo when Princess Grace officially opened the Lowe's Casino. She was a very funny lady, fiercely protective of Alard. Once after a midnight swim he came out of the water minus his toupée. Undeterred, Evelyn managed to procure a torch and at four in the morning armed with a spiked pole used for picking up litter, went beachcombing for his hairpiece.

I was delighted to take up their offer. La Costa has everything for the health and fitness freak, and for those who don't fancy starvation there are even alternative dining-rooms, graded into calorific potential!

Rich Americans have their own houses built on the edge of the golf course. Frank Fitsimmons, head of the powerful Teamsters' Union, has one, so does Richard Nixon.

I became friendly with the Fitsimmonses and was invited to watch a video of Frank playing golf. His wife is a nice Catholic woman who goes to Mass at six each morning. Frank gives the impression of being something of a thick Irish-American but in truth is the sharpest needle around, amusing and charming. His wealth and lifestyle are up there in the super super rich class with chauffeured limousine and private jet. I was amused comparing him with union leaders in England, where union philosophy considers wealth and any display of success to be somehow obscene.

We talked about that. 'I'm the president of their union, and those fellas like to know I'm living well. That means I'm successful, the union's successful and they can be successful too. I'm just one of them.'

While I was there, the Fitsimmonses' son came home after a long absence. He had the hippy hair, the unwashed jeans, the contempt for money that I have seen the world over among rich kids whose parents have made it.

They were giving a dinner party and asked me along. Pat and Richard Nixon were to be there.

I was now in a quandary. Did they know who I was – thirteen years after Profumo I still wondered if I was socially acceptable in certain circles. I didn't want to put anyone in an embarrassing position. Nixon had already fallen by this time (it was after Watergate) but still in the news. I kept quiet.

When the evening came I was excited. There were about fifteen of us having drinks. Frank said, 'Oh, incidentally he's not coming this evening because Pat doesn't feel too well.'

By the door was a big bouquet of flowers. When nobody was paying much attention, I wandered over to the flowers and looked at the note. It had, 'Sorry, Pat isn't feeling too well this evening. Regards. Richard.' I was in two minds to nick the card – it's the only thing in my life that I've ever had the desire to steal. But I didn't.

It was a disappointment. I was keen on meeting Nixon because I had read and heard so much about him, and I would have liked to have formed my own opinion. In a small party of people, it was just the right sort of atmosphere to have been able to assess him myself. But the opportunity was denied me.

24

I AM petrified of marriage. More afraid now than ever. I am not afraid of relationships, my affairs of the heart have been enduring, my lovers have remained friends.

Hoping to identify my deep-rooted fear of wedlock, which seemed somehow mixed up with my confused image of myself, I consulted a psychiatrist in Birmingham at the time that Rafi was pressurising me to name the day. Since Profumo, I had read everything ever written by Freud and Jung; now I decided to get in feet first, and made an appointment for a consultation. In the waiting-room a nervous little man sat fidgeting and picking his nose.

'What's wrong with you, then?' he asked. 'You look all right to me. My wife's in a mental home.'

The psychiatrist's first words were: 'You can't smoke in here.' He seemed coolly uninterested until I told him my name, then he really perked up, and gave me twenty minutes of rapt attention. I knew I was being marked down as a perfect specimen of guinea pig.

Finally, he delivered his advice. 'You must not marry. Instead you can stay in my clinic for a couple of months. You are in need of rehabilitation.'

I told him I'd think about it, walked sedately out of his office, through the front door, along the garden path and out of the gate. Then I jumped up and down shouting with delight. Anybody watching would surely have thought I needed treatment. I was just so happy to have seen the light.

I've come to know myself through experience. I'm afraid of marriage because I am a perfectionist and I'm afraid of setting myself high standards then falling short. I don't need a psychiatrist to charge me a couple of hundred pounds to tell me that. If I'd married all the men who asked me – and whom I've loved – I would have outscored Elizabeth Taylor.

I came close to marrying Pierre and being the Baroness de Cervello. He was such a funny guy, he had been in the Foreign Legion and had won the Legion d'Honneur. However, he could no longer visit France as he had blotted his copy book over the Algerian crisis.

Pierre was a difficult person to leave. I was constantly being met by friends of his saying how he missed me. Then there were his suicide attempts – terribly composed, lying on the bed. He had a baroque taste and there was a lot of gold, red and silver in his rooms, and a candelabra with ten candles beside the bed, where he would be stretched out with arms folded across his chest, carefully powdered to look paler.

'I'm glad you've returned just before I die.'

He had a great sense of the theatrical. Once in Germany, I said we should separate and he stepped through the window, took a leap and landed on the iron-grid balcony a few feet below. We were ten floors up at the time and he was clutching for safety on to the curtain. Just as well he was an authentic sportsman or he would have died a few times. I saw through his histrionics; at the same time it amused me, it was rather like watching a never-ending play.

He could do the most ghastly things, yet people the minute they saw him responded with a big smile. Everything forgiven. He was one of the most charming people I have ever met in my life. His combination of English schoolboy and aristocratic background was the secret. He was unscrupulous – there was always someone knocking on the door asking for Pierre de Cervello and he would say, 'Non, non, I am his brother.' He was a passionate gambler, and this led to problems. I felt a certain relief when we finally parted.

Werner, my lovely Swiss, came into my life after I left Rafi. He had been in our circle of friends, then when he heard we had parted and the club had burned down he asked me what I had planned.

I knew I could leave our dress business ticking over in the capable hands of my partner (later I sold my share), Dana was still a toddler, I had been happy in Spain, perhaps I'd go there and sit it out for a while. Werner owned a chain of discotheques in Spain and several apartments. 'Help yourself,' he said. When I told Rafi I was going to be away, in an attempt to find out whether he wanted us to get back together, his reply was non-committal, so I headed for Spain, and Torremolinos.

Living with Werner was blissful. He did everything for me and Dana, which was such a change after all I had been through. This was literally the first time in my entire life that I wasn't working. I had money of my own, even without Werner's support, enough to last a couple of months; it was then very cheap to live in Spain, and I had nothing to pay for the apartment. It was like falling into the laps of the gods. After Rafi I had a somewhat bruised ego – now somebody was building it up again.

He was a very special sort of person with a wonderful sense of humour. I remember once tearing to the airport in his Mercedes. The roads in Spain were awful in those days, and his exhaust system fell off. I heard the clatter and looking behind saw the complete exhaust system lying on the road.

'Werner,' I said, 'your exhaust has fallen off.'

'Oh, never mind,' said Werner, and just carried on. Nothing bothered him. The roof could fall in and all he'd say was 'tut tut' in that Swiss way.

We started an affair and lived together for two and a half years. He had a villa in Estartit, in those days the only big villa there with a swimming pool and panoramic view of the bay. I perched there on that mountain top for eight months, and it was one of the most wonderful times of my life. I painted and cooked – became very Spanish, taking home the live fish for lunch. When I decided I had had enough of my mountain, we headed for Zurich and spent the winter there, close to his family, who owned a huge chalet and a cotton-spinning factory with their own railroad. It was pleasant to be brought into this Swiss family; his mother saw me as having saved her son from his wild life of discotheques, women and drinking.

Werner wanted to marry me, and I agreed. But first I had to get divorced, which took some time to arrange and by then I realised I wasn't that keen to start again. I had just left a marriage – why go straight into another one?

I decided instead to return to Israel, buy my own apartment there, set up my own home and, from this basis of independence, make my choice. Werner accepted that. I sold my half of the factory to buy a small flat, and began collecting pieces to take to Israel, driving through Europe to England. I was leaving England, ready for the journey to Tel Aviv, when the Yom Kippur war broke out. After that war many things about me had changed, and marriage to Werner was one of them.

Around this time a new person came into my life. His name was Gorgio. He was the Argentinian Consul. We began a very difficult romance.

I am the last person who should get involved with politics and diplomacy. In Israel I am accepted, but where else in the world could I be quite so sure about attitudes? And in diplomatic circles one must be prepared to go to any one of a hundred countries. I was terribly worried from the beginning, it was all terribly serious, and we were deeply in love.

I knew many diplomats because most of them came to the club, though never the English ambassador or the American. Many came incognito, one ambassador was madly queer, and used to come in trying to pick up a boyfriend for the night. I was quite comfortable in diplomatic circles, but I hadn't been directly involved before. Then along came Gorgio, very handsome, very fast, crack sportsman, divorced, living in the chic area outside Tel Aviv with his two dogs.

From our first meeting, at a friend's birthday party, he was determined to get me.

'Look, I must take you out this evening. You must come over because I'm giving a big party in the house, please say you'll come.'

I agreed. He was very dishy, very entertaining, very nice, very funny and also quite mad. He once played Russian roulette and there was a bullet in the gun. He was also a poet – poets choose the diplomatic service as a cover it seems!

Once we got together it was instant, one hell of a love affair that boomeranged around Tel Aviv. Because his life was the diplomatic circle I became involved in Gorgio's dinners, going to his tennis and golf matches, mixing with his set.

I was concerned that by becoming deeply involved I would jeopardise his career as a diplomat. Being married to me could have been a nail in his coffin.

'OK, so I won't be ambassador in America or England,' he

said. 'They'll probably send me to Greenland and places like that.' He made it into a joke.

'I'm not sure I want to go to Greenland,' I said.

Gorgio and I discussed the alternatives. He'd give up his career, he said, buy a boat and sail round the world. He was a bit of an adventurer.

He was full of humour but I saw through it to the grain of truth. We discussed the problem and although it was spoken about in humour, he said, 'Look, here you are called the Queen of Tel Aviv. South American society is very snobbish, but if you win the emotions of the people in Argentina, you can do what you like there. They will never hold your past against you – you are only what you are. I will ask to be sent back to Buenos Aires and we will stay there for a couple of years.'

Apart from my loving concern for Gorgio's future, I knew a little bit about South Americans. He was mad for me while I was leading him a merry dance, but the minute you're married to them it's a different story – worse than the Spanish.

I declined to accompany him to social gatherings at the British Embassy. I knew the diplomatic staff socially and they were always very nice to me and I had no need to think that they would be otherwise, but I've always been very careful not to get into a position where I might be slightly embarrassing to somebody else. The French and Italians were continuously inviting me to parties and sometimes I accepted because I knew they had a different attitude.

Once I gave a diplomatic dinner in the Chinese restaurant and a group of us continued our conversation outside. One ambassadress wanted to borrow the *Oxford Dictionary of English Anecdotes*, which I had in my car. We said good night, I gave her the book and pulled the door shut and drove off. Suddenly there were screams – I'd dragged the ambassadress halfway up the street, her dress and coat caught in the car door. She was from a country very unpopular at that particular moment, and, as she was running hell for leather, I said to myself: 'I've given that government a run for their money.'

Our affair lasted eighteen months. Inadvertently he ended it – a Russian roulette that went wrong. He delivered an ultimatum: 'I can't stay here and let things drift along like this. I want to marry you. Either you marry me or I'm going to ask for a transfer.'

He hoped to push me into a decision, but there was no real rush, normally it took about six months for a transfer to come through. Not this time.

While I was spending a week in England, he phoned to say his transfer had come through, and he was leaving in a few days' time. 'Come back, we must talk.'

I rushed back to Tel Aviv, still in two minds. I had a long discussion with my mother-in-law, I really didn't know what to do. I loved him but I was still in control. I didn't let myself go.

The adventurous side of marrying Gorgio appealed to me. Had I not been Mandy Rice-Davies, being a diplomat's wife would have suited me down to the ground. I can't think of a better life for someone like me, who likes people, gets on with everyone, enjoys a slight element of something different around the corner and never having your life mapped out. I'm a good mixer. I decided to stall. I said that it was impossible to leave at once.

'Give me time to sort things out, and I'll follow you,' I said. 'Go to Argentina, you will be in central government there. You're going to have to find a flat and settle yourself. I can't just come over with a child in the middle of school – I will come over at Christmas and we'll spend a couple of weeks together. I'll have a look round.'

That seemed sensible. It was now late September.

After Gorgio left I felt very down. Next day I received a phone call from a director of the Israeli commercial theatre to offer me a part in a play. And I accepted. All those Iris Warren lessons were not to be wasted after all, all that Shakespeare sitting in the park practising with my tape-recorder. I was nervous, of course, but not dauntingly so. My whole life after all had been a stage. By accepting the offer, I couldn't go to Argentina at Christmas as planned and I wrote and explained. That was the end of the affair, as another phase in my life began.

For years I had been hearing about Joe Lewo, but somehow we never bumped into each other despite many mutual friends. Mostly he lived abroad. Just before the opening of the play, he and I met. I was delighted by him. He had a marvellous sense of humour – nothing in life was a problem to Joe. He was quick, positive and energetic. He was a Lithuanian, orphaned because of the war, and as a young boy ran with the Resistance. His parents were killed (like Peter's and many other Jews') and like Peter he overcame this. Joe was sent, as a child, to a camp in Canada, where many refugees were placed for adoption, but by the end of the war he was into his teens and rather past adoption. It seemed that nobody wanted him.

He started life wheeling and dealing, buying and selling, and actually made the beginning of his future with Cuba and Fidel Castro. He told me the story: he had a girlfriend and they wanted to go to the films but between them they hadn't the price of the ticket. So they bought a newspaper instead and went home. This was Montreal 1959. In the newspaper he read that America was breaking off all trade and diplomatic relations with Cuba. Joe made inquiries and found out that the Cubans needed chicken incubators. So he put a deal together that he would buy $10,000 worth of incubators and ship them over to Cuba. He had no money, so he went to the bank, had the luck to find somebody in the bank who had faith in him, and the bank put up the money for his first deal. This was the beginning.

Thereafter he wheeled and dealed in any commodity, anywhere, except arms. And he started to invest. He bought and still holds the largest block of private shares in Alliance Tyres in Israel, which, as well as making motor car tyres, are small enough to diversify into agricultural tyres, at a couple of thousand dollars each.

At once I liked Joe so much. He was a lot of fun.

Joe always lived in style – a gentleman to the nth degree, one of those marvellous people with many friends who sees any single occasion on the calendar as calling for a gift. He is always the first to mark any occasion.

Joe had never married or been engaged. When we met he was forty-three and had spent his youthful years getting rich and successful. He was obviously immediately attracted to me – I'm the tall blonde.

Joe chased me. He wouldn't give up, I was the woman that

he'd always wanted but couldn't quite get, which is always a challenge for the man who has everything. Not that we just sat in chauffeur-driven cars all the time, our best moments were sitting around at home drinking Dom Perignon and eating caviar. The simple things in life!

In the beginning I was not romantically inclined towards Joe. We'd go out together in a group, and Joe didn't rush it. He knew how to bide his time. Before the play opened we had a gap in rehearsals and Joe said, 'I'm giving a party for some of my business associates in Montreal, come over for dinner. Bring Avi too. And his wife. I'll arrange the tickets.'

I said, 'Look, I've only got two days before we open.'

'All you do', said Joe, 'is fly on the Monday, stay for dinner and go back the next day.'

It was quite a long way to go for dinner – Tel Aviv to Montreal. We stayed in the best hotel. A huge dinner was laid on at Joe's incredible penthouse, with a panoramic view. His furniture was priceless – French colonial stuff, Louis Quatorze, *objets d'art* in silver and gold lying around – like walking into the Louvre. We ate off Delft.

We were taken over, from the Rolls which met us at the airport, for the entire stay. Joe was not a jet-setter but a businessman, a serious person who at the same time enjoyed life, and he liked women. I like men who like women – who don't consider that loving a woman is a weakness. There are not many ambitious men like that. Find an ambitious self-made man, look at his wife and you'll always find she's quiet, some quiet, self-effacing creature who just blends into the woodwork.

The play opened and Joe sent hundreds of red roses, and gave a big dinner party afterwards. The play was very successful, so much so that Joe couldn't be too successful with me. I had too much on my mind. Joe became the man in my life. Having no family at all made him more appreciative of mine. He adored Dana and she him.

He was very generous. When it came to special occasions, there was always a beautiful diamond bracelet or necklace. I was very careful all my life not to be kept by a man in any real sense. Since Peter gave me the Jaguar on my seventeenth birthday no man has ever bought me a car or a house. I feel that these are the two things that by accepting you are tied to that person. Not all people would agree with this. Joe immediately wanted to buy me a villa, and I literally had to stop him.

When I was buying my first BMW he said, 'I'll buy you a Mercedes.' But I said, 'No,' and bought the BMW completely myself. When you are actually going out with a millionaire everybody thinks that he's bought you everything you own. It was a constant source of annoyance to me in Tel Aviv. People would say, 'Well, of course, she's got a BMW, Joe bought it for her.' Or, 'Of course, she's moving to a new penthouse . . . ' But whatever money I had I invested here and there and bought a bit of this and a bit of that and built up a little nest-egg.

The minute somebody knows you don't need or want their money, they can't wait to give it to you. No man, unless he is really in love with you and the relationship is long term, will buy you a mink coat in the first couple of months. That first mink coat is the most difficult mink coat to have. Because once you've got one the next person will say, 'I don't like that mink coat, let's go and buy you another one.' Or he won't like the diamond bracelet you wear all the time because he thinks some other man bought it. He can't just tell you to take it off and put it away. He will go out and buy you one six times better.

Cars and apartments are such private and personal things that you should only ever buy them yourself. A car is an avenue of escape. The apartment is your security. You can always earn a living – if you feel like escaping you get in your car and go. The apartment you need because you can lock the door. Even the smallest, most insignificant animal has a home. Nobody should be homeless, it's the root of self-respect.

Joe bought me masses of things and if I said, 'I don't think I like that, Joe,' he took it away again. (I wouldn't mind now all the things I've given him back. Just to put in the safe!) If I don't like something – it can be worth half a million dollars – I don't take it. If I had been calculating, loose – in other words the person most people imagine I am – I'd be worth millions today.

Joe was anxious for us to marry. I was enjoying my theatre work, but he said: 'You're not getting any younger.'

Over the years I had acquired a good reputation as an actress. I made my début with the English Theatre, playing such diverse parts as Odella in Lorca's *The House of Bernardo Alba*, where I played an innocent ('my daughter died a virgin' was the last anguished line of the play, and the fact that nobody laughed was an encouraging sign) and Cristal in Clare Booth Luce's *The Women*; and I'd made several films. After the Yom Kippur war, I launched myself as a 'serious' actress by performing in the Hebrew Theatre, speaking only Hebrew dialogue. My success surprised me. It was while playing the *Marriage Go Round* (in Hebrew) I had my first big hit, and decided that light comedy was certainly my métier. I'd moved from acting into the role of actor-co-producer (with *Move Over Mrs Markham*) when I met Joe. My film career was active, playing in bland, family-type films aimed at the young market, which meant my greatest following was among the under-tens. What a change in fan mail! At the same time I had retained my business interests, and at that point was also heading a promotional campaign for Helena Rubinstein cosmetics. The prospect that I was ageing fast and might soon be a back number hadn't occurred to me.

By this time I had decided to buy a bigger flat, a very beautiful penthouse in the best area of Tel Aviv, with a big roof garden, and you could see right over Tel Aviv to the sea. I was happy, but perhaps marriage would be better.

'I want to know now,' said Joe, phoning from Montreal, 'Will you marry me?'

'Yes,' I said. And from that moment things were taken completely out of my hands.

We had to find someone to take my part in the play because I couldn't wait until the end of the run, as we needed time to go to Montreal and from there look around and maybe buy a house in America. Then there were the wedding arrangements to be made.

He flew in immediately to give me my engagement ring, a famous eight-carat diamond which had belonged to King Farouk's mother. It was valued then at about $80,000, which is quite a nice little diamond, and in its Italian setting it looked very pretty on my finger. Joe had bought it when he first met me and kept it in the safe. He believed in being prepared!

I was making a film called *The Millionaire in Trouble* – the story of a millionaire and a chauffeur who change places. I played the American broad who was running after the millionaire.

I couldn't be sure that Joe had insured the ring and I figured it was safer on my hand than at home, so I wore it to work. I've always felt very safe in Tel Aviv. There is an underworld, a nasty one, they kill each other, but I have always felt secure there.

Joe went back to Montreal to arrange the marriage and I was invited to the opening of a new club in Natania, managed by Jean-Charles Lefevre, who had been working for us in Elat and managing our club in Tel Aviv.

In Israel everybody argues. You work for six months, have an argument, hate each other, then three months later back again all friends. Jean-Charles had argued with Rafi, taken off for Natania to open this new club, taking his sister with him, and, as I was quite friendly with her, when they invited me to the opening I agreed.

I was on stage that night, so after the play, taking another actress with me, I duly drove to Natania. We said good luck, stayed until three o'clock and they were shutting up for the night. I offered two girls a lift back to their apartment, which was on my way (my girlfriend having decided she would stay the night in Natania with her grandmother).

I had run out of cigarettes. One of the girls said, 'Come upstairs, I've got plenty.' I left the car, the keys in, the lights on, and went upstairs with her, picked up a couple of cigarettes, put them in my jacket pocket, lit one and took the lift down.

As I got to the ground floor, and went to push the lift door open, two guys thrust their way in wearing black masks, hats, black sweaters, black gloves, jeans, carrying two enormous guns. It all happened so quickly. Guns look much bigger when they are pointing at you.

They said in rehearsed English, 'Give me the diamond. I kill you.'

I was furious and thought: I'll be damned if I will. I don't care if I die, you're not getting it. So I said: 'Kill me, you'll never get the diamond.' I'd really lost my temper.

The guy on the right coshed me on the head, for which I had a line of stitches, and blood started to pour down my face. I know that if you concentrate your force you can be the strongest person in the world if you want to, and I decided that I would not open my hand, that the only way they would open my hand was if I died.

He coshed me again – I felt faint, already I was covered in blood down one side and slightly queasy, but I was determined not to give up.

The lift door was closed, and because it was so small we could hardly move, but nevertheless a struggle ensued. Blood was dripping down to form a pool on the floor. I kept trying to see the man on the right because I had a feeling that he might be somebody I knew, but every time I moved my head he punched me in the eye. I could see the eyes, like slits of ice, of the one guy on my left. Instinctively I felt I had a sporting chance that they would not kill me.

I didn't scream. For one thing I knew it was too late for me to be heard. Also I was concentrating my energies. I know too the worst thing in the world to do is scream; if you scream they either shoot you or knock you out just to shut you up. Stay conscious and someone might come in, the attackers might give up, might get panicky and leave. I was rapidly weighing all this in the balance. I wasn't going to give up until I really felt that I couldn't fight any more – again I was in a film. One attacker kept biting my hand (the scars go right down to the bone). I thought he was biting my hand to make me open it. But what he was doing was biting the diamond out of its claws. Suddenly they released me, he stopped biting and said, 'We're going now, don't scream.' That, I felt, was the moment *to* scream. I let out a blood-curdling scream – they ran for it. Now I couldn't see. I was covered in blood and one eye was completely closed. I pressed the lift button to the top floor. I didn't know they had the diamond and I thought they would come after me. I wanted to get as far away from them as possible.

On my way up in the lift I looked at my hand and there was no diamond. I've never felt so upset in my life. After my first feeling of elation that they didn't get the diamond and I'd beaten them, now I saw it gone I felt absolute cold anger. I pressed the lift to go down and ran out into the street. I could see them tailing off into the distance. If I'd had a gun I would have shot them. Of course, they were never caught. (After that I started wearing yellow diamonds – people think it's topaz.)

In Montreal, Joe heard the news. As I arrived back in my apartment after seeing the police he was on the phone. I told him what had happened. He took the first plane and arrived that evening, finding me in a nasty condition, my hair matted with blood, which I had to clean off before the evening show. I still had the empty setting. 'Sorry, Joe,' I said, 'this is all that's left of your diamond ring.'

He picked it up and threw it away. 'It was only a diamond,' he said. 'As long as you are all right.' He gave me another one immediately, round-shaped and weighing ten carats instead of eight.

Goodbye, Israel. Dana went to England to stay with my parents (Joe had already promised her a colour-television set, and a horse and ten dogs) while I went to Montreal to make the wedding arrangements.

We'd agreed we didn't want a big party, yet Joe was planning to have a plane fly in from here and a plane from there, and I was getting more and more worried about this. The last thing I planned was the society wedding of Montreal in the Palm Room of the Ritz Carlton Hotel, which is what it boiled down to in the end. Joe said, 'I've never been married. I'm only going to be married once in my life.'

I'd cut my hair very short, which is something I do at crucial times in my life. We were going to be married by the rabbi and went along to see him and fix a provisional date for the wedding. The Canadian press were making much of it. I was planning to fly into Paris, pick up a trousseau, have Yves St Laurent run me up a simple little outfit to wear for the ceremony.

The marriage settlement was being drawn up and there was several million involved. The lawyers got together and said, 'How much do you want?' Funny question to ask.

I said, 'What do you mean, I can't ask for money.'

They said, 'You have to.'

That worried me to death. I had a horrible feeling that I was being bought.

We flew to New York because Joe had business there, and arrived back both of us in a state of nervous tension, but pretending nothing was wrong.

Joe wanted to go to an ice-hockey game. I had a headache from the flight so I stayed at home, sitting in the study, looking out at the wonderful panoramic views over Montreal. Darkness was just coming down. I saw a plane going across the sky and thought, I'd like to be on that plane. I'd like to be going to England. I don't want to stay here.

In half an hour I had packed, ordered a taxi downstairs, sent the maid off for the night. One and a half hours later I was sitting on the plane for London.

I left him a note. 'Dear Joe, I've got cold feet. I'll be in London. Come over to London and see me.'

Joe came over on the next flight.

I told him, 'I've got in a panic about all this.'

He said, 'I know, me too. I'm such a perfectionist I wanted everything right. We should just go and get married. We're too old for all this nonsense about weddings. I just want to marry you. Let's just go get married.'

'No, Joe,' I said, 'Let's leave it awhile.'

25

RETURNING like a homing pigeon to Tel Aviv and the play (nothing cures a broken romance as effectively as work) I drove up to Natania to see my friends.

Jean-Charles asked me to dance. We had known each other for more than four years, in a completely detached way. I got up to dance with him. The song was 'Singing in the Rain'. As we danced I started to feel weak at the knees, my heart was beating faster, I could feel my face growing scarlet.

We looked into each other's eyes and I fell in love with him. It was ridiculous. It was like a blinding flash. He felt it too but he was suspicious of me, he thought I was playing some game with him. His suspicion struck me as coldness, I thought he wasn't interested in me.

There followed a courtship like something out of a Victorian romance. A beautiful romance, in every sense of the word. He would bring me flowers or a little gift. Come around to the apartment. There was no physical contact beyond a chaste goodnight kiss.

I began to get worried – that was fine for a week or so, but then I began to think maybe he didn't fancy me. Then I fell in with the game, went along with it, enjoyed the romance of being madly in love with each other.

We decided to motor across Europe to England. Driving across France he said, 'Let's get married.'

I said, 'I'm not sure I want to get married.'

'If you don't,' he said, 'I'm not coming to England with you.'

We reached England, arriving in Canterbury and went to apply to the registrar to get married. There was a delay while we produced divorce documents.

It was August Bank Holiday weekend, 1977. The day before I was supposed to get married, I panicked again.

'I'm sorry,' I said, 'I can't do it. I love you, adore you, you're marvellous, I worship the ground you walk on, let's live together for ever. I can't marry you.'

He had bought the wedding rings, one for me and one for himself the same, and he said, 'You will come with me in the morning and tell the registrar we don't want to get married.

Next morning I got up. I hadn't been to the hairdresser. I hadn't done my hair. I put on old shirt and jeans, no make-up, no eyelashes, quite deliberately, for I wasn't getting married, I was going to tell the registrar sorry but no.

We drove to the register office in my BMW.

Jean-Charles said, 'If you don't come in now I will drive this car into the wall.' He was in the mood to do it. I could imagine the scandal.

I thought I'd better get out of this car. Going up the steps I said, 'OK, let's get married then.'

By this time we were both completely white and shaky. We stopped two nice ladies with shopping baskets and asked, 'Would you like to be witness to our marriage?'

'Oh, how romantic,' said one, 'just like during the war.'

The registrar was obviously worried about the way we looked.

'Don't be so upset,' he said, 'it's only going to take a couple of minutes'.

Five minutes later we were married. Hand in hand we walked off to a bottle of champagne at the nearest hotel.

Most people go through life proving what they are. I go through life proving what I am not and I have to stop somewhere, but where? And what have I been doing all these years, caught up in a web of fate, not knowing who I really am. It is the oddest thing to experience in life, reading so much about yourself that often the line between fact and fiction is blurred.

I cannot afford to fail in what I do, because people will say 'Poor Mandy, she's come to a bad end.' I've been thrown off my path somewhere in life, and lost my sense of direction. I don't look at the roads ahead, I look for the escape routes off it.